The Gutsy Girl's Devotional

The Gutsy Girl's Devotional

6 MONTHS OF FEARLESS INSPIRATION

BARBOUR
PUBLISHING

ISBN 978-1-63609-453-3

Adobe Digital Edition (.epub) 978-1-63609-628-5

Published by Barbour Books, an imprint of Barbour Publishing, Inc., 1810 Barbour Drive, Uhrichsville, Ohio 44683, www.barbourbooks.com.

Our mission is to inspire the world with the life-changing message of the Bible.

Printed in China.

Are You. . .

GUTSY?
COURAGEOUS?
FEARLESS?
BOLD? . . .

The truth is, when you have the Courage-Giver Himself by your side, you *can* live each day fear-free.

Every devotion and prayer starter in this inspiring read will remind you of all the reasons it's possible (and important!) to be a gutsy girl of God. With each turn of the page, you'll clear a path to fearless living!

Light, space, zest—that's GOD!
So, with him on my side I'm fearless,
afraid of no one and nothing.
PSALM 27:1 MSG

THE GENESIS OF FEAR

The LORD God made garments of skin for Adam and his wife and clothed them.

GENESIS 3:21 NIV

Fear. It can grab you by the throat, raise your blood pressure, inhibit your walk with God, and so much more.

Fear didn't come into the picture until humankind took their eyes and hearts off God. It began with Adam and Eve in the Garden of Eden, the wonderful paradise God created just for them. God told Adam, "You are free to eat from any tree in the garden; but you must not eat from the tree of the knowledge of good and evil, for when you eat from it you will certainly die" (Genesis 2:16–17 NIV). God then created Eve and spent quality time with His loving and obedient children.

But then a sly, slithering snake came on the scene. Approaching Eve, he questioned God's rule about the tree. "Did God really say, 'You must not eat from any tree in the garden'?" (Genesis 3:1 NIV). The woman attempted to verify God's instructions but ended up skewing them by adding her own interpretation: "We may eat fruit from the trees in the garden, but God did say, 'You must not eat fruit from the tree that is in the middle of the garden, and you must not touch it, or you will die' " (Genesis 3: 2–3 NIV). The serpent then challenged Eve: "Surely you won't die. You'll just have a different perspective. You'll be like God, knowing the difference

between good and evil" (Genesis 3:4, author paraphrase).

Eve, unable to resist the luscious-looking fruit, took a bite and then gave some to Adam. They then realized they were naked and covered themselves. Hearing God walking in the garden, they hid. When God asked Adam where he was, the man's fear was uncovered: "I heard you in the garden, and I was afraid because I was naked; so I hid" (Genesis 3:10 NIV). Adam's next step was to blame Eve for his downfall. Eve, in turn, blamed the serpent.

God then cursed the serpent, Adam, and Eve. Yet He still demonstrated His unconditional love for His children, clothing them with animal hides before banishing them from paradise.

Thousands of years later, we're still dealing with desiring more than what we have with God, giving in to temptation, and quaking in fear—not just because we're ashamed of our missteps but because we don't trust our Creator or His Word.

Know this: God never changes. Just as He cared and provided for Adam and Eve, He cares and provides for you. So put your fear, shame, and imperfections aside. Open yourself up to your Creator and His love. As you do, your fear will vanish.

Lord, help me turn away from fear and to You. Amen.

IN GOOD HANDS

The Lord is my Shepherd [to feed, guide, and shield me], I shall not lack. . . . Yes, though I walk through the [deep, sunless] valley of the shadow of death, I will fear or dread no evil, for You are with me; Your rod [to protect] and Your staff [to guide], they comfort me.

PSALM 23:1, 4 AMPC

One of the most popular Bible passages is Psalm 23, for it provides the perfect picture of Jesus, the Good Shepherd. It exudes comfort, hope, safety, a positive attitude, and courage.

The Lord is my Shepherd. . . . God *is* your Shepherd, continually guiding you, feeding you, shielding you from danger. You have an ongoing relationship with the Creator of the universe, the Maker of the air you breathe, water you drink, and earth on which you walk. And because the Lord is your constant companion and guide, you can truthfully say. . .

I shall not lack. . . . That shall-not-lack principle applies not only to food, water, clothing, housing, and other material necessities but also to love, faith, hope, and other intangibles that you sometimes feel are beyond your reach. Yet those qualities are right there, in God's arms. All you have to do is ask for them. Then keep your eyes open as your Shepherd places them before you. Meanwhile, no matter how dark things look, you can proclaim. . .

I will fear or dread no evil. . . . You can live your life unafraid

for one good reason: God the Father is with you. He, the All-Powerful, is by your side. His Son, Jesus, is leading the way. And His Spirit is within you. With the Three-in-One covering you inside and out, you can walk unafraid. You need not fear anything that comes against you. The Father can erase your fears with a whisper. Jesus can still them with one motion. And the Holy Spirit can blow them away with one good exhale. Your Good Shepherd comes equipped with everything He needs to get you safely from one place to another. Even through the darkest of valleys, where shadows rise and fall, He extends His rod to protect you and His staff to guide you.

Today and every day, remember your Shepherd. Believe He's surrounding you with every step you take. Comfort yourself with the fact that He's equipped to keep you safe, no matter how dark things seem. You, little lamb, are in good hands.

Dear Shepherd, as I walk along the path You have laid before me, keep me aware of the fact that You are with me, guiding, shielding, loving, and feeding me. With You, I know I'm safe no matter how dark things get. In this truth I find not just courage and comfort but joy! Amen.

WHAT YOU NEED

"When you pray, do not say the same thing over and over again making long prayers like the people who do not know God. They think they are heard because their prayers are long. Do not be like them. Your Father knows what you need before you ask Him."

MATTHEW 6:7–8 NLV

There you are, ready to step out and do something for God. But then a sense of want arises in your heart. The what-ifs begin to ricochet around in your head. The idea of lack begins to weigh you down. You begin reasoning within yourself, thinking, *What if I step out, head in that direction, begin that work, and find I don't have everything I need to do what needs to be done?* Suddenly your feet are covered with hardened cement, and you find yourself anchored to the spot on which you stand, unable to move backward or forward.

Remember that human reasoning, secular logic, will only get you so far. It's faith that you need to overcome your fear. Faith is what you need to move forward. As Pastor E. W. Kenyon said, "Faith will lead you where you cannot walk. Reason has never been a mountain climber."

It's time you etched it deeply within your mind and wrote it indelibly upon your heart that God is ready, willing, and able to see you succeed in His plans for you. He wants you to use

the talents you possess to move His kingdom forward. He wants you to know, to realize, that He knows what you need now and in the future—"before you ask Him"! While you're doing what you're supposed to be doing in the moment, in the now, He is already down the road ahead of you, getting things ready for the next stage of your journey.

Realize that today God is saying to you, "Test Me in this. . . . See if I will not then open the windows of heaven and pour out good things for you until there is no more need" (Malachi 3:10 NLV)!

God is not one to leave you stranded, to leave things unfinished. You need to know that "He Who began a good work in you will continue until the day of Jesus Christ [right up to the time of His return], developing [that good work] and perfecting and bringing it to full completion in you" (Philippians 1:6 AMPC).

So, woman, trust God. Do not be afraid. He is committed to you even more than you are committed to Him. Test Him in this.

Sometimes, Lord, I feel so weighed down by the fear of lack. Help me remember that You will always take care of me. You will fill my every need before I even ask! Amen!

PRAYER, PRAISE, PATIENCE, AND PROCLAMATION

Anna the prophetess. . .never left the Temple area, worshiping night and day with her fastings and prayers. At the very time Simeon was praying, she showed up, broke into an anthem of praise to God, and talked about the child to all who were waiting expectantly for the freeing of Jerusalem.

LUKE 2:36–38 MSG

The prophet Anna hailed from the tribe of Asher. She had been married for seven years, and then her husband died. Instead of remarrying, Anna dedicated her life to God. She had been worshipping at the temple night and day, fasting and praying while she awaited the birth of the Christ, the One who was to save Israel.

Anna had total faith in God and His Word. In Him alone she trusted. The promises of His Word prompted her to pray for the appearance of God's Redeemer to her and her people. Her confident trust and faith in God gave her the patience to pray, fast, and praise every day.

Then one morning Anna appeared in the temple just as Simeon was praying over the baby Jesus. As soon as she came upon the scene, Anna began singing God's praises, thanking Him for the long-awaited Savior of her people. Then she went to talk to everyone she knew, so excited to share the news that the Messiah and Savior they had all been waiting for was finally here! The

flesh-and-blood Redeemer of Israel was now among them.

Anna's entire profile consists of just three verses. We aren't told the name of her deceased husband. We don't know her exact age. And we're not sure what spurred her on to dedicate her life to God. We do know, however, that as one of the only few named female prophets, Anna was the first to proclaim Jesus as the Christ, to spread the news to other people.

After these three verses, Anna is mentioned no more. Instead, she simply sinks into the background from whence she came. But isn't that what God's people are supposed to do? We are to take the attitude of John the Baptist, who announced Jesus but made sure his listeners knew, "This is the assigned moment for him to move into the center while I slip off to the sidelines" (John 3:30 MSG).

Anna slipped out of the picture, most likely dying before hearing Jesus preach and teach and seeing Him heal. Her God-given assignment in that regard was over. Yet she most likely continued to find her courage, hope, and relief in God as she prayed to and praised Him till the end her life, well and courageously lived.

Thank You, Lord, for the example of Anna. May I find inspiration in her fearless and patient dedication to You. Amen.

JUST PRAY

Is anyone among you in trouble? Let them pray.
Is anyone happy? Let them sing songs of praise.
JAMES 5:13 NIV

The first step you need to take when you find yourself feeling troubled by what's happening directly to you or what's going on around you is pretty simple.

Pray.

Now here's the funny thing. You're not going to want to do it. On your best days, you think you will. You think, of course, that when trouble comes, you'll pray. That makes all kinds of sense. Of course God wants us to bring Him our burdens. Of course we need to tell our heavenly Father what's going on. Of course.

But friend, you are not going to want to pray. You are going to want to fret. You are going to want to complain to someone. You are going to want to compare notes. You are going to want to take charge. You are going to want to take over. You are going to want to run away. You are going to want someone else to do it. You are going to want to hide under the covers. You are going to want to procrastinate. You are going to want to go to a movie. You are going to want to distract yourself. You are going to want to cry. You are going to want to get angry with somebody. You are going to want to eat chocolate.

You are not going to want to settle down and pray.

Why?

There could be all kinds of reasons. But the two that pop up most often are these: (1) You don't think you're good enough. (2) You doubt that God is good enough.

You know that "the prayer of a righteous person is powerful and effective" (James 5:16 NIV). But what about the prayer of a sometimes-righteous person? What about a pretty good person? What about a wannabe-righteous person? It's hard to imagine that your prayers will be all that powerful and effective. But what if they were?

You know the Lord can make the sick person well. You know God can offer forgiveness. In theory. But when it comes right down to it, you wonder—will God really bring about good in this situation? Or, perhaps, is God's idea of good here the same as ours?

And the answer to that last question is no. God's idea of good is much better than we can ever imagine. He is vastly more gracious than we have the capacity to be. He is more merciful. He is more generous. He is more faithful.

So go ahead. Are you in trouble? Pray. Are you happy? Pray and give thanks. Are you sick? Pray and ask for healing. Just pray, pray, pray.

Lord, hear my prayer. Amen.

SPEAKING UP

"The Lord is with us. Do not be afraid."

NUMBERS 14:9 NLV

The Israelites had already seen a lot of miracles, the work of an awesome God. He had given Moses and Aaron the power to bring plagues down on the Egyptians. His angel of death had spared His people's families during the Passover. With a pillar of fire, God had led His people away from Egypt. With His cloud, He obscured their presence from their enemy. Then God separated the Red Sea so His people could escape the Egyptian army and its chariots. *And* He provided the people with several laws and commandments to follow so they could live a right and good life.

Now the Israelites made their way to a place called Kadesh-barnea. From there Moses, at God's command, sent out twelve spies, one from each tribe, to scope out the Promised Land. His parting words to the scouts were "Be of good courage and bring some of the fruit of the land" (Numbers 13:20 ESV).

Forty days later, the spies returned, fruit in hand, to give their reports. Ten of them told Moses that although the land was wonderful, the people who lived there were too strong and big to defeat. In fact, they said, "We looked like grasshoppers in our own eyes, and we looked the same to them" (Numbers 13:33 NLV).

Two other spies, Joshua and Caleb, spoke up, ready to relate a different report. They agreed that the land was very good and

encouraged the Israelites, saying, "Do not be afraid of the people of the land. For they will be our food. They have no way to keep safe, and the Lord is with us. Do not be afraid of them" (Numbers 14:9 NLV).

Yet the people were poised to throw stones at Joshua and Caleb, more eager to believe and follow the way of fear than embark on the footpath of faith. But just then the Lord's glory appeared at the tent of meeting, staying their hands. And God spoke to Moses, wondering what He had to do to get the people to have faith in Him (see Numbers 14:11).

Because of their unbelief, God kept the Israelites wandering in the wilderness for forty years until the faithless generation died off. Only Joshua and Caleb, God's faith-filled followers, remained alive to set their feet in the Promised Land.

When you speak up, what do people hear? Are your words full of fear or faith?

Lord, may my vision be focused by faith and not obscured by fear as I seek to follow You. Amen.

BREAKING NORMS

The Master said, "Martha, dear Martha, you're fussing far too much and getting yourself worked up over nothing. One thing only is essential, and Mary has chosen it—it's the main course, and won't be taken from her."

LUKE 10:41–42 MSG

Martha and Mary of Bethany were sisters living together in the same house with their brother, Lazarus. One day Martha invited Jesus and those with Him home for dinner.

As soon as Jesus took a seat, Mary sat down at His feet. And there she stayed, listening to every word that dropped from His lips. Meanwhile, Martha was preparing and serving the meal—all by herself. For her, there was no time to listen—only to do! Yet there sat her sister at Jesus' feet.

So Martha decided to complain to Jesus, a move that seems totally justifiable. For she was experiencing a situation that many faith-filled women have found themselves in! They're running around like crazy women, trying to get things done, while others sit on the sidelines like pew potatoes!

Martha approached Jesus, putting her complaint before Him, saying, "Master, don't you care that my sister has abandoned the kitchen to me? Tell her to lend me a hand" (Luke 10:40 MSG). But Jesus said to her, "Martha, Martha, Martha, you're so frightened, worried, and anxious that things aren't going to work out right. But

that won't get you very far. What you really need to do is focus on one thing—the best thing—spending time with and listening to Me. That's the choice Mary has made. And it will never be taken away from her" (see vv. 41–42, author paraphrase).

According to Jesus, it's more important that you are attentive to Him and His Word than staying busy doing things that you, as a woman, are expected to be doing! This changing role of a faith-filled woman is confirmed in Luke's next chapter, where he reports on how a woman in the crowd yelled to Jesus, "Blessed the womb that carried you, and the breasts at which you nursed!" (Luke 11:27 MSG), to which Jesus responded, "Even more blessed are those who hear God's Word and guard it with their lives!" (Luke 11:28 MSG).

Jesus has made it clear. He wants you to have the courage to live a faith-filled life in a nontraditional way. Jesus wants you to add power to your life by making spending time with Him your main goal.

Show me, Lord, how to make spending more one-on-one time with You, sitting at Your feet, listening to Your words, my main aim in life. Amen.

A GREAT CALM

He got up, rebuked the wind, and said to the sea, "Silence! Be still!" The wind ceased, and there was a great calm. Then He said to them, "Why are you fearful? Do you still have no faith?"

MARK 4:39–40 HCSB

The people, standing on the shore while facing the sea, listened closely to Jesus' parables. As the crowd grew and began gathering around Him, Jesus stepped into a boat then sat down, continuing to teach.

When evening drew near, Jesus said to His disciples, "Let's cross over to the other side of the sea" (Mark 4:35 HCSB). So they headed out on the waters, as did the other boats with them.

While making their way across the sea, a windstorm blew in. Waves began breaking over the boat and swamping it. Meanwhile, their fearless Leader slept in the stern. In a state of panic, the experienced fishermen woke Jesus, yelling over the storm, "Teacher! Don't You care that we're going to die?" (Mark 4:38 HCSB).

Immediately, Jesus rose up and commanded the wind and waves to be still and *stay* still. After He spoke, "the wind ceased (sank to rest as if exhausted by its beating) and there was [immediately] a great calm (a perfect peacefulness)" (Mark 4:39 AMPC). Amid the great calm, Jesus asked His followers why they were so afraid. Where was their faith?

Jesus didn't just calm the wind and waves. He didn't just address

the situation that was happening around His followers. He took time to address their doubts within themselves.

When you don't trust God, when you lack confidence in Him, His power, His Spirit, and His Word, you find yourself becoming more fearful than faith filled. Yet even then, with one shout-out to Jesus, one question, one prayerful presentation of an issue, He moves on your behalf, transforming you and your world.

Jesus holds power over every crisis you face. All the natural forces in and out of this world are under His control. Just as He can still a storm, Jesus can calm your mind, soothe your soul, relax your body, and charm your spirit. No matter how big or small your faith, Jesus will still reach out and save you.

Read the story of the great calm (see Mark 4:35–41). Remind yourself of who Jesus is, what power He wields, and how He is always with you. Ask Him to give you the peace you need—within and without—as He continues to answer your cries and build your faith.

I know, Jesus, that sometimes I'm afraid, especially when I see no earthly way out of a situation. Help me face my fears and grow my faith. Come to me now, heavenly Lord. Make me be still and stay still in Your peace, protection, and love. Amen.

PAVE YOUR WAY

[Jesus said,] "Everyone who lives believing in me does not ultimately die at all. Do you believe this?" [Martha said,] "Yes, Master. All along I have believed."

JOHN 11:25–27 MSG

Once more, consider Martha and Mary of Bethany. From the biblical accounts of these sisters, Martha seems more intellectual, able to put things into words and speak them clearly when they're needed. Mary seems more emotional, expressing herself through physical means rather than words. Yet both find a way to live a life of faith and courage.

When Lazarus grew ill, the sisters sent word to Jesus. When Jesus received their message, He told those with Him that Lazarus's sickness wouldn't end with death but would be used to glorify God.

Yet Jesus stayed where He was for two more days. When He finally left to see Lazarus, He told His disciples that although Lazarus was dead, "for your sake I am glad that I was not there; it will help you to believe (to trust and rely on Me). However, let us go to him" (John 11:15 AMPC).

By the time Jesus arrived in Bethany, Lazarus had already been dead for four days! A determined Martha, hearing Jesus was near, went out to meet Him. Reaching Jesus, Martha told Him, "Master, if you'd been here, my brother wouldn't have died. Even now, I know that whatever you ask God he will give you" (John 11:21–22 MSG).

Jesus told her that Lazarus would be raised up—not later but now! He went further, telling Martha that anyone who believes in Him will never die. Jesus asked Martha if she believed that. Only then did Martha make the most wonderful testimony of faith that can be found in the New Testament: "Yes, Master. All along I have believed that you are the Messiah, the Son of God who comes into the world" (John 11:27 MSG).

Assured that Jesus would rouse her brother, Martha returned home and told Mary that Jesus was asking for her. Mary ran out and fell at Jesus' feet. Sobbing, she began saying the same thing as Martha: "Master, if only you had been here, my brother would not have died" (John 11:32 MSG). Then her voice trailed off as her sobs got the better of her.

Jesus Himself began weeping.

In the end, the Lord of the living raised Lazarus from among the dead. And many, seeing the glory of God, became convinced that He was the Messiah.

No matter what your makeup or circumstances, all Jesus asks is for you to have courage and believe. For both these things pave the way to miracles.

I believe, Lord! I believe! Amen!

FROM YOUR HEART

When the disciples saw what was happening, they were furious. . . . Jesus. . .intervened. "Why are you giving this woman a hard time? She has just done something wonderfully significant for me. . . . What she has just done is going to be remembered and admired."

MATTHEW 26:8, 10, 13 MSG

Six days before Passover, Jesus and His followers were in Bethany. So Lazarus and his sisters, Mary and Martha, invited him to dinner at their place. As usual, Martha served. The resurrected Lazarus was sitting at the table with Jesus.

Then in came their sister, Mary, with a jar of expensive and aromatic perfume, which she used to anoint her Lord's feet. She then wiped His feet with her hair. The entire house was filled with the aroma of liquid nard.

One simple act of love and devotion to her Lord, Master, Savior, and Friend Jesus. Somehow she knew His time was near. No words were exchanged between her and the others. Her eyes and mind were on one person and one person only—Jesus. What did she care for the threats, opinions, and criticisms of others?

Yet Jesus' followers were angered. They wanted to know why money was wasted on expensive perfume. The nard could have been sold and the money given to the poor.

Jesus came to Mary's rescue. He began to defend her, telling

them, "Why are you giving this woman a hard time? She has just done something wonderfully significant for me" (Matthew 26:10 MSG). Jesus told them that although they'd have the poor with them all the time, they would not have Him. So what Mary had actually done by this loving deed was anoint His body for burial. He ended His admonishment with "You can be sure that wherever in the whole world the Message is preached, what she has just done is going to be remembered and admired" (Matthew 26:13 MSG).

Mary was oblivious to all this back-and-forth. So intent was she on loving her Friend that all other voices, all other people, all other noises had been shut out. She only had eyes and ears for Jesus. In her silence, she let only her heart speak.

When you allow your faith to overcome your fear, when you focus on Christ alone, you find a new method of communication: you speak from your heart. You need say no words. Your actions and love speak louder than any words could. And what you do is remembered and admired by those you touch.

Lord, increase my faith so that I may overcome fear. Then help me to focus on You alone so that I may speak to others from my heart. Amen.

SALTY

"You are the salt of the earth. But if the salt loses its saltiness, how can it be made salty again?"
MATTHEW 5:13 NIV

Have you ever had to be on a low-salt diet? It's hard to do. Really hard. Salt is in everything. Even things you never would have thought about. Even things that don't taste remotely salty.

In the days before refrigeration, salt was often used as a preservative. Salt sucks the water right out of foods. When the water is gone, so is the happy environment for bacteria and mold, and thus the food is kept edible for a longer time than it normally would be.

Salt was sometimes used as a way of holding on to heat, as part of road surfacing material, in cleaning, as part of roofing material, and the list goes on and on. Several reports claim that there are more than fourteen thousand uses for salt. But as useful as it is, once salt has lost its ability to function, or once it has lost its flavor, it is no longer any good to be used as salt. It becomes just another bit of dirt. It becomes something other than what it was meant to be.

We who follow Christ have certain jobs to do. We are gifted by the Spirit and called by Christ to act in certain ways and to perform specific acts of goodness and kindness and faithfulness. We are to live lives that look different from the lives of those around us. We are to be pure and peaceful, to be merciful and meek, to be

righteous and poor in spirit, to mourn with those who mourn and rejoice with those who rejoice, and to keep on going and doing and being no matter what happens, or who hates us, or what is said about us because we love and serve Jesus.

If we lose our ability to be "salty"—to challenge people to enhance their lives with the Gospel and to preserve all that is good about the world—then we will have lost something of what it means to be a follower of Christ. We won't be the people God created us to be. But you don't have to be the most charismatic evangelist in the world; you don't have to be the most dynamic preacher; you don't have to be the wisest counselor in order to help people come to know Jesus. All you have to be is a little salty—be full of the Gospel, be truthful, be eager to show love and to serve others, and be well practiced in showing compassion. Be salty.

Jesus, help me to keep flavoring the lives of those around me with the goodness of Your love. Amen.

STANDING UP

The daughters of Zelophehad. . .stood before Moses, Eleazar the priest, the leaders, and the entire community.

NUMBERS 27:1–2 HCSB

During Old Testament days, women had few rights. They were considered more like possessions than people. Yet five daughters had the courage to stand up for their rights, benefiting themselves and all the women to follow.

Their years of wandering over, the Israelites were poised to enter the Promised Land. So a census was taken. And based on that census, the land was to be distributed.

Enter Zelophehad's daughters: Mahlah, Noah, Hoglah, Milcah, and Tirzah (see Numbers 26:33). Their father had died in the wilderness wanderings, leaving no sons. And under the current law, if a dad died leaving no male heir, his daughters could not inherit what he left.

Having been counted in the census, Zelophehad's daughters now approached Moses and company. They explained their situation then asked why their father's name should die out from his clan just because he had no sons. Couldn't they, his daughters, have his land?

Moses took their case to God. And God ruled that the five daughters were right. He made it clear that they were to receive their father's inheritance. Moreover, God determined that from

this time forward, the law was to be revised to include this new provision. From here on, if a man died without a son, his inheritance would go to his daughter. If he had no daughter, it would go to his brothers. If he had no brothers, it would go to his father's brothers. Finally, if the man had no uncles, it would go to the nearest relative so that the inheritance could stay in the family (see Numbers 27:8–11). Case closed.

Yet it should be noted that sometime later, the men of Israel considered that if the daughters married outside of their tribe, the land might be inherited by children of the father's tribe. So the law was tweaked to say that the daughters could marry whomever they wanted as long as they married within their father's tribe (see Numbers 36:3–9).

The amazing thing about Zelophehad's daughters is that they stood up for their rights while living in a patriarchal society. They considered their situation, saw the unfairness of it, and proposed a change in the law. Even more amazing is that Moses considered it important enough to take to God, that God Himself admitted the women were right, and that this case set a legal precedent that is still cited today!

When you see a wrong, ask God to give you the courage to stand up for your rights—or for the rights of others. Be confident that when you do, God will hear and help you if you're in the right.

When I stand up for the right thing, "LORD, don't be far away. My strength, come quickly to help me" (Psalm 22:19 HCSB).

WORKING IT OUT

The LORD God took the man and put him in the Garden of Eden to work it and take care of it.

GENESIS 2:15 NIV

Thomas Edison, the famous Midwestern inventor of the electric lightbulb and many other creations, is quoted as saying, "Opportunity is missed by most people because it is dressed in overalls and looks like work." He was certainly not a man who shied away from work. His life story is a tale of taking advantage of every opportunity he had to experiment and try out his new ideas—even when it sometimes cost him whatever current job he was employed at. He is a great example of the spark of the Creator that is in each of us—that desire within us to make things, to care for our world, and to figure out solutions to problems.

When we are in the middle of difficult times, it is good to remember who made us and what He made us to do. As Christians, we believe we were formed by God. God formed man from "the dust of the ground and breathed into his nostrils the breath of life, and the man became a living being" (Genesis 2:7 NIV). We are the work of God, and He created us in His image—in the image of the master craftsman, with skill in our hands and innovation in our hearts. It's no wonder that, especially when we are experiencing hard situations and complicated feelings, we feel better when we are doing productive work.

The first man and the first woman were no different than we are in this respect. Certainly they wouldn't have been content with just wandering about in the garden aimlessly. They must have been grateful to have been given a job to do. And what an honor! The Creator of all trusted them to take care of His creation. Not only did they enjoy the work of tending the garden, but God saw that humans would thrive in the work of tending relationships. He declared, "It is not good for the man to be alone" (Genesis 2:18 NIV). Men and women grow and flourish through relationships with one another—through the endless pursuit of understanding and learning from one another and figuring out how to live together.

But even after the Fall, when the man and woman had disobeyed God, God in His mercy did not take meaningful work away from us. It's true that with the curse came pain and sorrow—work would never be easy—but God in His wisdom knew that we would find blessings even within the curse.

Lord, when I don't know what else to do,
help me to work for You. Amen.

GETTING ON THE GOD TRACK

In Him the whole fullness of Deity (the Godhead) continues to dwell in bodily form. . . . And you are in Him, made full and having come to fullness of life [in Christ you too are filled with the Godhead—Father, Son and Holy Spirit—and reach full spiritual stature]. And He is the Head of all rule and authority [of every angelic principality and power].

COLOSSIANS 2:9–10 AMPC

When your anxieties begin to mount, your worries overwhelm, or your fears override all thoughts, fall into God's Word. There you will find all you need to get back on the God track, the right path, the narrow yet better way.

The father of lies loves to fill your mind with nonsense. To strike at your core. To get you so off balance that you begin to believe every word he says. But if you nourish yourself in God's Word, knowing that's what you need to flourish in this life (see Matthew 4:4), you'll find your anxiety abating, your worries waning, and your fears fading. For the Word will open your eyes to the truth of who you are in this world.

The entirety of God's being is found in Jesus. As well as His being fully human, He is fully divine. It may be hard for the mind to comprehend that Jesus is not just human—like you—but also the personification of God the Father, God the Spirit, and God the Word. Even more amazing is that because you are a believer and

therefore hidden in Him, you are *also* filled with God the Father, God the Spirit, and God the Word! Within you is all the "fullness of Deity," the head over all principalities and power!

Woman, daughter of the King, being who holds the Godhead—Father, Son, and Spirit—within her, you need not ever be afraid of anything. So, instead of shuddering in fear, trying to hide, or getting defensive, dig deep into God's Word. Remember that the power of the Godhead lies within you, and conduct your life accordingly.

Then, when trouble comes and you call on God, know that He will answer. Say, "God's now at my side and I'm not afraid; who would dare lay a hand on me? God's my strong champion" (Psalm 118:6–7 MSG).

Lord, so often I've run to a fellow human—a mom, sister, friend, or congresswoman—for help. I've reached out to her for a rescue. But now I realize that taking refuge in You is so much better. You, Holy Three-in-One, are all the power I could ever want or need. Amen.

GRACE AND FORGIVENESS

"My father, you have made a promise to the Lord. Do to me what you have promised you would do. Because the Lord has punished the people. . .who fought against you. But do this for me. Let me alone for two months. So I and my friends may go to the mountains and cry because I will never have a man."

JUDGES 11:36–37 NLV

Up until now, God had been raising up judges to help His people stave off their enemies. But now the men of Gilead (not God Himself) decided to call up Jephthah, a man they had once exiled, and asked him to lead them into battle against the Ammonites. After some discussion, Jephthah agreed to come and be their head man.

Yet later, instead of simply trusting God to help him win the battle, Jephthah made a rash vow before God to ensure his success: "If you give me a clear victory. . .I'll give to God whatever comes out of the door of my house to meet me when I return" (Judges 11:30–31 MSG).

Fortunately for the Israelites, the Ammonites were defeated. And a victorious Jephthah went home to Mizpah. But here's the snag. The first one who greeted him as he made his way up the walk was his only child, a twelve- to fourteen-year-old daughter.

When Jephthah realized what his rash vow to God now signified, he ripped his clothes and wailed about *his* misfortune. He blamed her for his having been brought "very low" and for her

being "the cause of great trouble to me" (Judges 11:35 AMPC). Only then did he tell her of *his* side of the bargain and his inability to take back his vow to God.

Jephthah's daughter was the gracious one. Instead of blaming her father, she reassured him, comforted him. Then, having accepted her fate, she asked him for only one thing. That she could go away with her girlfriends for two months, during which time she could have a good cry over never being able to be married or have children, remaining forever unfulfilled and being the last of her father's line. Most Bible scholars agree that Jephthah's daughter was not sacrificed as a burnt offering but instead dedicated her life to serving the Lord. Either way, kudos to her for being able to accept things as graciously as she did.

It takes scads of pluck to go on with your life after someone else's actions irreversibly alter the course of it. And it takes a lot of grace not to be bitter or unforgiving to that change agent. May Jephthah's courageous daughter be the example you find you can someday follow.

Show me, Lord, how to exhibit grace, forgiveness, and courage when the actions of others alter my present, and perhaps future, walk on earth. In Jesus' name I pray. Amen.

GOD'S FORMULA FOR SUCCESS

This Book of the Law shall not depart out of your mouth, but you shall meditate on it day and night, that you may observe and do according to all that is written in it. For then you shall make your way prosperous. . .deal wisely and have good success.

JOSHUA 1:8 AMPC

Moses had died, leaving Joshua to lead the Israelites into the Promised Land. And Joshua was totally up for the challenge, ready to take on guiding God's people—the mantle that Moses turned over to him (see Deuteronomy 31:7–8) and God affirmed (see Joshua 1:1–4).

Joshua's attitude and acceptance of his new position, his determination to be totally committed to God and His plan, were already habitual with him. Now Joshua was ready to hear God's formula for success to aid him in his quest.

Woman, understand this: the same formula for success that God outlined for Joshua (in 1:5–9) is yours as well.

Be confident knowing that you'll never walk alone, for God promises, "I will be with you; I will not fail you or forsake you. . . . The Lord your God is with you wherever you go" (Joshua 1:5, 9 AMPC).

Be confident knowing that you can do whatever God is sending you out to do. He's constantly encouraging you in this area. God

says, "No man shall be able to stand before you all the days of your life. . . . You shall cause this people to inherit the land which I swore to their fathers" (Joshua 1:5–6 AMPC).

Be confident knowing that God wants you to be strong, unafraid, encouraged, and courageous. In fact, He commands you to be so, saying, "Be strong (confident) and of good courage. . . . Only you be strong and very courageous. . . . Have not I commanded you? Be strong, vigorous, and very courageous. Be not afraid, neither be dismayed" (Joshua 1:6–7, 9 AMPC).

And finally, be confident knowing that God wants His Word to be an intricate part of your life. For when it is, you'll not only be unafraid but prosperous. God says,

> *Do according to all the law which Moses My servant commanded you. . .that you may prosper wherever you go. This Book of the Law shall not depart out of your mouth, but you shall meditate on it day and night, that you may observe and do according to all that is written in it. For then you shall make your way prosperous, and then you shall deal wisely and have good success.*
>
> Joshua 1:7–8 AMPC

Lord, make me a woman successful in Your eyes. Help me follow Your Word and way as I answer Your call. Amen.

THREE NAMELESS WOMEN

Faith comes from hearing, and hearing through the word of Christ.
ROMANS 10:17 ESV

Three nameless women came to Jesus for healing. One had a fever. One had been bleeding for twelve years. One had been bent for eighteen years. And Jesus healed all three.

The woman with a high fever was Simon Peter's mother-in-law (see Luke 4:38–39). Because she had been bedridden for quite a while, her family asked Jesus to help her. He stood over her, touched her hand, and told her fever to leave. And it did! Immediately afterward, Jesus "took her by the hand and raised her up" (Mark 1:31 AMPC). Once out of bed, to show her gratitude and perhaps to demonstrate her newfound health, she began waiting on everyone.

The woman who had been bleeding for twelve years had spent all her money on doctors, but none of them had helped. Now she was stealthily approaching Jesus, thinking that if she could just touch His robe, she would be healed. She did and was! Immediately! But Jesus felt the power leaving Him. So He stopped in His tracks and asked who had touched Him. The woman confessed it was she. Instead of admonishing her, Jesus said, "Courage, daughter. You took a risk of faith, and now you're well" (Matthew 9:22 MSG).

The woman with the back that had been bent for eighteen years was in the synagogue when Jesus was teaching on the Sabbath.

Seeing her there, Jesus called her over and with love in His eyes, said, "Woman, you are freed from your disability" (Luke 13:12 ESV). Then, after He laid His hands on her, she instantly straightened up and began praising God!

Unfortunately, the ruler of the synagogue became angry. Jesus had once again broken the rules, this time by healing on the Sabbath. Jesus responded by calling him a hypocrite! For, chances are, the man would have helped a donkey to water on the Sabbath. So why not help this woman, someone who was, in Jesus' eyes, of more value than any animal.

The experiences of these three women should tell you three different things. First, Jesus values you. He longs to help and heal you, wants to get you back on your feet. Second, Jesus doesn't want you just to be sneaking up on Him when you're looking for help. He wants you to boldly call out to Him and tell Him exactly what you need, taking a risk of faith. Third, Jesus is on your side. He, the ultimate authority in heaven and earth, sticks up for you.

And because you, like these women, are valued, emboldened, and defended by Jesus, you need never fear!

In You I trust, Lord. Amen.

THE WOMAN UNSHAKEN NOT STIRRED

The woman came and told her husband, "A man of God came to me, and his appearance was like the appearance of the angel of God, very awesome. I did not ask him where he was from, and he did not tell me his name, but he said to me, 'Behold, you shall conceive and bear a son.' "

JUDGES 13:6–7 ESV

Many biblical women remain unnamed. One such was Manoah's wife, a.k.a, Samson's mother. Yet although she was nameless, she is not to be forgotten.

Manoah's wife was barren, but the angel of the Lord appeared to her and told her that God was going to make it possible for her to conceive and bear a child, a son. She was to be careful not to drink wine nor eat anything unclean. His hair was not to be shorn because her son was to be a Nazirite. And he would usurp the Philistines oppressing God's people.

After this angelic encounter, the woman ran to tell her husband, Manoah. But for some reason, he wasn't confident in exactly what he and his wife were to do. So Manoah prayed for this man of God to return and explain how they were to raise this child.

Having heard Manoah's prayer, the angel returned—not to Manoah but to his wife alone. She ran to get her husband, who returned with her. The angel repeated the same instructions He

had previously given to Manoah's wife, making it clear there was nothing more that Manoah needed to know.

When Manoah proposed and then made an offering, he realized the supernatural being was the angel of the Lord. Mr. and Mrs. Manoah fell to the ground. He then panicked, telling her, "We will die for sure. For we have seen God" (Judges 13:22 NLV). But his unshaken wife told him they would be fine. God apparently had other intentions.

Being Manoah's wife may not have been easy. It's apparent that she was the stronger of the two, calmer, more levelheaded, faith-filled, and knowledgeable of God. And God surely knew that, for it was to her alone that He initially appeared not once but twice.

Her role as Samson's mother may not have been easy either. Yet she did what she could, following God's instructions and giving Samson her best motherly advice, knowing there was a good chance he would ignore it.

Even though you may be known only as someone's mother, wife, or daughter, don't despair. Don't give up hope on playing a big part for God. He sees you, knows your potential, and has a plan for you alone. Simply remain content, confident, and unshakable as you wait, hope, and expect His direction.

Give me the unshakable faith, strength, wisdom, courage, and contentment of Mrs. Manoah, Lord, as I await Your words of instruction. Amen.

ESCAPE BY FAITH

By an act of faith, Rahab, the Jericho harlot, welcomed the spies and escaped the destruction that came on those who refused to trust God.

HEBREWS 11:31 MSG

For Rahab the prostitute, it was business as usual—until two Israelite spies walked into her inn. They'd been sent by Joshua to scout out Jericho. But having somehow gotten word about the spies, the king of Jericho sent some of his men to check things out. His message for Rahab was clear: "Send out the men that are spying on my land."

Rahab had already hidden the spies beneath some stalks of flax on the roof of her inn. Having taken that treasonable step, Rahab took things further by not just lying to the king's men but sending them on a wild goose chase, saying, "Yes, two men did come to me, but I didn't know where they'd come from. At dark, when the gate was about to be shut, the men left. But I have no idea where they went. Hurry up! Chase them—you can still catch them!" (Joshua 2:4–5 MSG).

Once the king's men were off and running, Rahab went back up to her roof and told the spies that she already knew God had given them the land and that the inhabitants of her land were feeling fearful and hopeless against the mighty power of the God who parted the Red Sea. Rahab then asked the spies for mercy

and a promise that when they came back to destroy the city, she and her family would be spared.

The spies pledged that she and her relatives would come out alive—*if* she promised to hang a red rope outside her window. Promises offered and accepted, Rahab then used the rope to lower the spies out of her home and down the city wall.

Weeks later, Joshua sent the two spies into the now wall-less Jericho, commanding them to bring out Rahab and her family. Once they'd been retrieved, the Israelites burned down the city. But Rahab was "still alive and well in Israel because she hid the agents whom Joshua sent to spy out Jericho" (Joshua 6:25 MSG).

This woman's faith and courage stood up against not only her king but her community. Because Rahab believed in God, shared her testimony, and acted on His behalf, she was not only saved but became an ancestor of David and Jesus (see Matthew 1:5–6).

No matter who you are or what you've done, God can use you *if* you have the courage to trust God and step outside your comfort zone.

Your strength and power are proven, dear God. So I bring myself before You. Use me, Lord. Show me how I can serve You, and then give me the confidence and courage to do so. Amen.

THE COURAGE OF ONE

Pilate's wife sent him a message: "Don't get mixed up in judging this noble man. I've just been through a long and troubled night because of a dream about him."

MATTHEW 27:19 MSG

Jesus had prayed intensely in the garden while Peter, John, and James dozed. While Jesus spoke to His followers, Judas betrayed Him with a kiss. As He was being arrested, His disciples fled.

With no human companion, the Son of Man was brought before the high priest and elders of the Jews, the chosen ones, His people. There Jesus was spit on, struck, slapped, and mocked. In the distance, Peter denied Him as the rooster crowed.

As morning dawned, Jesus, bound and sentenced to death, was delivered to the governor, Pontius Pilate. At the same time, Pilate's wife awakened, sweating, sheets in disarray, her countenance strained. She shook her head in an attempt to erase the dream from her mind, but she could not. She bit her lower lip, summoned her courage, then hurriedly wrote a note to her husband, hoping he would receive it in time.

Judas, regretting selling His Savior for silver, tried to right his wrong. But the chief priests and elders refused to stand down. They were out for blood—the blood of Jesus. Filled with remorse, Judas hanged himself.

Jesus, standing before Pilate, was asked, "Are you the King of

the Jews?" He responded, "You have said so" (Matthew 27:11 ESV). Thereafter He remained silent.

At Passover, Pilate usually set free the people's prisoner of choice. He now had a decision to make: release Jesus, who had been convicted on trumped-up charges or release the notorious criminal Barabbas. As Pilate pondered, he received a note from his wife. "Don't get mixed up in judging this noble man. I've just been through a long and troubled night because of a dream about him."

Pilate looked over the crowd. He asked who they wanted. Jesus. Fearing for his political future and perhaps his life, Pilate met their demand: he released Barabbas. Jesus was scourged and delivered to be crucified. Pilate washed his hands to show that he was innocent of Jesus' blood. But was he?

Jesus' disciples had deserted and betrayed Him. His Father's chosen people had refused and abused Him. There was only one nameless person who bravely stood out from the rest, for Jesus, attempting to save His life: Pilate's wife.

When you're called to stand up for the innocent, to do the right thing, to speak the truth, to follow what may be God's leading to help another person, may you have the courage of Pilate's wife.

Lord, when it's needed, give me the courage to stand out from the rest, to speak Your truth. Amen.

AN AMAZING PILEUP

"Today I will begin to exalt you in the sight of all Israel, so they will know that I will be with you just as I was with Moses. Command the priests carrying the ark of the covenant: When you reach the edge of the waters, stand in the Jordan."

JOSHUA 3:7–8 HCSB

Sometimes what God calls you to do may make absolutely no sense at all, at least in your mind. That's when your trust in God has to kick in. That's when you courageously need to step in (or out) in faith, keeping your eyes on Him alone.

To reach Jericho, Joshua had to lead his people across the Jordan River while it was at flood stage. And God's method of crossing sounded a bit. . .strange.

As God instructed, Joshua told the priests to go ahead of the people and carry the ark of the covenant into the Jordan. He then told the Israelites that when the priests went into the Jordan, they would "know that the living God is among [them]" (Joshua 3:10 HCSB). He would drive out before them all the current inhabitants of the Promised Land.

Joshua then said something that seemed a bit far-fetched: "When the feet of the priests who carry the ark of the LORD. . .come to rest in the Jordan's waters, its waters will be cut off. The water flowing downstream will stand up in a mass" (Joshua 3:13 HCSB).

So the priests carried the ark into the river. And, unbelievably,

as soon as the soles of their feet hit the water, the Jordan did indeed stand still! The water stopped flowing and rose up in a heap! "The priests carrying the ark of the LORD's covenant stood firmly on dry ground in the middle of the Jordan, while all Israel crossed on dry ground until the entire nation had finished crossing" (Joshua 3:17 HCSB)!

As soon as the ark-carrying priests came out of the Jordan and their feet hit solid ground, the river went back to its normal flood-stage flow. What a miracle!

Every person in this story—Joshua, the priests, and the Israelites—had to have courage to do what God commanded, no matter how crazy it sounded. Because they obeyed unafraid, God was able to give them a sure sign, to do what seemed impossible. All so the Israelites would know that He was with Joshua.

When God is with you, anything can happen. With Him by your side, you can achieve the seemingly unachievable. By faithfully following the living God's directives, you can overcome any obstacle. With trust in Him, you can be courageous and experience the impossible.

Lord, give me the courage I need so I can, by trusting You, experience the impossible. In Jesus' name I pray. Amen.

SPEAKING UP

Speak up for those who have no voice, for the justice of all who are dispossessed. Speak up. . . and defend the cause of the oppressed and needy.

PROVERBS 31:8–9 HCSB

It's safe to say that most people find it easier to listen than to speak. Yet speaking up is just what God wants you to do when it comes to people whose voices are not being heard. He wants you to speak up for and "defend the rights of the fatherless. Plead the widow's cause" (Isaiah 1:17 HCSB). God also wants you to speak up for His Son, to tell others about Him (see Matthew 10:18).

So God has made it clear that He wants you to speak on behalf of Him and the voiceless. You open your mouth, but your mind goes blank. You have nothing, no words. You begin to panic. Next thing you know, fear shuts your mouth. With bowed head, you slink away, embarrassed, your tail between your legs.

Look to God. Get it into your heart, soul, and mind that you need not fear these moments. Instead, remember Jesus' words: "Don't worry about how or what you should speak. For you will be given what to say at that hour, because you are not speaking, but the Spirit of your Father is speaking through you" (Matthew 10:19–20 HSCB).

You need not rehearse anything. Just believe that "the Holy Spirit will teach you at that very hour what must be said" (Luke

12:12 HCSB). After all, that's what God did for the disciples. After Peter and John healed a man who was lame from birth, they were arrested. The next day, before the Jewish leaders, they were asked, "By what power or in what name have you done this?" (Acts 4:7 HCSB). It was at that moment that "Peter was filled with the Holy Spirit" (Acts 4:8 HCSB). Then and only then did he speak, answering, in part, "By the name of Jesus Christ" (Acts 4:10 HCSB).

So when it comes time for you to speak up—for God, for the helpless, for the voiceless, for yourself—leave fear behind. Don't worry about how you will be judged, what you will say, or how people will receive your words. Instead, take some time in the moment to pray, asking God what He would have you say—or not say. Believe His promise, trusting His Spirit to fill your heart, head, and mouth with His words. Speak, if that's what you're to do, slowly and clearly. When the Spirit has completed His work through you, stop speaking. And leave the results of your words in the hands of God.

Fill me with Your words, Lord. Give me the courage to be Your mouthpiece, using the words of Your Spirit to speak for the voiceless. In Jesus' name I pray. Amen.

FROM DREAMS TO REALITY

Without faith it is impossible to please and be satisfactory to Him. For whoever would come near to God must [necessarily] believe that God exists and that He is the rewarder of those who earnestly and diligently seek Him [out].

HEBREWS 11:6 AMPC

Sometimes life circumstances can give you the feeling that nothing is or ever will go your way; each day is just one more battle for survival. And then there are people like Joseph. . . .

Joseph of the Old Testament had been sold by his brothers, forced into slavery, and then imprisoned in a dungeon for a crime he didn't commit. These circumstances must have seemed very far removed from the dreams of his youth that had revealed his eventual eminence, predicting that someday his brothers and father would bow to him.

Yet no matter how bad things got, Joseph never lost sight of the fact that God was with him and would reward him—if only he maintained the courage to hang on to that hope. And he did—to the point where he became the number two man in Egypt, second only to Pharaoh.

It was Joseph who saved his father and brothers from starvation. Yet Joseph never tried to take revenge against his brothers nor held a grudge (see Leviticus 19:18). Instead, he told them, "Don't be afraid. . . . You planned evil against me but God used

those same plans for my good. . .life for many people. Easy now, you have nothing to fear" (Genesis 50:19–21 MSG).

Perhaps you are still holding on to some dreams God has given you for your life, but nothing seems to be working out. Instead of getting closer to their realization, you seem to be drifting further away. If so, get closer to God. Look to see what you can do to please Him, make Him smile. Forgive those who need your forgiveness. Believe that God really does exist and that He will someday reward you as you seek Him and His ways, day after day. Keep your hope alive. Obey Him in all you do and say.

Take to heart the idea, the fact, the promise that God does indeed have thoughts and plans for you—plans for your good, ones that give you hope for your future (see Jeremiah 29:11). Add to that the promise that God is able to and will do so much more than you ever "ask or think through His power working" in you (Ephesians 3:20 NLV).

Help me, Lord, to be brave, to continue to hang on to my hope in You and the dreams You've given me, no matter how impossible they might seem. In Jesus' name I pray. Amen.

NO MATTER

Laugh and sing for joy. Sing hymns to God; all heaven, sing out; clear the way for the coming of Cloud-Rider. Enjoy GOD, cheer when you see him! Father of orphans, champion of widows, is God in his holy house. God makes homes for the homeless, leads prisoners to freedom.

PSALM 68:3–5 MSG

One of the many great and special things about God is that He promises to stick with you through thick and thin. He's always there to back you up, bail you out, and be your advocate. No matter what comes into your life, no matter what challenge rises up before you, no matter what obstacle stands between you and your needs and desires, you never have to fear that you're alone, abandoned, or defenseless.

When you lose a parent, your grief may seem unbearable. Gone is that unconditional love, safety net, and support a good parent provides. When something wonderful happens in your life—a new job, baby, or career opportunity—you'll pick up your phone to call your mom only to suddenly remember she's no longer there to share in the joy. Or perhaps you're finally prepared to say "I do" to the man of your dreams, but your daddy is no longer here to escort you down the aisle.

Maybe you're already married, but the "till death do you part" portion of your vow comes up before you expect it. Or maybe you're

in the process of losing the home you and your loved ones built together. Or perhaps you find yourself imprisoned by an addiction you cannot seem to shake.

All of these scenarios can be scary. Perhaps you have already suffered one or more of them and are unsure of how you will pick up the pieces or deal with the situation. The future looks like a deep, dark abyss.

Now here's the upside of all this. When you suffer the loss of a parent, you need not fear. God the Father is here to take up that role. If you're a widow, God will be your champion and Prince Charming. Wondering what you're going to do now that you have no home or have lost your freedom? No worries. God is going to provide both.

The point is that no matter what happens, God is with you. He "bears our burdens and carries us day by day" (Psalm 68:19 AMPC). God is all the strength you could ever need. And He is pouring that strength into you (see Psalm 68:34–35).

Thank You, Lord God, for always being where I need You. Continue giving me Your strength and support today and every day. Amen.

A SHOW OF TALENTS

"Well done, good and faithful slave! You were faithful over a few things; I will put you in charge of many things. Share your master's joy!"

MATTHEW 25:21 HCSB

In Matthew 25:14–30, Jesus told His followers the parable of the talents. He said a man was going on a journey and called in three servants, and in accordance with their abilities, he entrusted the first with five talents, the second with two, and the last with one.

After their master left town, the servant with five talents made five more. The one with two made two more. But the one with one talent buried it.

When the master returned, he called his servants in. The first two servants had doubled the talents he had left with them. To each of them he said, "You have done well. You are a good and faithful servant. You have been faithful over a few things. I will put many things in your care. Come and share my joy" (Matthew 25:21 NLV).

Then the servant who had been given one talent approached. Fearing he would not be able to please his master, the last servant found a good place to hide his one talent, ensuring his ability to return it to its original owner, which he now attempted to do. But this servant was *not* rewarded. Instead, the master told the servant he should have at least invested his talent so that when the master came back, he would have a little something more.

As a result, the last man was not only severely punished, but his one talent was taken from him and added to the first man's ten. "For," says Jesus, "the man who has will have more given to him. He will have more than enough" (Matthew 25:29 NLV).

Jesus made it clear that God has entrusted to each of His followers a particular talent, opportunity, or resource. And each is to be used to serve God and His people, not hidden or neglected. As poet and pastor Henry Van Dyke said, "Use what talents you possess; the woods would be very silent if no birds sang there except those that sang best."

Today is your day to gather up your courage and step out of your comfort zone. Consider what talents you may have been neglecting or what gifts, opportunities, or resources you have put on the back burner. Dust off that guitar. Join that nonprofit organization. Or go up into your attic and see what you have that might better the life of another.

Be faithful with what you have been given, and God will give you more.

Show me, Lord, how You would have me better use my gifts, talents, and resources for You. Amen.

WATCH AND PRAY

"Watch and pray so that you will not fall into temptation. The spirit is willing, but the flesh is weak."

MATTHEW 26:41 NIV

Tired. That one word describes so many of us at so many points in our lives. For some of us, it's a daily state of being. And no matter what walk of life we come from, we can all understand this feeling. The mother of the newborn infant is tired. The late-night bus driver is tired. The high-powered CEO with a company in financial stress is tired. The cafeteria worker doling out dollops of mashed potatoes to loud-mouthed elementary-school kids is tired. The teacher working two jobs is tired. The single dad trying to take care of his three young boys is tired. The refugee trying to sleep in a crowded tent is tired. The soldier standing guard is tired.

None of us is meant to live as a tired person day in and day out. When we are tired, we are in a weakened state. Often our brains don't function quite as well. Some studies have shown that driving tired is actually more dangerous than driving drunk. Our reflexes are sluggish when we are tired. Our thinking is clouded. Our feelings sometimes get out of control.

If you are tired, you may be tempted to do something you wouldn't otherwise want to do.

Jesus knew His friends were tired. It had already been a long, emotionally charged day. And here He was, their Savior and the

Son of God, telling them that He would soon be betrayed and that He was going to have to die. The disciples were confused. They stayed close to Jesus, trying to make sense of it all and perhaps even trying to protect Him.

Jesus wanted to have some words alone with His Father. But He also cherished this time with His friends. Peter and James and John went with Jesus as He walked farther into the garden. They saw the shadow of sorrow pass over Jesus' face. Jesus asked them to stay and keep watch with Him as He went to pray.

But when He came back, He found that His friends had fallen asleep. It wasn't surprising. Jesus woke them up. "Watch and pray." Even in this moment of His great sorrow, Rabbi Jesus stopped to instruct His friends in a lesson for life. He indicated that prayer was a way to stay alert and not let ourselves fall, unwittingly or otherwise, into one of our temptations. Prayer can keep us on our toes even when we are weary.

Are you tired? Are you struggling to stay close to Jesus? Watch and pray.

Jesus, I ask You to help me be strong even when I have no strength left. Amen.

KEEPING YOUR COOL

"You are going to hear of wars and rumors of wars. See that you are not alarmed, because these things must take place, but the end is not yet. For nation will rise up against nation, and kingdom against kingdom. There will be famines and earthquakes in various places. . . . Heaven and earth will pass away, but My words will never pass away."

MATTHEW 24:6–7, 35 HCSB

News these days can be depressing. Nations are fighting one another. Weather extremes are wreaking havoc. Children are going hungry. Drugs are rampant. You name it, it's happening. And it can all be pretty scary.

Yet more than two thousand years ago, Jesus proclaimed that as the time of His return approached, these things would be happening. So you can expect an increase in violent weather: winds, rain, dust storms, hurricanes, tornadoes, and earthquakes will be swirling around you and shaking the earth. Nations will be warring with one another, and rumors of war will abound. But through all this, Jesus wants you to remain calm, cool, and collected, confident that Father God has all things under control. So even though it seems as if the entire world is going haywire, you're not to worry or be frightened.

The weather and the world, people and politics may seem to be erratic, untenable, and out of control. But there are three

persons you can always count on to remain the same and be there for you: God the Father, Jesus the Son and Word, and the Holy Spirit.

So the next time you sit down in front of the TV to watch your favorite news anchor or go for a jog while listening to your favorite newscaster, unclench your teeth. Take a deep breath. Pray for the people and places in the news, asking God what, if anything, you can do to help. Consider what part you can play to make this world a better place.

Then spend some time planting some verses in your heart to help you cope and leave your worries and fears behind. Remember that although the material world may pass through your fingers, God and His Word will never fade away. God and His love are eternally yours. He will never leave you. Say to yourself, "Relax and rest" (Psalm 116:7 MSG). Someday there will be a new heaven and a new earth, and God will be there with you, wiping away every tear from your eyes. There will be no more pain or crying (see Revelation 21:1–4).

Thank You, Lord, for Your promise that You will never leave me, that through this world and into the next, You are with me, helping me to find the goodness in You and this land of the living. In Jesus' name I pray. Amen.

DWELLING IN THE SECRET PLACE

He who dwells in the secret place of the Most High shall remain stable and fixed under the shadow of the Almighty [Whose power no foe can withstand]. I will say of the Lord, He is my Refuge and my Fortress, my God; on Him I lean and rely, and in Him I [confidently] trust! . . . You shall not be afraid.

PSALM 91:1–2, 5 AMPC

The most important aspect of your life is hidden from all eyes but God's. It's there, as you dwell in that secret place of communion with Him, that you find the protection you need to move forward, amass the courage to face unknown dangers, and receive immunity from evil consequences. What a privilege to abide in the almighty God—the One "whose power no foe can withstand."

Your safety, through good times and bad, is found within God's presence. You must go to Him. You must believe in Him. Begin by saying to yourself, "He is my Refuge and my Fortress, my God; on Him I lean and rely, and in Him I [confidently] trust!" Repeat those words to yourself over and over. Believe them. Get them firmly fixed in your mind. Carve them into your heart so that when trouble comes, you'll remain unafraid, calm amid the storm, confident that God will hide and protect you. Only within that secret place in Christ will you find the safety you crave.

God, your heavenly Protector, will cover you with His wings. Because of His presence, because He's your refuge, you need not

be afraid of anything, for nothing untoward can touch you. And it's not just God who is looking out for you. He's giving His angels orders to make sure you don't fall flat on your face!

Why is God doing all this for you? Because you love Him (see Psalm 91:14). That's why He's rescuing you from dangers seen and unseen. It's because you take the time to learn about Him, to understand Him, to know Him. You trust Him, relying on Him for everything from your breakfast to your dinner, from your job to your health. That's why, when you call on God, He answers you. That's why He sticks by you in times of trouble when others desert you. God is constantly watching, waiting, and helping, ever ready to beam you up into His arms, out of harm's way, above the fray.

Because of God, "You shall not be afraid."

Oh Most High, how wonderful to be in this secret place with You, my Refuge and Fortress. On You only do I lean. In You I trust. Because of You, I am not afraid. Amen.

THE ROAD HOME

Go, return each of you to her mother's house. May the Lord deal kindly with you, as you have dealt with the dead and with me. The Lord grant that you may find a home and rest, each in the house of her husband!

RUTH 1:8–9 AMPC

In the days of judges, when everyone did as they pleased (see Judges 21:25), Naomi lived in Bethlehem with her husband and two sons. To escape the famine there, the family went to Moab, where Naomi's husband died. Then her sons died, childless.

Hearing the famine in Judah was over, Naomi determined to return to Bethlehem. So she left Moab, her two Moabite daughters-in-law beginning the fifty-mile journey with her. . .on foot. . .through the wilderness.

Suddenly, Naomi stopped to tell Ruth and Orpah to go back home to their mothers. Then she prayed the Lord's blessing on the young widows, asking God to deal as kindly with them as they'd dealt with not just her but her sons. She asked the Lord to help the women find true rest and security in the homes of new husbands who could protect and provide for them.

After Naomi kissed them, the young widows began crying, refusing to leave her. So Naomi changed tactics. With a bit of tough love, she told her daughters-in-law they might as well go back home. "Even if I thought there was still hope for me to have

a husband tonight and to bear sons, would you be willing to wait for them to grow up?" (Ruth 1:12–13 HCSB).

Much has been said about Naomi. How she wanted Ruth and Orpah to leave her because they were reminders of all the mistakes she and her family had made by traveling to a pagan land. How she had gone to Moab with so much and was now going home empty-handed.

Yet one cannot help admiring this feisty, stubborn, mournful, strong, critical, and homeless widow. How unafraid she was to walk back home alone through the wilderness. And how even though she had felt as if God had deserted her, still she prayed for Him to take care of and bless her daughters-in-law. Although Naomi saw no future for herself, she requested a good future for them.

You may have times when you make mistakes and feel a bit bitter that life has treated you unfairly. But even during those times, may you have the courage to continue to be a loving example for younger women trying to find their own way home in the Lord.

Lord, help me to be a blessing to the women I meet on the road to my home in You. Amen.

EYES OF HOPE AND FAITH

Let us. . .throw aside every encumbrance (unnecessary weight) and that sin which so readily (deftly and cleverly) clings to and entangles us, and let us run with patient endurance. . .the appointed course of the race that is set before us, looking away [from all that will distract] to Jesus, Who is the Leader and the Source of our faith.

HEBREWS 12:1–2 AMPC

On His way to Jerusalem, where He would celebrate His final Passover and then be crucified, Jesus performed His last miracle of healing while on earth.

As Jesus was heading out of Jericho with His disciples and a crowd of followers, the blind Bartimaeus sat on the side of the road begging. He heard the healer Jesus was passing by. So Bartimaeus began yelling, "Jesus, Son of David, have pity on me!"

Some people told the blind man to be quiet. But the more they shushed Bartimaeus, the louder he yelled for Jesus to have mercy on him.

Then Jesus, the Son of God, on His way to being betrayed, deserted, beaten, and crucified, stopped. He told His followers to call the blind man. So they shouted out to Bartimaeus, "Take courage! Get up! He is calling you" (Mark 10:49 AMPC).

After throwing his coat off his shoulders, Bartimaeus jumped up and ran to Jesus.

Jesus, with His compassion and empathy, asked him, "What do you want Me to do for you?" (Mark 10:51 AMPC). Bartimaeus replied, "Teacher, I want you to give me sight."

Jesus said, "Go, . . .your faith has healed you" (Mark 10:52 NIV). At that very moment, Bartimaeus could see and began following Jesus down the road.

Author Elizabeth Gilbert said, "Faith is belief in what you cannot see or prove or touch. Faith is walking face-first and full-speed into the dark." Bartimaeus could not see, but he did believe. He had an unshakable faith in Jesus. And his persistence in calling Jesus paid off, stopping Jesus in His tracks. Those who had tried to silence him now encouraged him to be brave.

So Bartimaeus threw off his coat. Now free of any entanglements, unnecessary weights, the blind man flew to his Lord. He told Jesus exactly what he wanted—his sight—and gained it. Jesus' power and Bartimaeus's persistent faith had healed him.

Be as this blind man. Take courage. Throw away the unnecessaries, the distractions, the entanglements. Then walk face-first and at full speed to Jesus, keeping your eyes of hope and faith on Him.

Jesus, my Lord, help me to have no fear when I cry and You answer. Then may Your amazing power and my persistent faith work together to make a miracle. Amen.

LIKE A TREE

"But blessed is the one who trusts in the LORD, whose confidence is in him."

JEREMIAH 17:7 NIV

The pear trees grew golden as the air changed. Their fruit, filled with sweet goodness, swung heavy on the branches. When the winds blew in the late summer storm, the leaves held on for dear life—determined to finish their fuel-producing cycle before they gave up and began to fall. The trees stood tall and strong, with branches curving gracefully to the sky. Their roots grabbed tightly to the ground, spreading out and reaching for the nearby stream for refreshment. Year after year, the trees had grown and provided fruit for anyone who visited the farm. And year after year, their beauty blessed everyone who saw them.

But a few fields away, a once-beautiful pear tree stood on an abandoned estate. It had been planted in a container so it could be placed in a particular spot according to the grand design of the owner. Its growth had been stunted as a result. Then, when the owner's fortunes turned and he was no longer able to maintain the large gardens, he packed up the few belongings he could still call his own and went on his way, leaving all his beautiful plants to fend for themselves. It took only a few months for most of the estate to become an overgrown wilderness, and the poor trees and other plants in containers, without access to water (as the

season was a dry one), began to shrivel and bend themselves in grotesque curves.

So it goes with our hearts. As the Lord told the prophet Jeremiah, those who put their trust mainly in humankind—whose hearts turn away from the Lord and who depend on people for fulfillment and happiness—will not be strong but instead will suffer like bushes in a barren wasteland. Empty promises will disappoint such people, and they won't find solid ground in which to plant their hopes. There will be no steady source of food and refreshment for them, and thus they will be unable to bear fruit—to produce the kind of growth and behaviors that are needed to do good for others and for themselves.

But those who put their roots deep into the foundation of faith, hope, and love that the Lord provides us will have endurance and perseverance. Even when drought comes and hard times make it difficult to push through, their relationship with the Lord will help them be strong and confident. And they will never fail to bear good fruit.

Lord, thank You for being a never-ending source of refreshment and strength for me. Amen.

THE PROVIDER

So, my very dear friends, don't get thrown off course. Every desirable and beneficial gift comes out of heaven. The gifts are rivers of light cascading down from the Father of Light. There is nothing deceitful in God, nothing two-faced, nothing fickle.

JAMES 1:16–17 MSG

In this world, there are givers and there are takers. Jesus is a *major* giver.

C. S. Lewis said, "When we lose one blessing, another is often most unexpectedly given in its place." And that's what happened in Jesus' final moments.

After being scourged, beaten, and adorned with a crown of thorns, Jesus bore His cross to Golgotha. There He was crucified with a thief on either side. Above His head was a sign reading, The King of the Jews. By His cross stood four women: Mary, His mother; Mary's sister; Mary, the wife of Clopas; and Mary Magdalene.

Since Jesus' initial arrest, ten disciples had fled, and the disciple-betrayer Judas had killed himself. Only one disciple remained standing nearby: John.

Knowing His mother must be provided for, Jesus caught sight of Mary as well as John. He said, "[Dear] woman, See, [here is] your son! Then He said to the disciple, See, [here is] your mother! And from that hour, the disciple took her into his own [keeping, own home]" (John 19:26–27 AMPC).

Seeing her Son endure so much physical and emotional pain must have been torturous for Mary. When Jesus finally gave up the ghost, her grief must have been stifling. Yet when her grieving time ended, Mary most likely did not despair. For God had chosen an amazing woman to play a major role in His grand plan. This woman-child had the courage to birth then bring up God's one and only Son, to help guard and guide Him in His life on earth.

Mary was as courageous in the end as she had been at the beginning, for her Son had not neglected her. With His final breath, Jesus gave His mother another gift: a new home and a new "son" to provide for her.

Just as Jesus was there for His mother, He's here for you. Because you are a believer, a daughter of God the King, you will lack for nothing. Ever. So do not fear. Jesus has His eyes on you. He knows exactly what you need and will provide it exactly when you need it. Until then, continue to have courage and faith. Release your worries to God. And when you lose one blessing, keep your eyes open for the unexpected blessing that will take its place.

Lord, thank You for being my Provider on earth and in heaven. Because You are in my life, I know I will never, ever lack. Amen.

A FULL REWARD

"Where you go I will go, and where you lodge I will lodge.
Your people shall be my people, and your God my God.
Where you die I will die, and there will I be buried."

RUTH 1:16–17 ESV

The determined Naomi persuaded one daughter-in-law, Orpah, to go back to her mother's house in Moab. But she couldn't seem to get rid of the other, Ruth, the one who kept holding on to her, the woman as stubborn and determined as Naomi herself.

Ruth told Naomi that she was going wherever her mother-in-law was headed, that Naomi's people and God would be hers as well, and that wherever Naomi died, Ruth would die and be buried there with her. As far as Ruth was concerned, she and her mother-in-law were in a till-death-do-we-part relationship from here on in. So, Naomi, seeing that she wasn't going to change Ruth's mind, gave in. And the two women traveled through the wildness on their way to Bethlehem.

Upon their arrival, Naomi revealed her mindset to a crowd of women she once knew. She told them that because she left with so much and was now returning with so little, they should no longer call her Naomi, which means "pleasant," but Mara, which means "bitter." She confided, "The All-powerful has allowed me to suffer" (Ruth 1:21 NLV). Talk about a Debbie Downer! Negative Naomi truly seemed to believe she had no assets, no love, nothing

good in this life.

Meanwhile, we begin to see the error of Naomi's glass-half-empty mindset. For she did have one major asset, a huge blessing: Ruth. We see her courage to come to a land and live among strangers, her fortitude as she strived to find a way to feed, house, and otherwise support not only herself but her somewhat depressed (as well as depressing) mother-in-law.

Ruth's behavior and dedication to Naomi prompted the young widow's future husband to bless her, saying, "The LORD repay you for what you have done, and a full reward be given you by the LORD, the God of Israel, under whose wings you have come to take refuge!" (Ruth 2:12 ESV). And God did bless Ruth, providing her with a new husband and Naomi with a grandson from whom Jesus was descended.

When you are certain of God's path for you, have the courage to walk it. Be determined to take that narrow, least-traveled path. And take refuge where needed.

Under Your wings, Lord, I take refuge. Give me the courage of Ruth as I seek to walk Your way. Amen.

WHAT DO YOU WISH?

When Achsah came to Othniel, she got his consent to ask her father for a field. Then she returned to Caleb and when she lighted off her donkey, Caleb said, What do you wish? Achsah answered, Give me a present. Since you have set me in the [dry] Negeb, give me also springs of water.

JOSHUA 15:18–19 AMPC

In Numbers 13–14, ten of Moses' twelve spies came back shaking in their boots, telling him there was no way they could defeat the giants living in the Promised Land. But the other two spies, Caleb and Joshua, believed that with God's help they could successfully invade the land. Unfortunately, the people believed the report of the ten cowardly over the brave two. Because of their faithlessness, God sentenced His people to wander in the desert for forty years.

At the end of those forty years, only two men from the generation of wanderers were left to enter the Promised Land—Caleb and Joshua. So, when Joshua began dividing up the land, Caleb reminded him of their common history. How even though "my brothers who went up with me made the heart of the people weak with fear," he (Caleb) had "followed the Lord my God with all my heart" (Joshua 14:8 NLV). And because he had done so, Moses promised him a portion of land, a promise Joshua fulfilled.

Later, in the process of clearing his new land of unwanted residents, Caleb pledged to give his daughter Achsah in marriage

to whatever man captured Kiriath-sepher. The man who did so was Caleb's nephew Othniel.

Enter the cleverness and courageousness of the newly wed Achsah, a woman who found a way to prosper in the patriarchal society of her day. Just like her father, Caleb, she had no trouble speaking up. First Achsah asked Caleb for a field, which he granted her. Then, realizing how dry the field was, Achsah returned and asked her father for springs that could water that field. And Caleb once more granted her request.

The brave Achsah received what she and her family needed because she asked for it (see James 4:2). She took her courage and cleverness in hand and did what she could within the limits of the era in which she lived.

Perhaps there is something you need but have yet to ask for. If so, take some time to consider what you have and evaluate what you need. Then gather up your courage and ask God, knowing that if you do so, you will receive (see Matthew 7:7).

Father God, give me wisdom to figure out what I need and courage to ask for what I lack. Amen.

COAXED TO COURAGE

Some men brought to [Jesus] a paralytic lying on a mat. Seeing their faith, Jesus told the paralytic, "Have courage, son, your sins are forgiven. . . . Get up, pick up your mat, and go home." And he got up and went home. . . . Jesus turned and saw her. "Have courage, daughter," He said. "Your faith has made you well." And the woman was made well from that moment.

MATTHEW 9:2, 6–7, 22 HCSB

After preaching the Sermon on the Mount, Jesus ministered to the sick and demon-possessed. He performed some miracles on site, others long distance.

Awhile later, Jesus, pressed by the crowd, led His disciples to a boat so they could cross to the other side of the Sea of Galilee. Exhausted, He fell asleep. His followers, alarmed by a storm, woke Him, and He calmed the winds and waves. Ashore once more, Jesus cast demons out of two men then crossed back over the water with His disciples, landing in Capernaum.

They "were hardly out of the boat when some men carried a paraplegic on a stretcher and set him down in front of them" (Matthew 9:1–2 MSG). Jesus had preached, taught, healed, exorcised, and demonstrated His power over nature. And now, the minute His feet touched the shore, some men unceremoniously dropped a paraplegic at His feet.

The man was obviously somewhat frightened to be so abruptly

put before Jesus. But Jesus knew just what the man needed. The first words out of His mouth were words of encouragement and companionability. He told the man to "have courage" and called him His "son." Then Jesus gave the man what He needed, forgiveness of sins and healing of mind and body.

After healing this man, Jesus called Matthew to follow Him, answered questions about fasting, and received a request from a local ruler whose daughter needed healing.

As Jesus was traveling to the ruler's house, a woman who had been bleeding for twelve years touched Jesus' hem, saying to herself, "If I can just touch His robe, I'll be made well!" (Matthew 9:21 HCSB). Jesus turned. She, an unclean woman who had touched the Healer, trembled in fear. Yet Jesus did not reprimand her. Instead, once more He exuded encouragement and affection, saying, "Have courage, daughter. . . . Your faith has made you well." And in that moment, the woman was healed.

No matter where you are in your walk with God, no matter how you approach Jesus, brazenly or beggarly, He will not only heal you but, upon your approach, will put you at ease with words of encouragement and affection.

Lord, thank You for being ready, willing, and able to help me, no matter how I approach or where I am in my faith walk with You. Amen.

A RISK OF FAITH

[The woman who had been sick for twelve years with a flow of blood] told Jesus in front of all the people why she had touched Him. She told how she was healed at once. Jesus said to her, "Daughter, your faith has healed you. Go in peace."

LUKE 8:47–48 NLV

For twelve years, this woman who came to Jesus had an "issue of blood" (Matthew 9:20 KJV). For more than a decade, her menstrual period continued on and on, making her unclean, an outcast, unable to go into the woman's court at the temple. She lived on the edge of society, weak, helpless, and now poor because she had spent all her money looking for a cure from doctors but getting no relief. Truth be told, her condition had gotten worse not better.

She had heard about this amazing healer named Jesus, and she was determined to be healed, to find her way through the crowd. She told herself, "If I can just touch His robe, I'll be made well!" (Matthew 9:21 HCSB). Finally, she made her way to Jesus. As she reached out and touched His robe, she instantly felt her blood flow stop.

Yet she was not able to quietly slink away, for Jesus knew power had coursed out of Him. He stopped and turned and asked, "Who touched my robe?" as he scanned the faces in the crowd.

Finally, the woman healed of the issue of blood fell down trembling before Jesus. She told Him her story. Feeling shame

mingled with fear, she publicly revealed her condition. She told how she, an unclean woman, had entered the crowd and touched the Rabbi and how, in doing so, she had been cured. Then Jesus, lovingly, gently, assured her: "Courage, daughter. You took a risk of faith, and now you're well" (Matthew 9:22 MSG).

This account is unique. Here we meet the only woman Jesus addressed as "daughter." Here, in a society where women were the silent majority, Jesus prompted a woman to publicly tell her story. Here, in this account only, we read of Jesus feeling power leaving Him.

Just as this story is unique, so is every woman. Each woman has a unique issue she's dealing with. Yet each female follower can take comfort and strength from the fact that she has a loving Savior who considers her His daughter and wants her to recognize Him as her true Healer. One who wants her to take courage, take a risk of faith, reach out and touch Him, and tap into His power—and to share her story of transformation.

Jesus, I am once more amazed at the love You have for me, the concern You show for my issues. Fill me with courage, Lord. Help me, Your daughter, to take a risk of faith for You. Amen.

GOING DEEPER

Be not afraid. . .for I am with you. . . . I am alert and active, watching over My word to perform it. . . . Jesus came and touched them and said, Get up, and do not be afraid.

JEREMIAH 1:8, 12; MATTHEW 17:7 AMPC

Throughout His Word, God makes you myriad promises. He says He'll never leave you. He'll fight your battles. He'll be your Shepherd, and you'll never lack. He'll lead you to green pastures, give you rest beside still waters. He'll give you comfort, help, love, and guidance. In times of stress, He'll give you peace and rest. He'll give you wisdom when you're confused. When you have concerns, He'll keep you calm. When you are in the midst of a storm, He'll still the waves and wind. When you don't know what to say, God will give you the right words. If you ask, He'll answer. If you pray, He'll respond. If you speak, He'll listen. If you hurt, He'll heal. If you're weak, He'll strengthen. Do you believe God? Do you trust Him to do all these things and more?

If you find yourself afraid to go forward, to obey and honor God, to get out of your comfort zone, to walk where He would have you go, to say what He would have you speak, to help whom He would have you help, chances are you're doubting God's Word, His promises, power, and commitment to you as His beloved daughter.

If you do have any doubts about what God promised to do in your life, it's time to go deeper into not only His presence but

His Word. And to do so sentence by sentence, phrase by phrase, word by word.

In today's verses, God tells you to "be," to stand, to stay, to remain in a certain state. And that state is "not afraid." Why should you not be afraid? Because God is with you. But that's not all. His eyes are wide open, keeping track of everything that's going on within and around you. God is "alert and active, watching over" His Word. Why? To ensure that His "Word is completed" (Jeremiah 1:12 NLV). God says, "I'll make every word I give you come true" (Jeremiah 1:12 MSG).

To ensure that these facts are anchored in your heart, take some time to let these verses sink in today. Close your eyes, lean back, and hear God speaking His Word in that voice reserved just for you. Then imagine God's Son touching you, speaking to your heart of hearts, saying, "Get up, and do not be afraid."

Speak to me, Lord. Help me to take Your words to heart then to rise up in Your strength and courage. In Jesus' name I pray. Amen.

THROUGH FAITH

It was not through the law that Abraham and his offspring received the promise that he would be heir of the world, but through the righteousness that comes by faith.

ROMANS 4:13 NIV

In this text from Romans, Paul is referring to and reflecting on Abraham. Before the eyes of the world, Israel is the chosen people; Israel lives according to the law handed down from God by Moses. But something happened long before that, Paul teaches, that must be attended to. Long before the handing down of the law, there was a covenant between man and God; that man was Abraham. The first great promise that had been made by God with man and fulfilled was not the promise of the Promised Land, but the covenant made with Abraham. It was Abraham, wandering the earth, whose progeny went on to become the nation of Israel.

How is it that Abraham found favor with God? What virtue did he possess? Abraham had faith in God; he believed God and His promise. Accordingly, Paul teaches, the righteousness and justification that accrue to Abraham are due solely to that faith; or as Paul has it in other words, "Faith was credited to him as righteousness" (Romans 4:9 NIV). When did the birth of that faith occur? Paul tells us it occurred before the law was handed down; before the sign of circumcision came to be; and before his line was begun.

There is little doubt that Israel becomes the light of nations and does so through the law. However, Paul wants to emphasize that the covenant with Abraham comes well before the law, so that his righteousness comes through something else—not through words written down on tablets, or through animal sacrifices, or along with signs and wonders. God speaks, and Abraham believes. Indeed, it is that kind of faith that Paul wants to emphasize in the relationship of the believer with Jesus. For Paul, our inheritance from Abraham is not about being a nation that follows the law; it is all about being people who follow the Lord.

Paul's teaching attempts to preserve the righteousness of Abraham that was due solely to his faith; he teaches the followers of Jesus that there is a like righteousness that is due to them solely on account of their faith in Jesus. Those who persevere in believing in Jesus as the Son of God and in His resurrection will be credited with righteousness. And so we enter into a new covenant with the same God who spoke to Abraham under the same stars that shine on us now, and we listen for where God will send us.

Lord, I know my faith is the only thing that gets me through my days sometimes. Please increase my faith. Amen.

A CLOSE CALL

Hide not Your face from me in the day when I am in distress! Incline Your ear to me; in the day when I call, answer me speedily. . . . Have pity and compassion. . . . He will regard the plea of the destitute and will not despise their prayer.

PSALM 102:2, 13, 17 AMPC

Have you ever felt so removed from God that You couldn't feel His presence? That at some point you had gotten so distracted by other things and wandered so far off that you weren't sure how to get back?

In those horrifying moments when you can't seem to connect with God, don't fear. Instead, take to heart the words of writer Neva Coyle: "In those times I can't seem to find God, I rest in the assurance that He knows how to find me."

Hmm. God knows how to find you. Let's see if we can back that up.

God is with us even if. . .we're in a dungeon, like Joseph; floating in a basket, like Moses; wandering in the wilderness, like the Israelites; amid the crowd, like the woman with the issue of blood; hiding in a cave, like David; running to the desert, like Elijah; hidden in a palace bedroom then the temple, like baby Joash; in the midst of battle, like Deborah; in a harem, like Esther; in a foreign country, like Ruth; in a relative stranger's tent, like Rebekah; in a marriage with one husband and three other wives,

like Leah; in a pit, like Jeremiah; grieving in an ash heap, like Job; in a congregation, like the woman with the crooked back; amid the tombs, like the demon-possessed man; afloat on a boat, like Noah; in the belly of a big fish, like Jonah; amid the flames like Meshach, Shadrach, and Abednego; in the lions' den, like Daniel.

Know that wherever you go, whatever the circumstances, time, or place, God is with you. He hears your prayers. He knows your fears. He is with you, helping you, guiding you. You only need to trust that He's doing so—right now. You only need to lift your head, open your eyes, and look around you. Seek His face. Whisper into His ear. As pastor and author A. W. Tozer wrote, "We need never shout across the spaces to an absent God. He is nearer than our own soul, closer than our most secret thoughts."

There are so many ways You bless me, Lord.
Thank You for being nearer than I ever thought
imaginable, so close when I call. Amen.

THE HELPLESS AND THE HEALER

People came from the synagogue leader's house and said, "Your daughter is dead. Why bother the Teacher anymore?" But when Jesus overheard what was said, He told the synagogue leader, "Don't be afraid. Only believe."

MARK 5:35–36 HCSB

What do you do when all seems lost—including your courage?

Jairus was a synagogue leader. He had money, status, influence, and power, as well as a wonderful wife and a delightful daughter, both of whom he loved very much. But then, because no one is immune from heartache, something happened to turn this man's world upside down. His little daughter lay dying. His wife stayed by her side, feeling helpless, praying her husband's mission to Jesus would be successful, waiting for some word to come from Jairus before it was too late, hoping for some help, some remedy, some miracle.

Frantic to find the only One who could help his daughter, Jairus, now breathless, finally reached Jesus and threw himself down at His feet. He began pleading for his child's life: "My little daughter is almost dead. Come and put Your hand on her that she may be healed and live" (Mark 5:23 NLV).

Jesus said nothing, just began to follow the anxious Jairus home. The crowd around Him was growing, beginning to press in upon Him. It was then that He felt power leaving Him. He stopped

and asked who touched Him. Almost immediately some woman threw herself at His feet.

Jairus was wondering, *What's going on? Doesn't the Healer know time is of the essence?* They needed to hurry, or soon his little girl would be gone forever!

Moments later, one of Jairus's servants came to tell Jairus that his daughter had died. It was too late. Why bother the Teacher about it now? Jairus's heart sank. Tears flooded his eyes. And then, through his whirling thoughts, Jairus heard Jesus say five words—"Don't be afraid. Only believe"—words Jairus clung to as he found his way home.

Jairus, Jesus, Peter, James, and John arrived at the synagogue leader's home. All around them people were weeping and wailing. Jesus told them to stop—the little girl wasn't dead. She was only sleeping.

They laughed and made fun of Him. Jesus put them all out of the house. He then took Mr. and Mrs. Jairus, along with His three disciples, up to the little girl's room. As the parents tried to hold it together, determined not to be afraid but to believe, Jesus took their little girl's hand and told her to rise. And she did.

When you're feeling helpless, hopeless, and hapless, Jesus has five words He wants you to remember, to repeat, to write on your heart and mind: "Don't be afraid. Only believe."

When I feel helpless, Lord, help me not to be afraid. But to only believe. Amen.

AGAINST ALL ODDS

And Deborah arose and went with Barak to Kedesh. . . .
The villages were unoccupied and rulers ceased in Israel
until you arose—you, Deborah, arose—a mother in Israel.

JUDGES 4:9; 5:7 AMPC

Deborah had a lot of obstacles to overcome. First, she was a woman living in a patriarchal society. Men had many more rights than women, who were considered their property, mere chattel. Men typically ruled the day—and the nights.

Second, Deborah performed roles normally performed by men. In Judges 4:4 she is described as a prophet, a wife, and a judge. Later Deborah is revealed to be a fierce and brave warrior, a singer, and a *mother* in Israel, whose patience and trust in God led her to defeat an enemy against all odds.

For twenty years, God's people had been oppressed by Jabin, king of Canaan, and his army commander, Sisera. So the Israelites cried out to God, distressed by Jabin's nine hundred chariots of iron.

Up rose Deborah, ready to go into battle with her commander, Barak, who would not face the enemy without her. Once they got to Mount Tabor, she had Barak patiently wait until Sisera had gathered together his army. Then, with a heart, mind, spirit, and soul full of faith, she encouraged Barak, saying, "Up! For this is the day in which the LORD has given Sisera into your hand. Does not the LORD go out before you?" (Judges 4:14 ESV). And as it turned out, the

Lord had indeed gone out before Barak, pouring rain down upon the enemy army, bogging down the nine hundred iron chariots, transforming the enemy's assets into major liabilities, allowing Barak and his Israelites to annihilate the entire army except for one man: Jabin's chariot commander, Sisera. But even this man was later killed by a woman.

Like Deborah, you too are a woman who may have many obstacles to overcome. Like Deborah, you too may find yourself having to rise up, to become more courageous, to be a fierce warrior, as well as a fair judge, a fearless leader, and a good wife and mother.

In your quest to do as God wills, to live and lead as God calls you to, trust God to show you the way. Be patient as you wait for His direction. Then rise up quickly when He says the time is right, encouraging those you're leading. But most of all, remember that God is going before you. He is already transforming your enemy's assets into liabilities, clearing your path to victory.

Thank You, Lord, for always being with me. Help me to lead as You would have me lead, to go when You would have me go, to be who You would have me be. In Jesus' name I pray. Amen.

CALM, COOL, AND COLLECTED

The Lord is my light and the One Who saves me. Whom should I fear? The Lord is the strength of my life. Of whom should I be afraid? . . . Even if an army gathers against me, my heart will not be afraid. . . . I will be sure of You.

PSALM 27:1, 3 NLV

The level of calm you possess does not depend just on your trust and confidence in God. It also depends on your perspective.

In the verses above, David's words clearly reveal that he sees his world and his circumstances through God's eyes. Envisioning and trusting that God was by his side, David feared nothing. Because he knew he was walking with the Creator of the world, certain of His love, power, and protection, David could say, "When besieged, I'm calm as a baby. When all hell breaks loose, I'm collected and cool" (Psalm 27:3 MSG).

Just like David, his predecessors, Joshua and Caleb, also saw things from a heavenly perspective. When Moses sent them and ten others to spy out the Promised Land, he received two different reports. Although all agreed the land flowed with milk and honey, ten of the twelve spies said, "But the people who live in the land are strong. . . . All the people we saw in it are very large. . . . We looked like grasshoppers in our own eyes, and we looked the same to them" (Numbers 13:28, 32–33 NLV).

Yet Joshua and Caleb saw things differently, saying, "If the

Lord is pleased with us, then He will bring us into this land and give it to us. . . . Only do not go against the Lord. And do not be afraid of the people of the land. For they will be our food. They have no way to keep safe, and the Lord is with us. Do not be afraid of them" (Numbers 14:8–9 NLV).

Hearing this, the Israelites wanted to stone Joshua and Caleb. The only thing or person that stayed their hands was God, who came down in all His glory to annihilate His people. But because of Moses' intercession, God rescinded their death sentence. Their sole punishment would be never reaching the Promised Land they'd refused to enter.

Endeavor to see things from God's perspective every day. Know that no matter how great the danger is, you need not be afraid for God is with you. He's the stronghold, the refuge your heart seeks and your spirit longs for. No matter who comes against you, you're safe in the Lord's hands.

Because You're with me, Lord, I know I need never be afraid. Help me, my Protector, to see all things through Your eyes. In Jesus' name I pray. Amen.

TRAPPED IN DISCOURAGEMENT

I will be to you a God; and you shall know that it is I, the Lord your God, Who brings you out from under the burdens of the Egyptians. . . . Moses told this to the Israelites, but they refused to listen to Moses because of their impatience and anguish of spirit and. . .cruel bondage.

EXODUS 6:7, 9 AMPC

Four hundred years after Joseph's death, the Israelites living in Egypt had grown in number and unpopularity. Instead of looking at them as an asset to his country, Pharaoh considered them a threat to his people. So, to keep the Hebrew population down, Pharaoh ordered that their baby boys be killed at birth. And he forced God's people into slave labor.

In response to His people's cries and cruel treatment under Pharaoh, God sent Moses and Aaron to Egypt. During their first meeting, Moses asked Pharaoh to let the Israelites go away for three days to worship their Lord, but Pharaoh refused. To make matters worse, he then commanded the Hebrews' foremen to no longer give their workers any straw with which to make bricks. Yet the taskmasters were to require the same quota of bricks be made. Now the Hebrews had to gather their own straw, making their work even more onerous.

In response to their new duties, the Israelites came back to Moses, blaming him for increasing their fears as well as their

workload. In turn, a discouraged Moses went to God, asking Him, "Why did you ever send me? From the moment I came to Pharaoh to speak in your name, things have only gotten worse for this people" (Exodus 5:22–23 MSG).

So God told Moses to give His people a message: "You'll soon know Me as the God who, with power and might, rescued you from slavery in Egypt." Moses relayed God's words. But the people were so bowed down, so tired, overworked, frightened, discouraged, and dispirited that they didn't even listen to him.

Perhaps you can relate. Perhaps there have been moments in your own life when you were feeling oppressed, discouraged, overworked, tired, frightened. You were so busy trying just to survive that you felt you had no time for anything or anyone. Your life was joyless, filled with groans, moans, and heavy sighs.

Although tough life experiences are inevitable for most of us, each person does have a choice as to how she or he is going to live through them. You can choose to have courage or be discouraged, to focus on your problems or God's promises.

No matter how dark your circumstances, choose to remain confident that God is with you. That His light, love, and compassion are streaming down upon you. That He will rescue you with His might and miracles.

Help me keep my eyes on Your promises
and protections, Lord. Amen.

CALMER OF THE STORM

Immediately [Jesus] spoke with [His disciples] and said, "Have courage! It is I. Don't be afraid."

MARK 6:50 HCSB

Just when you think you can't take it anymore, that you're all alone, that your courage has not just waned but has become nonexistent, God shows up. He opens your eyes to His presence, love, strength, power, and peace.

All through the Bible there are numerous instances where people didn't recognize that God was—and in fact had always been—with them, helping them, watching them. When Jacob was running from Esau, he dreamed of the ladder from earth to heaven with angels ascending and descending on it. Seeing God standing above it, hearing His voice, then waking up from that dream, Jacob's first words were "*The Lord is in this place* and I did not know it" (Genesis 28:16 NLV, emphasis added). Jacob then marked that spot with the stone he had used for a pillow, renaming the place Bethel (House of God).

Years later, Jacob's sons destroyed and plundered Shechem in response to their sister Dinah's rape. Because of their reckless deed, Jacob and his family were in danger of being attacked. So God told Jacob to go back to Bethel and build Him an altar there. Relating God's command to his family, Jacob said, "Let us get ready and go to Bethel. I will make an altar there to *God*, Who answered

me in the day of my trouble, and *was with me every place I went*" (Genesis 35:3 NLV, emphasis added).

Thousands of years later, while on the sea, Jesus' disciples were being battered by a violent storm. Jesus was on the mountaintop where He had gone to pray. Seeing His followers in trouble, He headed toward them, walking on the water. Thinking He was a ghost, they became terrified. "Immediately He spoke with them and said, '*Have courage! It is I.* Don't be afraid.' Then He got into the boat with them, and the wind ceased" (Mark 6:50–51 HCSB, emphasis added).

Minister Lloyd John Ogilvie said, "Sometimes the Lord rides out the storm with us and other times He calms the restless sea around us. Most of all, He calms the storm inside us in our deepest inner soul."

No matter what storms you're trying to get through, you can remain unafraid. Simply remember that God is right here with you. He sees what you're up against. He has climbed into your boat. He's telling you how to navigate through rough waters. He's calming you within and without.

Thank You, Lord, for watching over me. I believe You are near. Calm my soul. Still my storm. Ride out the storm with me. Amen.

TOOLS AT HAND

"God will use a woman's hand to take care of Sisera.". . .
Most blessed of all women is Jael, wife of Heber the
Kenite. . . . She hammered Sisera, she smashed his
head, she drove a hole through his temple.

JUDGES 4:10; 5:24, 26 MSG

Deborah the judge and prophet had received God's plan, the one that would get His people out from underneath the oppressive hand of King Jabin of the Canaanites and his army commander, Sisera. She related that God-given plan to Barak, telling him to gather ten thousand men at Mount Tabor. From there God would lure out Sisera, his nine hundred chariots and charioteers, and "deliver him into your hand" (Judges 4:7 AMPC).

But Barak wouldn't go unless Deborah went with him. After agreeing to do so, she made it clear that "the Lord will sell Sisera into the hand of a woman" (Judges 4:9 AMPC). And, of course, her prophecy came true!

According to God's plan, Barak and his warriors had, with God's help, defeated Jabin's army, killing all men but one: Sisera.

Leaving his chariot behind, Sisera ran to the home of an acquaintance, Heber the Kenite. Heber was out, but his wife, Jael, was in. She went out of her way to greet him, telling him to come into her tent. She told Sisera, "Do not be afraid" (Judges 4:18 NLV), and covered the exhausted commander with a rug.

Sisera asked her for some water. She gave him milk to drink. He asked her to stand next to the door of the tent. He told her if anyone came by asking if anyone was in her tent, she was to say no.

And then, while he slept on her floor, "Jael wife of Heber took a tent peg and hammer, tiptoed toward him, and drove the tent peg through his temple and all the way into the ground. He convulsed and died" (Judges 4:21 MSG).

Later, when Jael met Barak, who was chasing down Sisera, she invited him into her tent and showed him the man he had sought. There lay Sisera, dead, her tent peg in his head.

Deborah's prophecy came true. And God's plan worked well, expediently, and efficiently because Jael summoned up her courage and used the tools she had at hand to do God's will.

In Deborah and Barak's song, Jael is labeled the "most blessed of women" (Judges 5:24 HCSB). All because she willingly and courageously played her part in God's plan.

When God calls you to action, be unafraid. Use the tools He has placed in your hands. And you too will be blessed.

Lord, give me the courage to answer
Your call and work Your will. Amen.

WONDER WOMAN

Hannah was very troubled. She prayed to the Lord and cried with sorrow. . . . "O Lord of All, be sure to look on the trouble of Your woman servant, and remember me."

1 SAMUEL 1:10–11 NLV

Hannah was one of two wives of Elkanah. Although more loved by her husband than Peninnah, Hannah remained childless while Peninnah did not. To make matters worse, Peninnah cruelly teased Hannah about her infertility, often reducing her to tears.

Then one year on their annual trip to the temple at Shiloh, Hannah tamped down her sorrow, plucked up her courage, and went to the temple. Bitterly distressed, she prayed to God through her tears, asking Him to look upon her, His handmaiden, not to forget her, and to gift her with her heart's desire: a son. In exchange for this precious gift, Hannah would give the child back to the Lord to serve Him all his life.

As Hannah was praying her heart out, the priest Eli took notice. Seeing her lips moving and no sound coming out, he asked if she was drunk. Hannah said, "Oh no, sir. . . . I haven't been drinking. . . . The only thing I've been pouring out is my heart. . .to GOD. . . . It's because I'm so desperately unhappy" (1 Samuel 1:15–16 MSG).

Relieved, Eli then blessed Hannah, saying, "Go in peace. And may the God of Israel give you what you have asked of him" (1 Samuel 1:17 MSG).

No longer sad, Hannah went on her way, confident that God would answer her prayer. And He did. Hannah went home, conceived with Elkanah, and gave birth to a boy she named Samuel. For the next several years, Hannah stayed home with her precious child, her heart's desire, until he was weaned. Then, true to her promise to God, Hannah brought Samuel to Shiloh and dedicated him to the Lord.

What made Hannah such a wonder woman began with her maintaining her grace while being cruelly taunted by a family member. Further, she was unafraid to ask God for her heart's desire. Through tears and pain, Hannah made clear that what she wanted most was a son. And God, obviously pleased with her, granted her heart's desire, fulfilling her request (see Psalm 20:4; 37:4). Even more remarkable, when the time came, Hannah courageously gave her most precious gift back to the Giver, who later blessed her with even more children.

You too have the seeds of a wonder woman within you. What are you unafraid to ask for and brave enough to give back to the Giver?

Lord, make me a wonder woman, unafraid to ask You for my heart's desire and then courageous enough to let it go. Amen.

MOVING FORWARD

"I have it all planned out—plans to take care of you, not abandon you, plans to give you the future you hope for. When you call on me, when you come and pray to me, I'll listen. When you come looking for me, you'll find me."

JEREMIAH 29:11–13 MSG

Jabin, the king of Canaan, was making life very difficult for the people of Israel. He was doing so with the help of his army commander, Sisera, who had nine hundred iron chariots. The Israelites had none.

So the Israelites cried out to God. God, in turn, spoke to Deborah, a very wise woman, judge, and prophet. Deborah then sent for Barak, telling him, "The God of Israel, commands you: Go to Mount Tabor and prepare for battle. Take ten companies of soldiers from Naphtali and Zebulun. I'll take care of getting Sisera, the leader of Jabin's army, to the Kishon River with all his chariots and troops. And I'll make sure you win the battle" (Judges 4:6–7 MSG).

But Barak would only move forward into battle if Deborah went with him. Otherwise, his feet were rooted to the spot. Fortunately for Israel, Deborah agreed to go with Barak but with a "but" in mind, saying, "But understand that with an attitude like that, there'll be no glory in it for you. GOD will use a woman's hand to take care of Sisera" (Judges 4:9 MSG). Of course, Deborah's prediction came true. The victory and glory were taken out of the hands of men

and put into the hands of women, namely, Deborah and Jael.

Someone once said, "You don't have to have it all figured out to move forward." All you need to do is trust God. Know that He has a plan for you, just as He had for Deborah, Jael, and His troops. When God chooses to glorify Himself through you, He will give you the resources, the knowledge, the time, the place, and the plan.

So ease off those lumps of clay that have hardened onto your feet. Wiggle your toes in the sands of God's time. Look for the place to which He's directing you. Believe with all your heart, soul, and mind that God is with you—not just today but every step of the way, leading you to victory.

Lord, help me be like Deborah. Fill me full of courage and faith, trusting in Your plan so that I can walk where You will, move forward step by step, my hand in Yours. In Jesus' name I pray. Amen.

COURAGEOUS ENCOURAGERS

When she heard the news about the capture of God's ark and the deaths of her father-in-law and her husband, she collapsed and gave birth because her labor pains came on her. As she was dying, the women taking care of her said, "Don't be afraid. You've given birth to a son!"

1 SAMUEL 4:19–20 HCSB

The priest Eli's sons, Phinehas and Hophni, were also priests—but very corrupt ones (see 1 Samuel 2:12–25). Their days were numbered. Here's how it happened:

After Israel lost a battle to the Philistines, the Israelite elders came up with an idea: "Let's bring the ark of the LORD's covenant from Shiloh. Then it will go with us and save us" (1 Samuel 4:3 HCSB). So Hophni and Phinehas brought the ark of God into battle against the Philistines. Israel lost anyway—and not just the battle but also the priests Hophni and Phinehas.

When Eli heard that Israel had been defeated, Hophni and Phinehas were dead, and the ark had been captured, he fell over and died. When Phinehas's pregnant wife heard about the ark's capture and the deaths of her husband, father-in-law, and brother-in-law, she went into labor. As she lay there dying, her midwives tried giving her a glimmer of light amid the darkness, saying, "Don't be afraid. You've given birth to a son!" But she made no response. In her last moments, she named her child Ichabod,

which means "Where is the glory?" for, she said, "The glory has departed from Israel. . .because the ark of God has been captured" (1 Samuel 4:22 HCSB).

Some things are still mysteries in this world, and one of them is childbirth. To this day, no one can predict the exact moment a woman will go into labor nor what the results of that process will be. Guesses can be made, but pregnancy and childbirth continue to carry with them many unknowns. Yet women continue to care for and be there for one another amid all the messiness, danger, and drama tied to the process.

In this scene, a few midwives were helping another woman birth a child into the world. They remained by her side to support, care for, and help her through this life-and-death effort. They encouraged their patient, their sister, to have courage. And in the end, they were once more reminded of the danger of their occupation. They were left with the tasks of finding a nurse to feed the newly born orphan and preparing the mother's body for burial.

May you too have the faith, fortitude, and courage to serve a fellow sister, bringing her a little light in the darkest of hours.

Lord, make me a courageous encourager,
one willing to step into the messiness, danger,
and drama of another woman's life. Amen.

LETTING GO

When Jesus heard this, he said to him, "You still lack one thing. Sell everything you have and give to the poor, and you will have treasure in heaven. Then come, follow me."

LUKE 18:22 NIV

We human beings are strongly attached to our material possessions, and so it was with the rich man in Luke 18 whom Jesus told to sell all his things: "When he heard this, he became very sad, because he was very wealthy" (Luke 18: 23 NIV). Indeed, Jesus' disciples are themselves flabbergasted by His comment about the difficulty the rich face in attaining the "kingdom of God"—that it's harder than passing a camel through a needle's eye. They ask, If the rich can't get into heaven, then who can? They still think that the worldly rich must enjoy God's favor. Jesus clearly thinks otherwise.

Oliver was a man of substantial gifts. By the time of his early middle age, he had amassed a considerable amount of wealth. Money was no obstacle between him and his desires. His success also secured other advantages for him. He had a beautiful wife and two daughters, he had rich friends, and he enjoyed the respect and adoration of many people.

Oliver went to church on Sundays because it was a thing to do. Yet he didn't feel much like he needed church. He donated money regularly, often joking to others that that was why the pastor wanted him there. But in truth, he looked down on faith, feeling it was a

crutch that some people, even many people, needed. But he did not. Oliver thought that all the credit for his success belonged to him. There were no miracles involved and never any experience that would make him think that God had anything to do with it. In his world, he was completely self-sufficient; really, he was God.

One Monday when he was reflecting on his outlook on life, he recalled hearing about the rich man. A little voice in his head prodded him, "You're not God, not even close. You're going to die one day and be forgotten in a short space of time. . . . If you want to be holy like God is holy, then give it all away." When he woke from his reverie, he realized that his fortune was *his* crutch and he would be terrified without it. He didn't give his riches away, but he did begin to see how hard it was for him to be closer to God. And he began from that day to pray earnestly for spiritual courage.

Lord, sometimes my troubles come not from what I don't have but from what I refuse to give up. Help me hold on to You instead. Amen.

BECAUSE GOD. . .

"Do whatever your circumstances require because God is with you.". . . Who is qualified (fit and sufficient) for these things? . . . Not that we are fit (qualified and sufficient in ability) of ourselves. . .but our power and ability and sufficiency are from God.

1 SAMUEL 10:7 HCSB; 2 CORINTHIANS 2:16; 3:5 AMPC

Because the people of Israel were clamoring for a king to lead them, God told the prophet Samuel to anoint Saul. After the ever-obedient priest did so, Samuel explained to Saul what would happen that day: "The Spirit of the LORD will control you, you will prophesy. . .and you will be transformed into a different person. When these signs have happened to you, do whatever your circumstances require because God is with you" (1 Samuel 10:6–7 HCSB).

All that Samuel predicted would happen came to pass. For a while everything went well under Saul's kingship—until he began relying on himself rather than God (see 1 Samuel 13:13–14; 16:14; 28:15).

Saul's first mistake was due to his impatience. Saul thought that if he didn't get back to his troops, they'd desert him. So, instead of waiting for Samuel to make an offering to God, as instructed, Saul did it himself—a clear sign that Saul didn't trust the Lord. Saul's second mistake was not following God's instructions in how to handle an enemy (see 1 Samuel 15:10–26). His third was violating

the law of Moses by going to a medium for battle advice.

The point is that when Saul began turning away from God, relying on himself instead of God, God turned away from Saul, looking to someone else to lead and care for His people.

When a challenge or obstacle looms in front of you, it's great to be confident and courageous because you believe God is with you and because you know that He will give you the power and strength to do what He's calling you to do. But keep in mind that major problems will arise when you start to take credit for what God is doing in and with you, when you begin to count on yourself, following your own wisdom, making your own rules, and taking matters into your own hands instead of trusting God and His wisdom, rules, and timing.

Remember, all your power and ability to be courageous, to step out of your comfort zone and do what circumstances require, are due solely to God's presence in your life. Count on Him alone. And as you do so, God will then be able to count on you.

Lord, all that I am, all that I do, is from Your presence and power working in and through me. Thank You for fitting me up to serve You alone. Amen.

LIGHT OF THE WORLD

"I am the light of the world. Whoever follows me will never walk in darkness, but will have the light of life."

JOHN 8:12 NIV

On foggy mornings, the sun rises as usual—just like any other day. But instead of the world waking up and acknowledging its arrival, the low, thick clouds blot out its light. But the light is still there. The world is not dark. Light scatters through the particles of the clouds, blanketing the world in gray. As the sun rises and the temperature of the air grows warmer, the clouds begin to move, rising away from the earth. Soon, shafts of light come breaking through the clouds, dazzling us with a golden glow.

The light of our world is sometimes hard for us to see, but it is always there, and it never leaves us in darkness.

Jesus claimed to be the light of the world. The Pharisees He spoke to were blinded by the clouds of their own pride and knowledge—they wanted to be right. They wanted to be in control. So they tried to challenge Jesus' authority. But they ultimately failed because the light of Jesus' truth shone through their questioning.

It was Jesus' light that shone down on the woman caught in adultery—putting her in the spotlight not to shame her but to feature her as a symbol of the hypocrisy of those standing ready to accuse her (John 8:1–11). He shone on her to give her grace. He shone on her to warm her in His light and let her know He would

not condemn her.

It was Jesus' light that drew people to Him in the temple courts, where He taught about who He was and about the Father who had sent Him. He taught that He would soon have to leave this world, but those who would follow Him, who would keep seeking the light of life, would not be left to die in the darkness of their sins.

It is Jesus' light that shines in our lives still today. It is His light that draws us to Him. It is His light that we stand in to confess our sins and be forgiven. It is His light that sets us free. We may not see it clearly. At times we may even get caught up in our own confusion and pride and impatiently claim we do not see it. But in those times, we have to hold on to the knowledge that His light is always there, ready to break through our clouds.

Lord, be the light in my darkest moments. Amen.

STRONGER

He gives strength to the weary and
increases the power of the weak.
ISAIAH 40:29 NIV

We humans are not all that hardy at times. We tire easily. And there is much about the world these days to make us tired.

We might find ourselves weary of watching celebrities preen and push their images while so many around the world are healing from the wounds of war. Or we might grow weary of hearing about the hard times some people are having in selling their mansions when so many millions of people are right now trying to stay warm in makeshift shelters and plastic tents in the refugee cities.

We easily might become weary of hearing politicians squabble about and position themselves on issues that seem important, while ultimately they can make no progress past their opinions to get much accomplished for anyone's good. We might become weary of watching people protest and make elaborate signs to voice their opinions about issues of justice and civil rights while conversely seeing low voter turnouts for elections that could make a real difference.

We might become weary of listening to fundraising campaigns for all kinds of good causes while at the same time realizing how much is being spent all around us every day on luxury cars, designer clothes, and fancy cups of coffee. We might become weary

of people saying they want to do good but time after time choosing self over others.

We might become weary of ourselves when we intend to follow God and do what's right yet get sucked into sins that hurt us and the people we love. It's not just those of us who are older who become cynical and sorry about the world we've created for ourselves; young people also stumble as their steps slow with fatigue. We are all vulnerable to the kind of world weariness that sets in over time.

Thankfully, we have a source we can go to when we become so tired that we find it hard to stand on truth, to act in love, and to extend grace. We can go to God Almighty, whose strength is everlasting and who never tires of loving us. We can ask for help and for wisdom from the One who has a limitless supply of both. We can ask for refreshment and innovation from the Creator God who formed this world from end to end. When we are at our weakest, He can make us stronger. When we are without hope, He can renew our vision. When we cannot walk, He can make us fly.

Lord, I owe everything to You. Please lift me up. Make me stronger. Amen.

IN THE DARK

"Lord," they answered, "we want our sight."
MATTHEW 20:33 NIV

Sometimes, we just make things difficult. We are so wrapped up in our wrongheaded desires, we can't see straight. We hide behind lies. We cover up our ambitions. We put more distance between ourselves and the people we've already pushed away. We disobey God and then keep running from Him.

In Matthew 20, we see two sets of two men asking for different things. One set blindly asked for something they couldn't even handle. And one set openly begged for a gift of mercy that they very much wanted.

God is not blind. He sees our motives. He sees our needs. He knows exactly what we want before we even figure out the words to ask—before we even realize what we want. Even when we are smack dab in the middle of our sin and trying to hide away from the God of the universe, He sees us and knows what's on our hearts.

Zebedee's sons, James and John, wanted more authority. They wanted to be something great in the kingdom of heaven. Apparently, they hadn't been listening all that well to Jesus' sermons. They didn't realize that to be great, they had to be willing to be small. They were blinded by pride and ambition, and they couldn't see what Jesus was trying to tell them—that to sit at His right and left meant they would have to drink from His cup—a cup full of suffering.

As Jesus and the disciples were leaving that area, two men who were physically blind heard that Jesus was passing by, and they shouted out to Him with no shred of shame, "Lord, Son of David, have mercy on us!" (Matthew 20:30 NIV).

Jesus heard them—of course He did! "What do you want me to do for you?" (Matthew 20:32 NIV).

The men asked for their sight. That's all. They just wanted to be made well again—to be healed so they could look on the face of the Son of God. They had no ulterior motives (that we know of). They just wanted to see.

And Jesus, seeing their need, realized that these two men knew exactly what they were asking for, though they didn't know how it would change their lives. "Jesus had compassion on them and touched their eyes. Immediately they received their sight" (Matthew 20:34 NIV). But that wasn't the end of their story. They could have gone anywhere, done all sorts of things they hadn't been able to do before. What did they do when they could see again?

They followed Him.

Because when you finally can see, you don't want to waste any more time in the dark.

Lord, help me to see You clearly. Amen.

GOOD TO GO

"The LORD who delivered me from the paw of the lion and from the paw of the bear will deliver me from the hand of this Philistine."

1 SAMUEL 17:37 ESV

Jesse sent his youngest son, David, to check on three of his older brothers fighting in Saul's army against the Philistines. That's when David heard the giant Goliath taunting the Israelites. Even worse, David saw no one from Israel brave enough to face the giant. Then he heard the king's reward for fighting Goliath: riches, Saul's daughter, and a tax exemption. Yet David was less concerned about the reward than he was about Goliath's defying God's army. So David volunteered to battle the Philistine trash-talker.

The first to oppose the idea was Eliab, David's oldest brother. With anger, he told David to mind his own business and go back home. But David refused to be discouraged and repeated his willingness to face the Philistine.

The second naysayer was King Saul. He thought David was too young and too inexperienced to fight Goliath. Once more David refused to give up the idea. Being a shepherd, David had defended his sheep, occasionally killing a bear or lion to keep his lambs safe. Besides, David told Saul, God would help him now as He always had in the past. Saul finally agreed, saying, "Go, and may the LORD be with you" (1 Samuel 17:37 HCSB).

The third impediment was Saul's insisting the boy don his (the king's) own armor. But after dressing in battle gear, David told Saul, "I can't walk in these. . .I'm not used to them" (1 Samuel 17:39 HCSB). So David removed the king's armor and took up his own shepherd's staff, five smooth stones, and his sling. Then he went out to face Goliath.

Imagine being in a situation where people you know and love are working against you. First your family misreads your intentions and becomes angry at your bravely pursuing your calling. You brush that off only to face someone you respect, someone in authority, who says you have two strikes against you: you're too young and you don't have enough experience. After you shrug that off, someone insists that you take up unfamiliar tools, ones you know will only trip you up!

God knows you. He knows your intents. And if they're aligned with His, you're good to go. No matter what anyone else thinks or says, you're well equipped in Him to face whatever challenges He's calling you to face. As Bernice King, Martin Luther King Jr.'s youngest child, said, "Refuse to be disheartened, discouraged, distracted from your goals in life." Instead, pick up your tools and face your challenges unafraid, knowing that God will give you victory.

Thank You, Lord, for equipping me for and being with me in all challenges. Amen.

FREE ME

Who will free me from this life that is dominated by sin and death?
ROMANS 7:24 NLT

You know you've felt it. You've been sitting at that traffic light, waiting for the green, and staring out at the horizon. And the thought has gone through your head, *What if I just kept going? What if I just kept driving straight ahead. . .out of town, out of the state, all the way to the ocean? What then?*

We all want to escape our lives sometimes. Usually, when the mountain of life's details feels too heavy to manage, or when bigger troubles are sitting like stubborn storm clouds over our households, or when we're so stressed and exhausted we can't even define what's bothering us, that's when the escape plan seems particularly attractive. And it's never that we want to leave our loved ones behind. We don't really want to shake up our entire lives. We just want a break. Really, we just want a vacation from being. . .us.

Paul understood this feeling. He had felt frustrated and confused by his own jumbled mixture of motivations, intentions, and actions. "I don't really understand myself, for I want to do what is right, but I don't do it. Instead, I do what I hate" (Romans 7:15 NLT). He recognized the strength of the sinful nature within him—how it kept blocking him from his desires to do good.

The power of this sinful nature is what makes us feel so trapped

in our lives. It's not that anything happening around us is overwhelming. When we sit down and put it all on paper, we can see what's right to do. We can find at least a few potential solutions to our complex problems. Often our troubles are not at all the things that are happening outside of us. It's the trouble inside that keeps us tied in knots. And we can't escape ourselves.

Being a slave to our sinful nature keeps us from enjoying all the good gifts God wants us to have. But thanks be to God, He can free us. *How do I get free from myself? How do I break the cycle of sin and shame?* The answer is always Jesus. We can't do it on our own. We can't even do it together. And we can't do it just by obeying a set of laws. We have to have Jesus.

"Because you belong to him, the power of the life-giving Spirit has freed you from the power of sin that leads to death" (Romans 8:2 NLT). The next time you are sitting at that light, waiting for go, don't dream about getting away. Dream about getting closer to God.

Lord, free me from the hold of sin. Amen.

ALL THE DIFFERENCE

"You come against me with a dagger, spear, and sword, but I come against you in the name of Yahweh. . . . Today, the LORD will hand you over to me. . . . Then all the world will know. . .that it is not by sword or by spear that the LORD saves, for the battle is the LORD's."

1 SAMUEL 17:45–47 HCSB

Imagine being a bystander seeing David facing off against Goliath.

On the side of the Philistines is a people-taunting, trash-talking giant with an abundance of battle experience. You can see it by the numerous scars on his face. Almost ten feet tall, he's wearing a bronze helmet and a 126-pound coat of mail. Bronze armor shields his legs. Across his shoulders is a bronze sword. His spear's iron point weighs 15 pounds. And a man walking in front of him bears his shield.

On the side of the Israelites is David, a young shepherd boy who has seen some battle experience—against lions and bears. He wears no armor and bears no shield. All he has is his shepherd's staff, five smooth stones that he puts in his shepherd's pouch, and his sling.

But wait. He has one more thing. Although it's unseen in this scene, this "thing" is a powerful weapon *and* shield with vast experience in warfare. It's Yahweh. And He makes all the difference in the world.

Just as David was a rescuer of his sheep, God was a rescuer of David. And David knew God was mighty enough to deliver him no matter how impossible the situation appeared to human eyes. And that's just what happened to everyone's surprise—except David's!

Although Goliath looked imposing, the weight and quantity of his gear, the things he thought would protect him, made him an easy target for David. David's one smooth stone, slung from a distance, hit the giant's forehead and felled him immediately. David then ran up to the giant, lifted Goliath's sword, and finished him off. When the Philistines saw Goliath fall, they ran off only to be chased down and killed by the men of Judah and Israel.

When facing obstacles, David walked by faith not by sight. He disregarded the comments and opinions of others because he knew God was with him. David trusted that God would rescue him in the present as He had in the past and would continue to do so in the future.

Each day you have the choice of walking by faith, seeing things from God's perspective, and making that your reality instead of walking by sight and seeing things from a limited human perspective. Today—and every day—remember David and Goliath. And walk by faith. Then you too will fell your giants.

Lord, help me walk by faith not by sight. Amen.

BUOYED BY FAITH

Instantly Jesus reached out His hand and caught and held [Peter], saying to him, O you of little faith, why did you doubt? And when they got into the boat, the wind ceased. And those in the boat knelt and worshiped Him, saying, Truly You are the Son of God!

MATTHEW 14:31–33 AMPC

Fear. It can come upon you so suddenly. You're minding your own business, whistling a happy tune, and *boom!*—something unexpected happens. Filled with uncertainty, you look for a way to save yourself, a way to "fix" your situation. But then, eyes off God, you begin to sink. You reach out your arms, you cry for help amid a perceived sense of hopelessness. And the next thing you know, Jesus sweeps you out of danger and into His embrace.

Fear is easy to sink into. Even Jesus' disciples suffered from it. On one occasion, Jesus had the Twelve—four of whom were seasoned fishermen—get into a boat and head across the Sea of Galilee. Meanwhile, He went up on a mountain to pray. Alone.

For nine hours, Jesus' crew battled strong wind and waves. And then, through the darkness and splashing water, they saw someone or something coming toward them—not in a boat but on the surface of the sea. It was, of course, Jesus walking on the water. But, mistaking Him for a ghost, they screamed in fear. Only Jesus' words, "Take courage! I AM! Stop being afraid" (Matthew 14:27 AMPC), calmed them.

A now confident and reassured Peter decided he wanted to walk on the water with Jesus. He dared to step out of the boat and onto the sea. Yet once he had answered His Lord's command to come, he took his eyes off Jesus. When "he saw the strong wind" (Matthew 14:30 NLV), fear entered him. And Peter began to sink.

Note that fear came on Peter after he "*saw* the strong wind." Yet no one can "see" the wind. So it seems his imagination overrode his faith in the One who had called him.

God hasn't given you a spirit of fear. That's something you yourself have developed over time. But what God *has* given you is a spirit of power, love, and self-control (see 2 Timothy 1:7). And you need all three to buoy your faith—"the leaning of your entire personality on God in Christ in absolute trust and confidence in His power, wisdom, and goodness" (2 Timothy 1:5 AMPC). That's something worth praying on and working toward.

Lord, I don't want to give in to the spirit of fear. So help me buoy my faith. Help me tap into my God-given spirit of power, love, and self-control. In Jesus' name I pray. Amen.

IT'S ALL ABOUT TRUST

When I am afraid, I will trust in You. In God, whose word I praise, in God I trust; I will not fear. What can man do to me? . . . This I know: God is for me. In God, whose word I praise, in the LORD, whose word I praise, in God I trust; I will not fear.

PSALM 56:3–4, 9–11 HCSB

While in Philippi, Paul and Silas were heading to a place to pray when they met a slave girl. Her owners were profiting from her psychic and fortune-telling abilities. She began following Paul and Silas, announcing to whomever would listen that they were God's servants.

After a few days of this, Paul had had it. He turned and commanded the spirit within the girl to depart. And it did—along with her money-making abilities. Her enraged owners grabbed Paul and Silas, roughed them up, and dragged them to the magistrates, saying, "These men are disturbing the peace—dangerous Jewish agitators subverting our Roman law and order" (Acts 16:20–21 MSG).

The judges, swayed by her owners and the bloodthirsty crowd, ordered Paul and Silas to be stripped of their clothes, beaten, and thrown into jail. There they were to be held under heavy guard, their feet tethered by chains.

About midnight, Paul and Silas began praying and singing praises to God. Suddenly the earth shook, the prison doors flew open, and all the prisoners' bonds came loose. When the jailer

woke and saw the destruction, he assumed all had escaped. He grabbed a sword to kill himself, but Paul stopped him, telling him all the prisoners were still there and accounted for.

The jailer bowed down before Paul and Silas, trembling with fear. He took the men outside, asking what he needed to do to be saved. They answered, "Put your trust in the Lord Jesus Christ."

The jailer did. So did his family. All were baptized and "full of joy for having put their trust in God" (Acts 16:34 NLV).

Woman, it's all about trust. When you're afraid, trust in God—the God whose Word you praise for its power to strengthen, soothe, and settle. Trust *that* God. Then you won't fear, because you'll understand that God is not against you but for you in every way, every day. *That* God, the One on your side—trust Him.

To help you move from fear to trust, consider memorizing today's lead-in verses—or any other verse that better suits you. Or memorize this paraphrase of Teresa of Avila's prayer and repeat it over and over to soothe your soul: "Let nothing disturb you. Let nothing frighten you. Everything passes away except God. Whoever has Him lacks nothing. God alone is sufficient."

Lord, You are all I need. Amen.

STRAIGHT PATHS

So David went back to GOD in prayer. GOD said, "Get going."

1 SAMUEL 23:4 MSG

King Saul was chasing David down, seeking to kill him. You would think that such a circumstance would have consumed all of David's thoughts and plans. Yet even while literally running for his life, David was concerned about the Philistines fighting against the people of Keilah. So, rather than relying on his will, David inquired of God: "Should I launch an attack against these Philistines?" (1 Samuel 23:2 HCSB). And God said yes. Go. Do.

It sounds like a done deal. But when David told his men of his God-confirmed intentions, they made it clear that they didn't think this was a good idea. After all, they were already afraid of Saul's chasing them. And now David wanted them to go to battle with the Philistines? If they did, they might be caught between Saul's army and the Philistines! David's six hundred men had their eyes on their problems instead of on God and His recommendation.

David now had two choices. He could either give in to the fear of his men and lose Keilah to Israel's enemy, or he could go back to God and confirm His will. Refusing to catch the contagion of fear, David went back to God. He asked and God answered: "Get going. Head for Keilah. I'm placing the Philistines in your hands" (1 Samuel 23:4 MSG). So David and his now more-motivated men fought the Philistines and rescued Keilah and its people.

Later, when Saul heard that David was in Keilah, he decided to go there to trap David and his men. David prayed to God again. He told God what he had heard of Saul's strategy. He wondered if the rumors about Saul's plans were true. He asked if the leaders of Keilah would turn him, their rescuer, over to Saul. God said yes to both questions. So David and his men got going, managing to escape before Saul and his men arrived.

Throughout his life, David continually consulted the Lord (see 1 Samuel 23:1–5, 10–14; 30:8–9; 2 Samuel 2:1–2; 5:17–25; 21:1), asking Him what he should do. Even when he became the king of Israel, David understood that he was, after all, only a man. And men have limited knowledge. But not so of the Lord God, whose thoughts are so much higher than those of any man or woman (see Isaiah 55:8–9).

One way to fight the fear that arises up within or without is to "trust in the LORD with all your heart, and do not lean on your own understanding. In all your ways acknowledge him, and he will make straight your paths" (Proverbs 3:5–6 ESV).

I'm coming to You, Lord, for wisdom and courage.
Tell me, what should my next steps be? Amen.

GET UP AND GO

I will trust and not be afraid, for the Lord God is my strength and song. . . . The Lord. . .has done excellent things [gloriously]; let this be made known to all the earth. Cry aloud and shout joyfully, you women. . .for great in your midst is the Holy One.

ISAIAH 12:2, 5–6 AMPC

After Jesus ascended into heaven, His twelve apostles chose seven men to help them minister to the growing church. Among those seven men "of good repute, full of the Spirit and of wisdom" (Acts 6:3 ESV) were Stephen and Philip.

Shortly after the apostles had prayed over the new ministers, asking God to align their wills with His, Stephen was killed (see Acts 7:58–60). This prompted many followers of the Way to scatter.

So Philip headed to Samaria, where he preached, taught, and healed. Then one day an angel of the Lord told him to "get up and go" (Acts 8:26 NLV). The amazing part isn't the angel's specific message. It's Philip's *response* to that message: "He got up and went" (Acts 8:27 AMPC). Philip had no fear, no excuse, no hemming and hawing, no buts. He was given an instruction, an order, a direction, and off he went.

Meanwhile, an Ethiopian eunuch who had come to Jerusalem to worship was heading back home. He, an official from Queen Candace's court, was sitting in his chariot, reading Isaiah 53:7–8, where the prophet predicted the circumstances of Jesus' demise.

Arriving in Gaza, Philip heard the Holy Spirit's instructions to climb up into that eunuch's chariot. The ever-obedient Philip ran up to the eunuch and asked if he understood what he was reading. The eunuch responded with "How can I unless someone shows me, teaches me, guides me?" He then invited Philip to join him in the chariot.

Perhaps Philip was an answer to the eunuch's prayer. Who knows? All we really do know is that Philip showed up at the right time to help this seeker and that their in-depth conversation about Isaiah's prediction opened the door for Philip to tell the eunuch all about the Man who had saved the world.

After Philip's teaching, the eunuch asked to be baptized. When they came up out of a nearby stream, "the Spirit of God suddenly took Philip off" (Acts 8:39 MSG).

If you want to be used by God in unique circumstances, pray—not to pull God to your will but to align your will with His. That way, when God does call, you won't be afraid. You'll just get up and go.

God, give me the courage to get up and go when You call. Amen.

A FREED WOMAN

Jesus said to her, . . ."Go to my brothers and say to them, 'I am ascending to my Father and your Father, to my God and your God.' " Mary Magdalene went and announced to the disciples, "I have seen the Lord."

JOHN 20:17–18 ESV

Joyce Meyer says, "Only God can turn a mess into a message, a test into a testimony." That's just what Jesus did with Mary Magdalene. A bit of a mess before she met Jesus and later tested, her life became a message and a testimony.

Jesus had freed Mary Magdalene from seven demons (see Mark 16:9). Now, a blank slate before Him, He was free to fill her cleared-out mind with His wisdom, tenets, and lessons. She was free to become the woman God wanted her to be. Free to support and minister to the Teacher and Healer she loved before and after His death. Free to have a new beginning and witness a new ending.

Mary Magdalene was there when Jesus was on the cross and laid in the tomb (see Matthew 27:56; Mark 15:47). She was one of the first to find the stone on Jesus' tomb rolled away (see Mark 16:1–4). And she was the first to see and talk with Jesus after His resurrection—not that anyone believed her report (see Mark 16:9–11).

In John's Gospel account, Mary was standing outside Jesus' tomb weeping. As her tears flowed, she stooped to look inside the tomb. There she saw two angels, one of whom asked her why she was crying. She told him, "They took my Friend, my Teacher, my Jesus. And I don't know where they've put Him" (see John 20:13, author paraphrase). She turned, and there stood someone she thought was a gardener but who in reality was Jesus. He asked why she was crying. Rather than directly answer Him, she asked, "Have you taken my Jesus? If so, where? I'll take Him away" (see v. 15, author paraphrase).

Then Jesus gently said her name: "Mary."

She cried out, her heart bursting with joy, "Teacher!"

Jesus told her not to hold Him there but to tell the others. And Mary did.

Mary had voluntarily gone to the garden, watching for and weeping for Jesus. When others had denied Him, she proclaimed Him. When others deserted Him, she remained near Him. When others left the empty tomb, she remained, watching, waiting, until she met Him once more.

Because of Jesus, Mary's life was forever changed. She was no longer afraid but trusting. No longer broken but whole. No longer a mess but a message.

Lord, free me for You. Change my fear to trust, my brokenness to wholeness. Make my mess a message. Amen.

STUMBLING

To him who is able to keep you from stumbling and to present you before his glorious presence without fault and with great joy—to the only God our Savior be glory, majesty, power and authority, through Jesus Christ our Lord, before all ages, now and forevermore! Amen.

JUDE 24–25 NIV

A stubbed toe. Dropped papers. Spilled coffee. These are all likely results of stumbling. Usually, stumbling does not result in any horrible, life-changing consequences.

But it all depends on where you stumble, doesn't it?

Stumbling up a flight of steps might leave you with a bruised shin or two. Stumbling down a flight of steps might give you a broken neck.

Stumbling along an uneven sidewalk might result in a bruised ego—especially if people are watching. Stumbling along an uneven path on the side of a mountain could lead to your death.

The stumbling Jude was referring to when he wrote to believers was a serious matter with serious consequences. It was a spiritual stumbling, the kind that could lead a person to fall into eternal fire. The examples he gives as reminders are of those who were destroyed for their lack of faith, of angels who rejected their places and are now bound in darkness, and of those who succumbed to immorality and perversion and now suffer punishment forever.

People who stumble in this way and who keep walking on bumpy roads on purpose are those Jude describes as "clouds without rain, blown along by the wind; autumn trees, without fruit and uprooted—twice dead. They are wild waves of the sea, foaming up their shame; wandering stars, for whom blackest darkness has been reserved forever" (Jude 12–13 NIV). In other words, they are people who seem at first as if they have something to offer—people who may appear to be friendly, or wise, or charming, or good—but then turn out to care only about themselves and their desires.

We've probably all met people like this—perhaps we've even been hurt by them. But there is a way to protect ourselves from getting entangled with toxic men and women who try to make us fall. We can build ourselves up in our faith by reading God's Word and listening to Him every day. We can pray in the Holy Spirit. We can love others and learn to love them well, following the example of Jesus. We can be aware of and express gratitude for the mercy of God and offer mercy to others who are in danger of stumbling too—extending a hand to help them find their balance again.

God, my Savior and King, I'm so thankful not only that You are able to keep me from stumbling, but that You are willing to do so. Amen.

DARING THE CONSEQUENCES

Joseph, he of Arimathea. . .daring the consequences, took courage and ventured to go to Pilate and asked for the body of Jesus.

MARK 15:43 AMPC

Joseph of Arimathea, a good and righteous man, wealthy, and an esteemed member of the Jewish council (see Luke 23:50–51), was waiting for the kingdom of God. He was a follower of Jesus. But because of his fear of the Jews, he had kept his allegiance to Jesus secret.

And now here hung his Master. Alone, except for some women standing and watching nearby. It was his moment to step forward. If he was going to serve Jesus one last time, that time was now.

Finally, heedless of the consequences, Joseph gathered up all his courage. He went to see Pilate and asked for Jesus' body. Once assured that Jesus was already dead, Pilate granted Joseph's request.

Joseph carried Jesus to his own tomb. Nicodemus came by, bringing a mixture of myrrh and aloes, about seventy-five pounds in all (see John 19:39).

Silently, the men worked together, reverently, mournfully, honored they could perform this one last duty for the Teacher. They gently wrapped Jesus' body in a linen shroud with the spices and carefully laid Him in Joseph's tomb. With all their strength, they rolled a stone against the tomb's entrance. Their hearts broke

when they looked up to see the women who had followed them there—Mary Magdalene and Mary the mother of Jeses, quietly watching and weeping from a distance.

There are times in our lives when, like Joseph, we at last receive the courage we need, the boldness to do what we know God would have us do. It happens when we speak up for the speechless, help the helpless, love the unloved, provide for the poor. With no regard for the consequences, we find a way to venture forth and do what we never before had the confidence to do. God molds us, raises us up for times such as these, just as He raised up Joseph of Arimathea on this specific occasion.

God put Joseph in his position on the council, allowed him the necessary riches, and gave him the courage he needed to do what God wanted done. For Joseph to publicly display his allegiance, adoration, and affection for a man who had just been mocked, beaten, spit on, stripped, and crucified was indeed a risk—but one God gave him the courage to take.

May God do the same for you, giving you the courage to risk all for Him.

Lord, may I one day have the courage to risk all I have and am for You. Amen.

A LONE WOMAN, UNAFRAID

She saw David and his men coming toward her and met them. . . . When Abigail saw David, she quickly got off the donkey and fell with her face to the ground.

1 SAMUEL 25:20, 23 HCSB

No word describes Abigail so well as *unafraid*. She, a lone woman, faced an enraged David and his army of four hundred men with only servants, food, drink, and wisdom. And she did so without her husband's consent. Here's how it happened:

David was still on the run from the murderous Saul. While out in the wilderness, he shielded the sheep of other men, one of whom was Nabal.

This man Nabal (meaning "fool") was a very rich, evil, and harsh drunkard, whereas his wife, Abigail, was gentle, beautiful, and wise.

One day David sent some men to Nabal with a polite greeting, reminding Nabal that David and his men had defended the man's sheep. David then asked if Nabal would be so gracious as to repay their efforts by providing them with food and drink.

Nabal not only denied the request but couched his refusal with insults aimed at David and his men. Enraged, David told four hundred of his men to strap on their swords and be ready to kill Nabal and his household.

When Abigail learned what had happened, she immediately

gathered supplies, sent them ahead with her servants, and then came herself, riding on a donkey. Once face-to-face with David and his four hundred warriors, Abigail dismounted and fell prostrate on the ground. She begged David to ignore Nabal and his words; to spare her husband, herself, and her household; and to accept the supplies she had brought. Abigail complimented David, calling him God's mighty servant whom God would make king over Israel. She then said, "When the LORD does good things for my lord, may you remember me your servant" (1 Samuel 25:31 HCSB).

David—thrilled with Abigail's speech, wisdom, and supplies—told his men to stand down and allowed Abigail to go home in peace. She did so, returning home to a very drunk Nabal. She told her husband nothing about her encounter with David until the next morning. At daybreak she shared her news, which shocked the now sober Nabal, who suffered a stroke and died ten days later. When word of Nabal's death reached David, he proposed to Abigail and married her.

God knows there will be times when, like Abigail, we need to stay calm, cool, and collected when called to protect our household. We need to find a way of making peace with others while trusting God to guard and guide us as we seek His wisdom and grace. In doing so, we can have confidence that God will reward our courage in ways beyond our imagining.

Show me, God, the way of peace and courage. Amen.

GROUNDED ON THE WORD

Put out into the deep [water], and lower your nets for a haul. And Simon (Peter) answered, Master, we toiled all night [exhaustingly] and caught nothing [in our nets]. But on the ground of Your word, I will lower the nets [again].

LUKE 5:4–5 AMPC

One day a crowd was pressing in on Jesus as He stood by the Sea of Galilee. So He stepped into Peter's boat and asked him to draw it away from the shore. Then He sat down and continued to teach.

When He was done talking, Jesus told Peter to pull the boat into the deep water and lower his nets. Peter, an experienced fisherman, knew that in the Sea of Galilee the best time to fish was at night and in shallow water. He told Jesus that they'd worked all night long and had caught nothing. "But," he said, "on the ground of Your word, I will lower the nets [again]." After doing so, the men caught so many fish, their nets were at the point of breaking.

That's when Peter was "gripped with bewildering amazement [allied to terror]" (Luke 5:9 AMPC). As he trembled, Jesus put him at ease, saying, "Have no fear; from now on you will be catching men!" (Luke 5:10 AMPC). When Jesus said, "Follow Me" (Matthew 4:19 NLV), Peter did not hesitate.

For three years Peter journeyed with the Master. During that time he grew in wisdom and faith. Yet at the same time, Peter also yelled at Jesus when he should have supported Him, fell asleep

when he had been told to stay awake, and deserted and denied his Lord instead of sticking by Him. Yet Jesus still loved, cared for, and provided for Peter. For Jesus saw Peter not as he was but as the man he would become, the rock on which He would build His Church.

In one of their last encounters, Peter and several other disciples were once more fishing. They'd been out all night and had caught nothing. The resurrected Jesus, standing on the shore, said, "Cast the net on the right side of the boat" (John 21:6 AMPC). They obeyed, and once more their net was at the point of breaking with fish. And once more Jesus invited Peter to follow Him (see v. 19).

Jesus continually seeks, finds, encourages, calls, and commissions. And though you may fail, fear, or falter, Jesus continually returns, ready to forgive and forget. For Jesus sees you as the woman you will become.

Never fear or falter. Ground your life on the Word, knowing that no matter what, Jesus will always seek your company, still care and provide. Still tell you to have no fear but simply to follow Him.

Lord, on the ground of Your Word, I come. Amen.

NEVERTHELESS. . .THROUGH FAITH

The Jebusites, the inhabitants of the land. . .said to David, You shall not enter here, for the blind and the lame will prevent you; they thought, David cannot come in here. Nevertheless, David took the stronghold of Zion, that is, the City of David.

2 SAMUEL 5:6–7 AMPC

The eleventh chapter of the New Testament book of Hebrews is called "the Hall of Faith." In it you'll find a summary of people who experienced miracles in response to their faith. David is mentioned in a list near the end, but no specifics are covered. The writer says he didn't have the time to tell about all the ways people such as David "through faith conquered kingdoms, enforced justice, obtained promises" (Hebrews 11:33 ESV). Nor is there space to do so here. Nevertheless, we can slip in this one story. . . .

In 2 Samuel 5, all the tribes of Israel came under one king: David. Finally, the shepherd God had equipped to lead His people, the man called the apple of God's eye, was on the throne. Now king, David and his men marched to Jerusalem to rout out the city's occupants, the Jebusites.

Upon David's arrival, the Jebusites, thinking their city impregnable, mocked him, saying, "You might as well go home! Even the blind and the lame could keep you out. You can't get in here!" (2 Samuel 5:6 MSG). Apparently, the Jebusites knew little of David and his God.

The next verse in this account (2 Samuel 5:7 AMPC) begins with a very powerful word: *Nevertheless*. For, regardless of the Jebusites' thoughts, perspective, and opinion, "*Nevertheless*, David took the stronghold" (emphasis added)! Once the Jebusites were routed and the city conquered, David lived there, named it the City of David, and "became greater and greater, for the Lord God of hosts was with him" (2 Samuel 5:10 AMPC).

David conquered the city because his power source was God. David knew and trusted in God's Word. He had a determination to see that Word fulfilled. He "did as the LORD commanded him" (2 Samuel 5:25 ESV). And because David trusted God's words over those of men, he had the courage to do what others said he couldn't or shouldn't do.

Of course, David sometimes messed things up. After all, he was a mere man. Nevertheless, more often than not, David and God were very much on the same page.

You too can live a "nevertheless" kind of life. You too can muster your courage to follow God's will and Word and conquer those who criticize. For in the same way the Lord, His power, and His Word were with David, they are with you.

When I'm challenged, Lord, help me remember the power of a "nevertheless" action in You. Amen.

SUPERNATURALLY ENCOURAGED

But David encouraged and strengthened himself in the Lord his God.

1 SAMUEL 30:6 AMPC

God knows there are days when we need all the encouragement we can get.

Such was the case with David. Because Saul was out to get him and his men day after day, they "kept moving, going here, there, wherever—always on the move" (1 Samuel 23:13 MSG). While David was hiding in the wilderness of Ziph, his good friend Jonathan showed up and "encouraged him in his faith in God, saying, 'Don't be afraid, for my father Saul will never lay a hand on you. You yourself will be king over Israel'" (1 Samuel 23:16–17 HCSB). Prince Jonathan's words undoubtedly gave David more confidence, strength, and energy to move forward in God while he was being chased from behind.

Several chapters (and miles) later, David, still on the run from Saul, found even more encouragement. This time, he searched for it and found it—in God.

David and his men had been away from home. Upon their return, they found everything—including their wives and children—gone, their homes burned down to the ground, and their families taken by the Amalekites. Seeing the devastation, David and his men were crushed, weeping until they had no more tears

left. Then, when the men started talking about stoning David, his distress grew even more. Not one man seemed to be on his side. No one was giving him any support. He had no one to lean on.

Yet David refused to give in to fear, panic, or grief. Instead, he found a way out: "David encouraged *and* strengthened himself in the Lord his God." He spent time in God's presence. He prayed, asking God if he should pursue the men who raided their homes and took their families. God's answer was yes. Go. You'll catch up to them and "without fail recover all" (1 Samuel 30:8 AMPC).

Refreshed, renewed, and reinvigorated, David and his men went after the Amalekite raiders and recovered not just what they'd initially lost but even more (see 1 Samuel 30:19–20).

During those times when you fear that everyone is against you, that there's not a friend to be found, go to God. Spend time in His presence. Ask Him what your next steps should be. Allow God to reenergize you, to give you the strength and courage you need to do whatever He would have you do. And you'll not just recover what you've lost but come away with even more.

I come to You, Lord, for strength and encouragement.
What would You have me do? Amen.

FEARLESS DO-GOODERS

You are now her true daughters if you do right and let nothing terrify you [not giving way to hysterical fears or letting anxieties unnerve you].

1 PETER 3:6 AMPC

When writing to believers who had been scattered, the apostle Peter told Christian women they could be considered Sarah's children if they did what was right and good and weren't frightened by anything, not letting the storms without disrupt the calm waters within. But how does a woman get there from here?

Sometimes it seems impossible to stay calm in this world. After all, Sarah didn't have to face the issues and worries we do. She didn't have to be concerned about losing her job, paying back educational loans, commuting through increasing traffic and aging infrastructure, learning new technology, listening to bickering politicians, keeping a roof (that doesn't leak) over her head, raising kids in an increasingly immoral world, and so much more. No. She had a successful well-to-do husband. She was amply provided for, taken care of. Her worries were few.

But wait. Hang on. It's true that Sarah had all the material goods and security she could want. But what she didn't have was a child. God had made promise after promise that she and Abraham would have many descendants. But years passed and still no little bump appeared beneath her dress.

So *that* was Sarah's concern—that she had yet to have a child, the one thing that completed women in her day. It's true that she did try to fix her situation by getting a child through a surrogate mother. But that endeavor backfired.

Then, finally, God was ready, and so was Sarah. God, in effect, had readied Sarah by growing her faith. "Because of faith. . .Sarah herself received physical power to conceive a child, even when she was long past the age for it, because she considered [God] Who had given her the promise to be reliable and trustworthy and true to His word" (Hebrews 11:11 AMPC).

How wonderful for Sarah—and Abraham! At long last God had granted them a child.

You can be like Sarah and "be not afraid of sudden terror and panic, nor of the stormy blast or the storm and ruin of the wicked when it comes" (Proverbs 3:25 AMPC). You can do that by making "the Lord. . .your confidence, firm and strong," for He "shall keep your foot from being caught [in a trap or some hidden danger]" (Proverbs 3:26 AMPC).

You, Lord, are my confidence. In You I trust and believe, knowing that You will always be true to Your word. Amen.

THE COURAGE TO WAIT

[What, what would have become of me] had I not believed that I would see the Lord's goodness in the land of the living! Wait and hope for and expect the Lord; be brave and of good courage and let your heart be stout and enduring.

PSALM 27:13–14 AMPC

Sometimes the most courageous thing you can do is wait—as you trust and hope in the Lord.

Rizpah had been King Saul's concubine. By him she had borne two sons, Armoni and Mephibosheth. But now Saul was dead. And King David was praying to God, looking for answers as to why a famine had come upon his kingdom. God said, "It is because of the blood shed by Saul and his family when he killed the Gibeonites" (2 Samuel 21:1 HCSB). So David asked them what he could do to make atonement for Saul's misdeeds. The Gibeonites requested that seven of Saul's male descendants be hanged. So David had Rizpah's two sons (Armoni and Mephibosheth) and five of Saul's grandsons handed over to the Gibeonites, who hanged them in the first days of the barley harvest on a hill.

And that's where Rizpah spent the next five months. Beside seven dead bodies. She spread a cloth on a rock where she laid. She shooed away the birds during the day and chased away the beasts that came at night. But she never gave up hope. Even as the days melted into the nights and the nights into the days, Rizpah

maintained her vigil. And she kept her courage, hoping and expecting she would see God's goodness in the land of the living. With an extreme amount of patience during what to others may have appeared to be a hopeless situation, Rizpah waited for God to act.

Finally, Rizpah's faith, hope, courage, and patience paid off. King David heard what she was doing. So he had the bones of Saul and his son Jonathan gathered together with Saul's other sons and grandsons. They were buried in the family tomb by his command. And then the rains came.

No matter how bleak things look, no matter how hopeless the situation, no matter how difficult the circumstances, be sure God sees what's happening. Know that He will bring His loving-kindness your way. Your job is to wait patiently—and be strong and hopeful, knowing that God has a plan. And part of that plan is that you *will* have an answer to your prayer.

Help me, Lord, on those days when I seem to lose hope, when one day runs into the next as I wait on You. Show me what You would have me do, Lord. Help me to be brave, to be filled with expectation and strength, looking forward to seeing Your goodness in the land of the living. Amen.

ONLY A WOMAN

Do you not discern and understand that you [the whole church at Corinth] are God's temple (His sanctuary), and that God's Spirit has His permanent dwelling in you [to be at home in you, collectively as a church and also individually]?

1 CORINTHIANS 3:16 AMPC

Are you afraid to step out of your comfort zone or traditional role because you're "only a woman"? Are you afraid no one will listen to you or think you have anything important to say because you're "only a woman"? Are you afraid to stand up and speak the truth because you're "only a woman"?

It's time to put those fears to rest. To replace them with the power of God's Word.

Although most of the stories in the Bible are about men, women still played a pivotal role, especially in the New Testament. Consider the following:

- The first person to be told that Jesus would be the Messiah was mother-to-be Mary (Luke 1:30–33).
- The first person who realized Mary was carrying the Son of God was Elizabeth (Luke 1:39–45).
- The first person to spread the Good News about the newborn Jesus being the Messiah was Anna the prophet (Luke 2:36–38).
- The people who, out of their own resources, financially supported Jesus and His disciples were Mary Magdalene, Joanna (the only woman married), and Susanna (Luke 8:1–3).

- The people who anointed Jesus were Mary of Bethany and the unnamed, sinful woman (Matthew 26:6–13; Mark 14:3–9; Luke 7:36–50; John 12:1–8).
- The people who remained with Jesus at the cross were all women (Matthew 27:55–56; Mark 15:40; Luke 23:49; John 19:25).
- The people who witnessed Jesus being placed in the tomb by Joseph of Arimathea and Nicodemus were all women (Matthew 27:61; Mark 15:47; Luke 23:55).
- The people who came back to the tomb after the Sabbath were all women (Matthew 28:1; Mark 16:1; Luke 24:10; John 20:1).
- The first person to see the resurrected Jesus was Mary Magdalene (Mark 16:9; John 20:14); Matthew says Jesus first revealed Himself to Mary Magdalene *and* the other Mary (Matthew 28:1–9).

Daughter of God, sister of Jesus, you need not be afraid to step out, to do what God calls you to do. God is with you. He will never leave you. He will fulfill His promises to you when you step out in faith, in Him (see Luke 1:45).

Lord, I feel Your presence. I know You are with me as I, in the tradition of all the faithful women who have gone before me, step out to keep in step with You. Amen.

DEFENDING THE DEFENSELESS

"Enough! . . . You're here to defend the defenseless, to make sure that underdogs get a fair break; your job is to stand up for the powerless, and prosecute all those who exploit them."

PSALM 82:2–4 MSG

King David had many wives by whom he fathered many children. Three of those children were Absalom, his beautiful sister Tamar, and their half brother Amnon.

It so happened that Amnon was sick with love for his half sister. Yet he could see no way to "get his hands on her" (2 Samuel 13:2 MSG). Then Amnon's crafty cousin Jonadab suggested that Amnon pretend to be sick. When his father, David, came to visit him, Amnon could request, "Have my sister Tamar come and prepare some supper for me here where I can watch her and she can feed me" (2 Samuel 13:5 MSG).

Amnon followed through with Jonadab's plan. As instructed by her father, Tamar went to Amnon's house and prepared food in front of him. But after she served him, he refused to eat. Instead, he told everyone to leave the room and then insisted that Tamar go with him to his bedroom.

There Amnon forced Tamar into bed, disregarding her pleas for him not to hurt her, not to do this terrible thing that would bring her shame and him disgrace. She ended with "Oh, please! Speak to the king—he'll let you marry me" (2 Samuel 13:13 MSG). But her

pleas fell on deaf ears. Being the stronger of the two, Amnon raped his sister. Immediately afterward, his hate for her was more than his former love for her. Tamar was left in ruin, her head covered with ashes, her face with tears, her gown torn.

Although outraged at the news of what happened to his sister, Absalom waited two years and then killed Amnon.

Betrayed, abused, and abandoned by all the males in her family, Tamar was now damaged goods. Her future was bleak. Her innocence gone forever.

Stories of rapes and abuse (physical, mental, and emotional) of women and young girls are all too common. Yet some victims are beginning to find the courage to speak out, to tell their stories in hope of receiving justice. Perhaps you have your own story to tell.

Either way, God commands each of us to find a way to help "defend the defenseless. . .stand up for the powerless, and prosecute all those who exploit them." Doing so will take courage. A first step may be to pray . . .

Lord, comfort all the women and girls who have been abused by others. Give them strength, courage, and love. Most of all, Lord, show me how You would have me and others stand up for them. Amen.

FROM STORM WIND TO WHISPER

He quieted the wind down to a whisper,
put a muzzle on all the big waves.
PSALM 107:29 MSG

Praise our God, the God who makes unions out of contradictions and knits peace out of warring factions. Praise our God for finding a path through extremes that somehow manages to be more radical than any side could imagine. And praise our God for drawing to Himself all things, small and great, known and unknown.

Psalm 107 is a psalm of praise, thanking God for the myriad ways He brings His people out of trouble. It's a beautiful, rich song that reminds us again and again that no matter where we are, what we've done, or what kind of hardship we are facing, God can rescue us. He will save us. All we have to do is call out to Him.

If we've been left high and dry by desperate times and are struggling just to get by, God will resettle us in the land of plenty. He will satisfy our thirst and feed us more than we need.

If we've been walking through a dark valley for our souls, caught up in our own rebellion and fleeing the hard work of following God's commands, God will hear our cries for help. He will grant His "miracle mercy" (Psalm 107:15 MSG) and save us from the prisons we put ourselves in.

If we've suffered physically because of bad decisions and failure to care for our bodies, God can heal us with a word—He can quiet

our restlessness and give us the will to overcome our addictions.

If we've experienced a whirlwind of emotions, riding a roller coaster through personal drama, God will still our storms. He will hush the hysterical outpourings of our hearts and turn down the volume on the drama. He will quiet our wind to a whisper so we can finally hear Him speak.

This is our God—who humbles proud princes and sets them to wander without a home while lifting up the oppressed and establishing them as overseers of flourishing estates. This is our God, who has a wisdom that confounds the scholars of this world and who has followers who seem foolish in their acts of kindness toward a world that rejects them.

"Good people see this and are glad; bad people are speechless, stopped in their tracks. If you are really wise, you'll think this over—it's time you appreciated GOD's deep love" (Psalm 107:42–43 MSG).

God, I want to swim in the depths of Your love and experience the stillness of Your peaceful waters. Amen.

NOT FORGOTTEN

Are not five sparrows sold for two pennies? And [yet] not one of them is forgotten or uncared for in the presence of God. But [even] the very hairs of your head are all numbered. Do not be struck with fear or seized with alarm; you are of greater worth than many [flocks] of sparrows.

LUKE 12:6–7 AMPC

Imagine you're a child. Your mom drops you off at camp then forgets to pick you up. . . . You're a student in school. The teacher never calls on you. . . . You've worked at your job for three years, and you still don't get the same pay or respect as your male coworker in the next cubicle. . . . It's your wedding anniversary. You make a fancy dinner. Your husband, oblivious, calls at the last minute and says he'll be working late. . . . It's Mother's Day. Not one child has called or sent a card. . . . You've said something without thinking. Now all your friends seem to have deserted you. . . . You're getting into the later years. One day you look in the mirror and note how much the wrinkles have increased and the hair decreased. . . .

Sometimes it can be difficult to be a daughter, student, employee, wife, mom, friend, or senior. Some days you may feel forgotten, neglected, underpaid, and taken for granted. It's almost as if you're slowly fading away, wondering if anyone cares anymore. You fear no one values what you have to say, what you know, what you can do, who you are.

Here's the good news. There's Someone who knows exactly who you are. And He still loves you. Always has, always will. He knows every detail about you—even the number of hairs you have (or don't have) on your head.

That one person is God. And He is eager to be all you need. He's the Father you never had, the One filled with compassion for you (see Psalm 103:13). He's the comforting Mother you need (see Isaiah 66:13). He's your Teacher, showing you the way to go (see Psalm 32:8). He's your Boss, the One who will give you your real reward (see Colossians 3:23–24). God is your Husband (see Isaiah 54:5). He's also your Son (see Matthew 12:47–49). He's the Friend who sticks closer to you than a brother—or a sister (see Proverbs 18:24). God will even care for and carry you as you become a woman of mature years (see Isaiah 46:4).

So, woman, what's to fear? God is with you. He values you, knows you like no other.

When you're feeling afraid, alone, deserted, ignored, unfriended, neglected, and rejected, get closer to God. Value Him as much as He values you.

No fear when You're here, Lord. No fear. Amen.

KINGDOM SEEKERS

"Do not seek what you are to eat and what you are to drink, nor be worried. For all. . .seek after these things, and your Father knows that you need them. Instead, seek his kingdom, and these things will be added to you. Fear not. . .for it is your Father's good pleasure to give you the kingdom."

LUKE 12:29–32 ESV

Life can be exhausting, especially when you're frightened or worried about your life and the lives of those for whom you're responsible.

You look at your checkbook balance and shake your head, wondering how you're ever going to make ends meet. What food and drink will you be able to afford this week? How much more wear will you be able to get out of your current wardrobe before you start looking like a rag lady? How much higher will your health insurance premiums go before you can no longer afford any coverage at all? How long will your car be roadworthy? How will you ever plan for retirement when you have diapers to buy, college loans to pay off, and a house that needs a new roof?

These are the kinds of questions that can keep you up at night, especially when there seems to be no man-made solution in sight. Fortunately, you're a believer. You don't have to live this kind of life. You can choose another path: the one Jesus provides. Jesus tells you that you don't need to be worried about what to eat and drink. Nor are you to be anxious about insurance, paychecks,

clothes, cars, IRAs, student loans, and houses. Life is worth more than all those things.

Look at the birds. They don't go to a job from nine to five. They don't store extra feed in their garage. They simply tweet their praises to God, and He provides all they need! If God does that for a flock of birds, He'll do even more for you!

Besides, worrying adds nothing to your life. Well, it will add more worry lines in your face and give you more acid in your belly. But those are things you really don't want (or need) more of.

Jesus' cure for your anxiety is to seek God. Seek His kingdom. Then all you need will be supplied. But what does it mean to seek God's kingdom? It means to make God a priority in your life, to seek Him early in the morning through prayer and reading of the Word. To search for His presence, wisdom, will, and way. As you do so, worries and fears will fade away, and faith will take center stage.

Lord, in this moment, I draw near to You, seeking Your face, wisdom, and light. Lead me where You would have me be. Amen.

A WISE WOMAN FROM TEKOA

Joab sent for a wise woman from Tekoa, and said to her, "Pretend to be filled with sorrow. Dress as if you were filled with sorrow, and do not pour oil on yourself. . . . Then go to the king and speak to him in this way."

2 SAMUEL 14:2–3 NLV

Everyone knows of the New Testament wise men, the ones who visited and brought Jesus gifts. But not many people know of the wise *women* of the Bible, particularly this one from Tekoa.

Here's the scenario: Absalom had killed Amnon, the half brother who raped his sister Tamar. Immediately afterward, Absalom ran to his grandfather's house, hoping the anger of his father, King David, would eventually cool down enough so he could come back home.

Finally, that day came. Joab, the commander of David's army, noticed that David had finished mourning Amnon and begun yearning for Absalom. So, wanting to help David see sense, Joab sent for the wise woman of Tekoa. He told the old woman to dress in mourning and tell David a story.

Once in his presence, the wise woman told David that she, a widow, had two sons. One day one killed the other. Now her entire clan wanted to kill the killer, which would leave her with no son at all! She knew this must be wrong because, she reasoned, "God does not take away life. He works out ways to get the exile back" (2 Samuel 14:14 MSG).

David, perceiving the injustice of the woman's only surviving son being killed, soon saw the similarity between her situation and his. Beginning to suspect her story was fictional, David asked if Joab put her up to coming to see him. She bravely admitted that Joab had indeed given her these words to say, but then worked to assuage the king's potential anger by appealing to his ego, saying, "It was because he wanted to turn things around that your servant Joab did this. But my master is as wise as God's angels in knowing how to handle things on this earth" (2 Samuel 14:20 MSG).

Thanks to Joab's plan and this wise woman's courage, King David instructed Joab to bring back Absalom, which, for better or worse, Joab did. And the woman? She returned home, having kept her cool while playing a part in the machinations of two men—one her king, the other a commander—and reconciling members of the royal family.

Someday you too may be called to use the power of story to help someone see the error of his or her ways or to right a wrong. In any case, keep your cool, knowing that God will give you the wisdom and courage to do both.

Give me the wisdom and courage I may need, Lord, to right a wrong. Amen.

JESUS IS CALLING

"I have not come to call the righteous, but sinners."
MATTHEW 9:13 NIV

Who's on your list? What list? Well, the list of people you would rather not have to deal with. Maybe it's a list of people you'd rather not sit next to in church, or on an airplane, or at your dinner party.

We all have people who make us feel uncomfortable just by their very existence. Sometimes we have legitimate reasons for feeling this way, but more often than not, we just have prejudices. We make up our mind about some people before we even set eyes on them. And there are whole categories of sinners that we think we know all about, aren't there?

We know why they sin. We know how often they sin. And we know what their sin has done to their hearts and minds. And we don't want anything to do with them.

Because maybe we think those people should be someone else's problem. We have been put on this earth to love everyone—except those people. Someone else is in charge of loving those people. We did not sign up to love them. We signed up to love cute little babies or nice old folks or the kind of people who smell good and wear their Sunday best to church. We did not sign up to love people who. . .sin.

Maybe we look at certain sinners and we see what we once were or what we easily could become. Or maybe we see them and

realize that they are just like us. And for various reasons, that makes us feel uncomfortable.

And that's what's funny about Jesus' response to the Pharisees when they wondered why this Jewish teacher would want to be seen with tax collectors and sinners. They figured that if He was legitimate, if He really knew the law, He would know that He was risking His reputation. He was risking being made unclean.

But Jesus said, "It is not the healthy who need a doctor, but the sick" (Matthew 9:12 NIV). And then He went on to tell His hearers to go brush up on their scriptures—to go learn what this means: "I desire mercy, not sacrifice" (Matthew 9:13 NIV).

Do you see what Jesus did there? He turned the tables on them. He said: The sick people are the ones who need a doctor. And guess what—if you don't get that God wants you to show people mercy instead of offering your oh-so-holier-than-thou worship to Him, then you are the sick ones. You are the ones who need a doctor. So get in line.

Jesus is calling sinners. Don't you want to answer Him?

Lord of all, help me to love all. Amen.

GET GOING

He answered me, "I am all you need. I give you My loving-favor. My power works best in weak people." I am happy to be weak and have troubles so I can have Christ's power in me.

2 CORINTHIANS 12:9 NLV

Some people's knees start wobbling when they find themselves in small, confined places. Some feel their legs turning into jelly when they have to climb a ladder. Others find their hands shaking when they have to give a speech.

What situations make your knees knock together? What challenges bring your fears and weaknesses into focus?

Consider Moses. God wanted him to lead His people out of Egypt. To do that, Moses would have to go to Egypt and talk to Pharaoh. But Moses was reluctant to go, in part because he wasn't a good speaker. He told God, "Master, please, I don't talk well. I've never been good with words, neither before nor after you spoke to me. I stutter and stammer" (Exodus 4:10 MSG).

Moses had the wrong mindset. He was seeing every challenge before him as something he had to face and overcome in his own power. Like many of us, he was thinking only of what he could do in his power, not what God could do through him. He was self-reliant rather than God-reliant. So God let him know where his true power and abilities lay, telling Moses, "Get going. I'll be right there with you—with your mouth! I'll be right there to teach you what to say" (Exodus 4:12 MSG).

God is all you need to meet any and every challenge you face. He promises to be right there with you. He wants to be your "[strength and defense] every morning" (Isaiah 33:2 AMPC). Through Isaiah, God said, "Energize the limp hands, strengthen the rubbery knees. Tell fearful souls, 'Courage! Take heart! GOD is here, right here, on his way to put things right and redress all wrongs. He's on his way! He'll save you!' " (Isaiah 35:3–4 MSG).

Remember that God knows exactly who you are and what you need. He knows your weaknesses and fears, your assets and your liabilities. And God will use all those things to demonstrate His power and strength as He works through you! So, woman, no need to fear. God is with you—today and every day!

Lord, You know exactly where I falter, what I fear, when I fall. Be with me in those moments, Lord. Work Your power and strength through me. Amen.

FROM ORDINARY TO EXTRAORDINARY

God is in the center of her. She will not be moved. God will help her when the morning comes. . . . The Lord of All is with us. The God of Jacob is our strong place.

PSALM 46:5, 11 NLV

Sometimes things don't go at all as planned. . . . Even though Joab and the wise woman convinced David to allow Absalom to return home, the father-son reunion never really gelled. Their disunion morphed into an outright coup as Absalom sought to dethrone David.

Now David was once more on the run. Yet amazingly, his kingdom was saved in part by the courage of a calm, cool, and collected servant girl and a housewife. Here's what happened:

Two of David's men, Jonathan and Ahimaaz, were hanging out at En Rogel, for it was there that a female servant was to pass on information that they'd relay to King David. This line of communication worked out well until a boy spotted David's men and reported them to Absalom.

Knowing that they had been identified, the two men hurried out of En Rogel and arrived at the house of a man in Bahurim. As quickly as possible, they climbed down into the well the man had in his courtyard. The man of Bahurim's wife threw a cover over the well's opening then spread ground corn on it. Just as she had

done so, Absalom's servants appeared on the scene. They asked her, "Where are Ahimaaz and Jonathan?"

The calm, quick-witted woman answered, "They were headed toward the river" (2 Samuel 17:20 MSG). Taking her at her word, they followed her directions but didn't find the men. Afterward, they simply headed back to their master in Jerusalem.

When the woman of Bahurim determined the coast was clear, she removed the cover, signaling to the men it was now safe for their escape.

Thanks to the efforts, calm, and courage of a servant girl and a housewife, David received vital information that not only saved his life but his kingdom.

God works His will in amazing ways. He designs his plans so that ordinary people are provided an opportunity to play extraordinary roles in His story.

Perhaps God is preparing you, an ordinary woman, to play an extraordinary part. In doing so, He wants you to learn how to keep calm amid chaos, to be steadfast when trouble comes, to be ready to take unusually brave actions in common places such as a backyard, the market, or on a side street. With God at your center, you will not fail.

Lord, thank You for writing someone as simple as I am into Your story. Grow me into a woman of strength and confidence, Lord, so I'll be ready when You need me. Amen.

AND YET. . .

"So I say to you, keep asking, and it will be given to you. Keep searching, and you will find. Keep knocking, and the door will be opened to you. For everyone who asks receives, and the one who searches finds, and to the one who knocks, the door will be opened."

LUKE 11:9–10 HCSB

In Luke 18:1–8, Jesus told His followers "a parable to the effect that they ought always to pray and not to turn coward (faint, lose heart, and give up)" (Luke 18:1 AMPC). The fascinating thing about this parable is that the protagonist (the main character, often also the hero or the "good guy") is a poor widow, the least powerful and most vulnerable person in society at that time.

Because she is a woman—typically not allowed to appear in public much less testify in court—her rights are few. Because she is a widow, she has no male to be her advocate and speak for her in court. And because she is poor, she has no money with which to bribe the judge (her antagonist) to rule in her favor. To make matters even more difficult, the judge hearing her case is one "who never gave God a thought and cared nothing for people" (Luke 18:2 MSG).

And yet here she is, a poor widow, coming into court, breaking all the rules of society. She tells the judge her rights are being violated. She demands he protect her! The judge refuses. Nevertheless, she keeps

on coming. . .and coming. . .and coming to court, pleading her case.

Finally, the widow wears down the judge. She shatters his resolve. He says, "Because this widow won't quit badgering me, I'd better do something and see that she gets justice—otherwise I'm going to end up beaten black-and-blue by her pounding" (Luke 18:5 MSG).

Jesus told His listeners, "Do you hear what that judge, corrupt as he is, is saying? So what makes you think God won't step in and work justice for his chosen people, who continue to cry out for help? Won't he stick up for them?" (Luke 18:6–7 MSG).

Jesus wants you to know, to get it straight in your head, that when you continue to come to Father God, to ask, seek, and knock on His door, "He will not drag his feet" (Luke 18:8 MSG) to help you. So don't "turn coward (faint, lose heart, and give up)" (Luke 18:1 AMPC). Keep on asking, searching, and knocking, knowing that God will, in His perfect time, answer the prayer of the persistent.

I come to You now, Lord, asking, seeking, and knocking for Your answer to my plea through prayer. Hear me, O Lord. Amen.

SURE UNSEEN

Our life is lived by faith. We do not live by what we see in front of us. . . . Now faith is being sure we will get what we hope for. It is being sure of what we cannot see.
2 CORINTHIANS 5:7; HEBREWS 11:1 NLV

Pastor and teacher Andrew Murray once said, "We have a God who delights in impossibilities." That's an amazing claim. Yet it is backed up again and again in the Bible. Story after story shows believers what happens when God's people are motivated by faith instead of fear.

By faith Abraham went when God called him to go—even when he had no idea of where he was going (see Hebrews 11:8). He blindly followed his promise-making God and so received all he had been promised.

By faith Sarah was able to conceive and give birth—even though both she and her husband, Abraham, were well past child-bearing age. She received that miracle child because "she had faith to believe that God would do what He promised" (Hebrews 11:11 NLV).

By faith Moses' parents hid him from the infant-killing Pharaoh. "They were not afraid of the king when he said that all baby boys should be killed" (Hebrews 11:23 NLV). Because of his parents' faith and his own faith, Moses left Egypt, unafraid of the king's rage. "Moses did not turn from the right way but kept seeing God

in front of him" (Hebrews 11:27 NLV).

Because God's people had faith, they went through the Red Sea, just as if it were dry ground. Decades later, because of their faith, the walls of Jericho fell.

Because Rahab the prostitute had faith, she hid Joshua's spies from the king of Jericho. Therefore she and her family weren't killed when God's army attacked. Rahab later reformed—and became an ancestor of Jesus!

All these stories, about how people walked by faith and not fear, are listed in Hebrews 11. In each situation God did something amazing, something that seemed impossible. Consider the military conquests of Gideon, Barak and Deborah, Samson, and David; the miracles of Elijah and Elisha; Daniel in the lions' den; Shadrach, Meshach, and Abednego amid the furnace flames; the healings, prophecies, and powers of Jesus; and in the end, the amazing works of Jesus' disciples.

You too can be part of God's amazing story if you replace your fears with faith. If you live focused on the unseen rather than the seen. If you become sure of receiving the things you hope for, certain they exist even though you cannot yet see them. Believe. And God will do something amazing.

I want to become a part of Your story, Lord.
Help me be sure of what I cannot yet see. Amen.

DESIRE AND POWER

For God is working in you, giving you the desire and the power to do what pleases him. Do everything without complaining and arguing, so that no one can criticize you. Live clean, innocent lives as children of God.

PHILIPPIANS 2:13–15 NLT

We can't do this without God. That's all there is to it.

What is "this"? "This" is everything—anything that's worthwhile, anything that can make a difference in the world. "This" is how we are meant to shine brightly for Christ.

No complaining? No arguing? No one criticizing you? In most households with teenagers, this by itself would be some kind of miracle. Can you imagine being able to go about your daily routine, making plans for where you need to go, what you need to buy, and what you are making for dinner, without someone trying to negate your votes? Can you imagine making it through a day in which you yourself don't complain about something?

Living a clean, innocent life? So we shine like a bright light "in a world full of crooked and perverse people" (Philippians 2:15 NLT)? Does that sound anything at all like something you could achieve on your own? Does that even sound like something you'd choose to do on a normal day?

How about rejoicing even if we lose everything? Does that sound like an achievable goal for most of us? How do we even

begin to learn how to do that? How do we make our service an acceptable offering to God? Should we make a practice of losing things just so we can experiment with personal failure?

Can you hold firmly to the Word of life? Can you obey the Creator's words—the words of the One who made all things well and designed them to function together in a beautiful harmony? Can you listen to where He leads you so that your work will not be useless? Can you follow in His steps, looking out for ways to solve problems creatively and to work together with others in wisdom and grace?

We *can* do all of "this." We can do these things because the One who made us *is* working within us and through us, not just to make us capable and competent but to make us *want* to do what pleases Him. And when we have the desire to please Him and the power to please Him, we will be able to meet the goal of pleasing Him. And then we will certainly rejoice.

Creator God, thank You for the wonderful working You perform in me! Amen.

THE POWER TO CHANGE EVERYTHING

As for God, His way is perfect; the word of the Lord is tried. He is a Shield to all those who trust and take refuge in Him. . . . God is my strong Fortress; He guides the blameless in His way and sets him free. He sets me secure and confident upon the heights.

2 SAMUEL 22:31, 33–34 AMPC

Nothing compares with the power of prayer. As one person wrote, "Sometimes, all it takes is just one prayer to change everything." Oh, so true.

Consider Elisha's servant. An army surrounded him and his master. He cried to Elisha in fear, wondering what they were going to do. Elisha told him, "Fear not; for those with us are more than those with them" (2 Kings 6:16 AMPC). He then prayed for God to open his servant's eyes. And God did just that, allowing the young man to see a mountain full of horses and chariots of fire, banishing his fear.

After Jacob had cheated his brother, Esau, out of his inheritance and his father's blessings, he ran away from home to escape his brother's anger. Years later, when the brothers were to see each other again, Jacob asked God to deliver him from Esau (see Genesis 32:9–12). And God did.

When Moses asked for help at the edge of the Red Sea, God

separated the sea so His people could walk between walls of water (see Exodus 14:15–25). Later, because of Moses' prayer, God changed the water at Marah from bitter to sweet (see Exodus 15:25) and brought water out of a rock at Horeb (see Exodus 17:5–7).

Amid a battle, Joshua prayed for the sun and moon to stand still, and God granted his request (see Joshua 10:12–13). Samson's dad, Manoah, prayed for an angel to come back and give him and his soon-to-become-pregnant wife some direction, and the angel did (see Judges 13).

Elijah asked God to bring a boy back from death, and God did (see 1 Kings 17). Soon after, Elijah asked God to bring down fire from heaven. Once more, it was a done deal (see 1 Kings 18)!

The list goes on and on about how people in the Bible pray to God and everything changes.

The thing is, God is *still* in the business of answering prayers. And right now He's waiting for yours. So take to God all your worries, concerns, and problems—big and small. Cry out to Him with groans, moans, or words, and know that He will hear. He will answer. And He will change everything.

Thank You, Lord, for the privilege of prayer.
Help me, Lord. Here's what's happening. . . .

A WOMAN WARRIOR'S WISDOM

The woman went to all the people with her wise counsel.

2 SAMUEL 20:22 HCSB

Having just staved off one rebellion, that of his now deceased son Absalom, King David was facing another. This one was being led by a man named Sheba. Second Samuel 20:1 gives the reader a good picture of this Benjamite, describing him as "base and contemptible" (AMPC), "worthless" (ESV), "good-for-nothing" (MSG), and "wicked" (HCSB). Because of Sheba's claim that there was no future for Israel with David, all but Judah deserted the king and followed Sheba. So David, back in Jerusalem, sent his men to chase down the rebel.

After a side skirmish along the way, David's nephew Joab arrived in Abel where Sheba had taken refuge. As the king's men worked to besiege the city and batter down walls, the residents behind those walls began to panic. When battering rams began to strike the city walls, the voice of a wise woman was heard above the din. From behind the city walls, she asked people to listen and to tell Joab she would like to speak to him. Once Joab came near, she asked him to confirm his identity—it was no use negotiating with someone other than the top man. He said he was Joab.

Then this lone woman simply asked Joab to listen to what she had to say. He patiently replied, "I am listening" (2 Samuel 20:17 ESV).

She spoke of how people used to come to Abel for wisdom, and they'd get it. That its people were peaceful, faithful. Why would Joab want to mess around with this God-blessed place?

Joab explained that he had nothing against the city. He didn't want to destroy it or its people. All he wanted was one resident: Sheba, the man who revolted against King David and was now hiding behind Abel's walls. If the citizens handed him over, Joab would leave in peace. That sounded like a fair deal to the wise woman: the life of one "base and contemptible" (AMPC), "worthless" (ESV), "good-for-nothing" (MSG), and "wicked" (HCSB) man in exchange for the city and its people.

So she presented the idea to her fellow citizens. Soon after, Sheba's head came over the wall and landed at Joab's feet.

What a wise woman warrior! She lifted her voice when others were panicking. She stood toe-to-toe with the king's military man while others shook in their boots. She negotiated a deal and came up with a plan and a compromise with a man who was a born strategist. She saved her city by sacrificing one life. May you one day prove to be just as wise.

Give me the courage, Lord, to be wise, to speak when others remain silent, to stand when others shake. Amen.

MY ROCK

"The LORD is my rock, my fortress and my deliverer;
my God is my rock, in whom I take refuge."
2 SAMUEL 22:2–3 NIV

The little boy curled his fingers around the edge of what to him seemed like a small mountain. With every bit of strength he had in his chubby legs and sweaty hands, he pushed himself up on his toes and pulled his body up, up, up on top of the large, sun-warmed rock. At last. He let out a whoosh of relief and spread himself out on the massive flat face of the stone, face up, eyes closed, soaking in the golden light.

Up on the rock, he didn't worry about the neighbor's scary miniature poodle that always nipped at his heels when he ran too close to it. He didn't have to be afraid of anything. And he didn't even have to think too much about being tagged "it." No one could see him there on the rock, especially when he made himself as flat as could be. The rock was his safe place. It was where he liked to come when he thought his parents were being unfair. It was where he came when he felt sad or alone, like when his favorite goldfish died. No one would have guessed how comforting a giant rock could be, but this little boy knew.

Have you ever found comfort and rest in an unlikely place? Maybe you have a friend who's gruff and intimidating on the outside but has a heart of gold on the inside. Maybe you have a

favorite spot in your town that seems ugly to anyone else but gives you peace. Maybe you have found quiet in the middle of chaos or found refreshment in a desert landscape. Maybe you find soothing in a storm.

David had known a lot of storms. He described the "waves of death" circling him and the "torrents of destruction" overwhelming him (2 Samuel 22:5 NIV). But then he called out to God, and what was God's response? "The earth trembled and quaked, the foundations of the heavens shook; they trembled because he was angry" (2 Samuel 22:8 NIV). But God was not angry with David—no, God rebuked David's enemies, using all the imposing gloom of thunder and the echoes of His might. Because David was faithful, God showed faithfulness to him. And because God is the almighty, all-powerful rock of a God that He is, His faithfulness is strong and loud and formidable. And in that, we can find comfort.

Lord, when I am shaken, help me hold tight to the solid reality of You. Amen.

THE REAL MOTHER

The mother of the living child had much pity for her son and said to the king, "O, my lord, give her the living child."
1 KINGS 3:26 NLV

Just after Solomon became the new king, the Lord came to him in a dream and said, "Ask what you wish Me to give you" (1 Kings 3:5 NLV). The young and inexperienced king asked for wisdom so he would know "the difference between good and bad" (1 Kings 3:9 NLV).

God was so pleased that Solomon asked for wisdom instead of riches and long life that He gave Solomon all three—riches, long life, *and* wisdom. But it was the wisdom that came just in time. For the very next day, Solomon found himself having to resolve an argument between two female prostitutes.

The first woman told Solomon that she and this other woman lived in the same house. One day the first woman gave birth to a son. Three days later the other woman delivered her own son. But that night, when they were alone, the second woman rolled over on her son and he died. So she got up in the middle of the night and switched her dead son for the first woman's live one. The next morning, when the first woman woke to nurse her child, she found the boy was dead. That's also when, upon closer inspection, she realized the boy was not her child!

The second woman protested the first woman's account, telling

Solomon the live child was hers. Both cried out for Solomon to resolve the situation. And he did, merely by asking someone for a sword so that he could cut the child in two, giving each woman one half.

The first mother courageously revealed she was the true mother, saying to Solomon, "O my lord, give her the living child. Do not kill him," whereas the second woman said, "He will not be mine or yours. Divide him" (1 Kings 3:26 NLV).

The wise Solomon then said, "Give the first woman the living child. Do not kill him. She is his mother" (1 Kings 3:27 NLV).

Solomon isn't the only wise person in this story; the wisdom, bravery, and self-sacrifice of woman number one is clearly revealed. For one of the hardest things a mother could be called to do is let go of her child. And that's where God came in.

God alone can give a mother the strength, wisdom, and courage she needs to do the right thing at the right time for her little (or not so little) ones, no matter how heart-wrenching it may be for her.

Help me be brave, Lord, when my love for my children is put to the test. Amen.

LOSING OR KEEPING

"Anyone who loves their life will lose it, while anyone who hates their life in this world will keep it for eternal life."

JOHN 12:25 NIV

Do you love your life? Do you look forward to every day? What about your job? Do you hold on tightly to your work, counting every hour, checking off every achievement? Are you stashing away funds and gathering possessions? What about your family? Are you planning every moment and hanging on to each memory?

If you are finding all your fulfillment in your earthly minutes, if you are getting caught up in the daily grind, you may want to check your goals. This life is, after all, temporary. Our days on earth are just a blip on a very wide screen. It's hard to remember this in the moment, though, isn't it? Some days seem to last forever. And some days we wish would last forever.

But that feeling, that longing for forever, is exactly the glimpse of heaven we need to hang on to. We need to remember that every bit of goodness, every bit of love, every bit of joy and glory and hope that we experience here on earth is just a taste of what we are designed to feel in the kingdom of heaven, when we are living there with God.

When Jesus said, "Anyone who loves their life will lose it," He wasn't predicting that all the happy people would die young. Nor was He saying that you need to walk like a grumpy old man

through your days, hating every minute, in order to gain eternal life. He was instead commenting on our priorities. Those who are wrapped up in their lives now will find it very hard to let go of any of that earthly happiness in order to serve the Lord. Those who, on the other hand, look forward to heaven and put serving Christ first, before all the rest of their worldly desires, will find themselves ready at any moment to walk into eternal life.

It's not wrong to enjoy our lives. But focusing too much on what happens to us in the here and now may result in our losing sight of the yet to come. And God has so much more in store for us!

Lord, help me not to get so distracted by the nearest parts of my life that I forget what You have promised for me. I want to serve You well, Lord. Show me how. Amen.

LOOK AGAIN

I have been cast out of Your presence and Your sight; yet I will look again toward Your holy temple. The waters compassed me about. . .the seaweed was wrapped about my head. . . . When my soul fainted upon me [crushing me], I earnestly and seriously remembered the Lord; and my prayer came to You.

JONAH 2:4–5, 7 AMPC

In the first two verses of the book of Jonah, God is telling Jonah what to do ("Go to Nineveh"). The third verse records Jonah doing the exact opposite: "Jonah got up *to flee* to Tarshish *from the* LORD*'s presence*. He went down to Joppa and found a ship going to Tarshish. He paid the fare and went down into it *to go* with them to Tarshish, *from the* LORD*'s presence*" (Jonah 1:3 HCSB, emphasis added). Jonah thought he was fleeing from God, but he quickly found out he couldn't because God is everywhere, seeing and hearing everything.

Jonah was on the ship when God whipped up a big storm. Jonah, knowing he was the problem, told the sailors to throw him into the sea. Reluctantly, they did. The storm calmed, but Jonah was eaten by a huge sea creature.

There, in the belly of the fish, Jonah had time to think and pray. Jonah recounted his harrowing ordeal, telling how he cried out to God and God answered him. How his eyes and his focus were now back on the Lord. Jonah praised God, thanking Him for saving his life, after which God commanded the great fish to spit Jonah out on dry land.

Later what Jonah had feared would happen did indeed happen: God spared Nineveh (see Jonah 4:2). So although you're left wondering if Jonah learned a lesson, you realize you have picked up a few of your own.

The first big takeaway is that there is no way you can ever run from God. He sees and hears everything. He knows where you are and what you're doing. So remove that option from the table when God calls you. Instead, keep your eyes on Him. The second is that what God wills will be done, whether you're on board with it or not. The third is that if God calls you to do something that seems scary, don't flee or freak out. Instead, be still, resting in His presence. Wait patiently for Him to equip you. As you focus on Him alone, He'll instill you with the strength and encouragement you need.

In You, Lord, I am waiting and still. Fill me with Your strength and courage. Show me where You would have me go. Amen.

PRETENDERS

You are following a different way that pretends to be the Good News but is not the Good News at all.

GALATIANS 1:6–7 NLT

Now, perhaps more than ever, we are living in a time when it is hard to figure out who is a trustworthy source. Some people say follow *this* person. Others say you can trust *that* person. We can do some research and find some answers but not all, and then it's hard to trust the source of those answers.

But does that mean we should give up trying? Should we just shrug our shoulders and say it's impossible to trust anyone? Should we just blindly follow whoever has the strongest voice? Should we stop seeking the truth?

Surely the answer to these questions is no. We are called as children of God to be seekers of the truth and to be speakers of the truth. How do we do that?

The best way is to start and end with the Word of God. If we hear someone claiming to preach the Gospel of Jesus, it's not hard to compare their words to the story of Jesus in the Bible. Even in matters that are more flexible to interpretation, we can look in God's Word to see if all the threads of the message line up with the statements of Jesus and with the story of God's people.

For instance, if a speaker claims to be preaching the Gospel of Christ, yet they leave out the need for people to come to

repentance, we can look in God's Word and clearly see repentance being preached. We can conclude that the speaker either is not a reliable source for wisdom or has made a grave oversight in preaching the Word of God.

Or if a speaker claims to be preaching the Good News but then talks about the resurrection of Jesus as only a symbol and not a reality, we can go to God's Word and contrast its truth with the message we heard.

Or if a speaker claims to be telling us about anything—how to love others, how to know God's will, how to receive Jesus' salvation—and yet that speaker lives in a way that is contrary to everything that is spoken, we can go to God's Word and see the inconsistencies being presented and conclude that the speaker does not seem to know the truth of Jesus.

We should not condemn any speaker, however. We are not the distributors of condemnation and judgment—God will do the judging. But we can and should be discerning seekers of the truth.

God of the Good News, help me to be a truthful speaker of that Good News to everyone I see. Amen.

KING OF THE FLOOD

The LORD sits enthroned over the flood; the LORD is enthroned as King forever. The LORD gives strength to his people; the LORD blesses his people with peace.

PSALM 29:10–11 NIV

Drip. Drop. That's how it started—just a sprinkle. Then the sprinkle turned into a steady rain. Then torrents of rain beat down on the community. The creeks spilled over. The rivers burst out of their banks. And the water kept coming.

There is little peace when the floodwaters are rising, the rain is still pouring, and your front steps are just feet away from trouble. Little peace and yet so little you can actually do. You can't stop the rain. You can't hem in the rivers. You can't build a wall to keep the waters out of your house.

All you really can do is pray.

Floods are one kind of trouble. But often our troubles come in floods. The old saying "When it rains, it pours" rings true more regularly than we'd like. And in those times when the accidents and mistakes and bad luck and disappointments pile up one on top of another like some giant totem pole of misfortune, it's easy to feel forgotten. It's easy to believe God has left the building. Maybe He's on vacation or just busy with another mess somewhere else in the world. Or maybe He's just mad at us.

But when torrents of trouble come, the best thing we can do

is take shelter under the One who "sits enthroned over the flood." No matter how we feel about the situation, no matter how helpless we are, and no matter where we think God may have gone off to, the fact remains that He is the best person in our lives to help us.

People may try to help, and we definitely should try to lift one another up. We especially should protect the weaker ones among us and look out for those who are alone or abandoned. But we cannot depend on humans to give us everything we need. And when those floodwaters of strife begin to recede, the real work of healing and cleaning and rebuilding begins.

Our Lord is mighty and powerful. He can give us strength. He can reach into our hearts and mend our wounds. He can see into our minds and help us untangle the knots we get ourselves tied up in through poor decisions or negative patterns.

God will not always stop the floods from coming. But He will always be with us in the water.

God of the flood of my troubles, wash over me. Let my stress and my pain bring me humbly to the shore of Your peace. Amen.

THE WIDOW OF ZAREPHATH

Elijah said to her, "Don't be afraid; go and do as you have said. . . . For this is what the LORD God of Israel says, 'The flour jar will not become empty and the oil jug will not run dry until the day the LORD sends rain on the surface of the land.' "

1 KINGS 17:13–14 HCSB

In 1 Kings 17, the prophet Elijah told wicked King Ahab that Israel was going to suffer a drought. Soon afterward, God told Elijah to hide by the Cherith River. There he would have food and water. So Elijah went to Cherith, and God sent ravens to bring him bread and meat twice a day. When the brook eventually dried up, God told Elijah, "Get up, go to Zarephath. . .and stay there. Look, I have commanded a woman who is a widow to provide for you" (1 Kings 17:9 HCSB). So Elijah went to Zarephath, a city of Gentiles.

When Elijah arrived at the city gates, he saw a widow collecting sticks of firewood. He called to her and asked for some water. As she went to get it, he asked for her to give him some bread as well. Unfortunately, she said, she had nothing but some flour in a jar and a little oil in a jug. The sticks she had been gathering were what she was going to use to make a last meal for herself and her son before they died.

Elijah told the woman not to fear but to make him a small loaf of bread and then some for herself and her boy. God would more than replenish her supplies.

The woman obeyed Elijah, and true to His word, God continually refilled her jar of flour and jug of oil. Happily, all three of them ate bread for many days.

Yet then something horrible happened. Instead of putting on pounds and becoming healthier, the widow's son got so sick he died. After she cried out to Elijah, Elijah in turn cried out to God, praying for Him to return the boy to the land of the living. And God did! Elijah then brought the boy downstairs and handed him over to his mother. The woman said to Elijah, "I see it all now—you *are* a holy man. When you speak, GOD speaks—a true word!" (1 Kings 17:24 MSG).

This Gentile widow saw a bit of God in Elijah. Because of that, she trusted him and found the courage to feed him before herself or her son.

Be as the three members of this unlikely trio. Trust God to provide, to be true to His word, and you'll find the courage to comply.

Lord, as I trust in You to provide,
grow my courage to comply. Amen.

COURAGE AND CAUTION

"I brought you out of the land of Egypt. . . .
And I sent Moses, Aaron and Miriam to lead you."
MICAH 6:4 NLV

Imagine hiding near the banks of the Nile. Your mother has just put your baby brother (later named Moses) in a basket among reeds then walked away. Although tears stream down her face, you see your mother's faith keeping her back straight, her footing firm. She has put her precious babe in the hands of God, believing the Creator and Maintainer of the universe can best protect her child.

You witness all this. You would like to follow your mother home, but you can't. No matter what the danger, you have to see what happens to your little brother. Out of the corner of your eye, you see Pharaoh's daughter appear with her maids. Your breath catches in your throat as her eyes light upon the basket. Your heart beats wildly as you watch her direct a maid to retrieve the little ark. You breathe a sigh of relief when the princess sees the little boy's face and smiles.

Somehow your feet find their way to the princess's side. You ask if she would like you to find a nurse. She nods, and you run off, soon towing your mother, her breasts still full of milk, along behind you. The princess hires your mother, and you're a family once more. At least for now.

Years later your brother Moses is called to lead the Israelites

out of Egypt and into the Promised Land. Your brother Aaron is chief priest. God works miracle after miracle, even parting the Red Sea! And soon you find yourself the first female prophet, dancer, singer, leading other women along to join in praising God (see Exodus 15:20–21).

Flash-forward to years later. You're on the Wandering-in-the-Desert Tour with the rest of the Israelites. Your initial courage and contentment have whittled down to criticism and discontentment. You speak out about your brother Moses' marriage to a woman you don't approve of. Next thing you know, you're thinking God has slighted you. Aren't you just as good as your brother Moses (see Numbers 12:2)? Suddenly God is calling you out. Such thinking and outspoken criticism provoke Him into cloaking you in leprosy. Aaron pleads with Moses to pray for you. Moses does, and God heals you.

The lesson? God loves it when you're trusting in Him, following where your curiosity leads, being fearless in new situations. What God hates is when confidence turns to criticism or cockiness. Today, examine your own walk with God. Where might He want you to be humbler and more encouraging? How might He be leading you to be not just a leader but a follower as well?

Show me, Lord, how to be fearless and yet humble as Your forever female follower. Amen.

NEVER SEPARATED

For I am convinced that neither death nor life, neither angels nor demons, neither the present nor the future, nor any powers, neither height nor depth, nor anything else in all creation, will be able to separate us from the love of God that is in Christ Jesus our Lord.

ROMANS 8:38–39 NIV

Imagine for a minute that you live in a world of fear. Imagine that every bump in the night, every problem in your path, every bad thing that happens—no matter how big or small—seems to be one more bit of evidence of not just bad things happening to you, but bad spirits out to get you. Imagine that every day you struggle just to step outside your door because you are so afraid of what might happen.

Anxiety can be a powerful force. It can tie people up just as surely as if heavy chains were locked around them. It can make people feel as if they are physically heavy. It can trap people in their homes as if boulders have been moved in front of their doors. It can imprison people inside their own minds.

But God is stronger. And God can set people free.

Many people are trapped within themselves due to anxiety, and they don't even know it. It's important for this reason for all of us to keep reaching out to each other. It's important for us to care for one another and be in each other's lives enough to be able to

ask, "Are you okay?" And it's important for us to be able to know when the answer to that question is truthful or not.

It can be messy to be in each other's lives. It can be extremely difficult to help someone suffering with a mental illness. But it is also one of the most beautiful things to see someone who was once a slave to fear be freed and able to live again. Wise treatment plans will include not only medicines but also the assurance of support—the acknowledgment that other people need to stay in the patient's life.

Truthfully, we all need to be reminded that we are not alone. That we are never ever alone. That nothing can separate us from the love of good people, and nothing can keep us away from the love of Christ. No troubles. No bumps in the night. No bad people. No illness. No persecution. No physical conditions. No mental conditions. No demons. No distance. Absolutely nothing can keep us from God's eternal, powerful, pure, forgiving love.

Lord, help me reach out to others and remind them that they are never far from You. Amen.

OUR STRENGTH

God is our refuge and strength, an ever-present help in trouble.

PSALM 46:1 NIV

When the storm rages and the winds blast, the shingles come ripping off the roof and the trees go crashing to the ground; when the river rises or the tide surges and the overflow rolls into your basement or your living room or your kitchen; when the cyclone winds lift up a host of objects that are never meant to be airborne and hurl them ever so violently back to the ground; when fire in a blind rage ravages the earth, turning miles and miles of beautiful forest into a blazing inferno; when boiling rock overflows the mountaintops or the muddy earth slides thunderously down a mountainside to meet its victims; then it is that we learn that neither princes nor horses nor swords nor money can help us: God and God alone is our refuge and our strength.

About one o'clock on a Friday night, Judy and Charles got a phone call from the nearby university where their nineteen-year-old son, Tim, was enrolled. He had fallen from a wall somewhere on campus and had to be flown by helicopter to the nearest hospital. So the couple sped into the night to get to the hospital and to Tim.

"This is crazy," Charles said. "The last thing I want is to get pulled over, but I'll be darned if I'm not going to go as fast as I can." Then after a few minutes, he said, "The fact is that we're not going to be able to do anything when we get there. I just want to

see him." Judy sat in silence, frozen with fear.

When they found the trauma department, they sat for several minutes waiting to see their son. A nurse came and began to talk to them about the measures that had been taken for Tim's safety. She told them calmly that their son had broken his neck in the fall, but he was stable. At that point a door to a room opened, and Tim was being rolled by them. He was still conscious, but only barely, because he was sedated. When he was taken off to be settled for the night, the tearful parents sat together, holding hands and praying. "Dear Lord," Charles prayed, "in times past I know I've said that I needed You, but this night, Lord, You are all that the three of us have. Please stand by Tim and give him the strength to get through the night. But whatever happens, dear God, I know that You are with us, our refuge and our strength."

Lord, I know I can depend on You
in every time of trouble. Amen.

UNLOVED, BELOVED

I will call Not My People, My People,
and she who is Unloved, Beloved.
ROMANS 9:25 CSB

The mutt sat shivering in the corner, on the edge of a puddle of his own making. From his looks, he seemed to be one weird mixture—part chihuahua, part pug, part lab, and part some kind of terrier, perhaps? It was anyone's guess. One snaggle tooth protruded up over his top lip, where a wiry set of whiskers gave him the quirky impression of having a mustache. His eyes bulged out from his tiny head. He snuffled and sputtered as he breathed. One leg stuck straight out from underneath his belly, as if even his own limbs were trying to escape this creature.

His coloring was mottled—some combination of black, gray, and brown that made him look as though he had just bathed in a mud puddle. But he hadn't bathed at all—maybe ever. The stench of wet dog rose up from him like the mushroom cloud of an odor bomb.

And all around him bounded a family of happy, fluffy, handsome golden retriever pups.

He was definitely not the pick of the litter.

He wasn't even from this litter.

But the little girl who walked into the shelter that day saw him all alone in the corner and walked right over to him, not paying

attention to the bouncy balls of golden fur running all about. She held out her hand, and the unlovely creature snuffled, stuck out his tongue, and licked her fingers, then looked up at her with his big eyes and wagged his tail.

"This one, Mommy!"

Maybe you feel like you aren't exactly the pick of the litter. Maybe you feel left out and unloved. Maybe you feel that way because that has been part of your experience.

But our God delights in the lesser things of this world. He takes pleasure in exalting the humbled. He enjoys shining a spotlight on what has previously been hidden in the shadows. He makes "known the riches of his glory on objects of mercy" (Romans 9:23 CSB). God takes the forgotten ones of the world—the broken, the unholy, the used up, the horrid, the ugly—and He remembers them, heals them, sanctifies them, restores them, and transforms them. He uses unexpected people to bring to fruition the fruits of His glory.

God can and will use you—no matter what you look like or feel like or what your life has been like to this point. And not only will He use you to do great things in His kingdom; He will love you.

Beloved God, thank You for loving me even when I feel unlovable. Amen.

FEARS VS. DREAMS

What time I am afraid, I will have confidence in and put my trust and reliance in You.

PSALM 56:3 AMPC

Motivational speaker Les Brown said, "Too many of us are not living our dreams because we are living our fears." That statement makes one pause and ponder, *Am I living my fears and not my dreams?*

Consider Kings Saul and David. After the prophet Samuel privately anointed Saul, God "changed his heart. . . . Then the Spirit of God took control of him" (1 Samuel 10:9–10 HCSB). Yet even then, in the very beginning of his kingship, Saul stumbled. First, when he lied to his uncle instead of admitting Samuel had just privately anointed him king; then again when Saul hid among the luggage, just as Samuel was looking for him, ready to publicly announce his kingship (1 Samuel 10:14–16, 21–22).

Later Saul made some fear-based choices. One led him to make an unauthorized sacrifice (see 1 Samuel 13:7–15) and another led him to order the slaughter of eighty-five priests (see 1 Samuel 22:6–19). The worst fear-based choice Saul made was after Samuel died. When the Philistines were once more gearing up to fight the Israelites, Saul was afraid to the point of trembling physically. He asked God what to do, but "the LORD did not answer him in dreams or by the Urim or by the prophets" (1 Samuel 28:6 HCSB). So Saul sought out a medium so he could ask the late prophet Samuel for

advice. No good news came from that quarter either.

When we look at David's kingship, we see a much different story, for David, even before he took the throne, lived according to the Lord's ways. Even though he was by no means perfect, David based his life on trusting and relying on God alone. Because of that trust, David faced and defeated the giant Goliath whom Saul had feared (see 1 Samuel 17:11, 32). Because of his complete trust and belief, David "was successful in everything Saul sent him to do" (1 Samuel 18:5 HCSB).

You're a daughter of the King. He's the One you can trust, count on, have confidence in. Because He's your Rock, Shield, Protector, and Fortress, you need never quake with fear.

Jesus has told you that "God will help you deal with whatever hard things come up when the time comes" (Matthew 6:34 MSG). So give God all your fears, worries, and problems (see 1 Peter 5:7). And take Corrie ten Boom's advice: "Never be afraid to trust an unknown future to a known God."

Lord, I want to live my dreams not my fears.
Help me trust You with my unknown future. Amen.

A SOFT WHISPER

The Lord *was not in the wind. After the wind there was an earthquake, but the* Lord *was not in the earthquake. After the earthquake there was a fire, but the* Lord *was not in the fire. And after the fire there was a voice, a soft whisper.*

1 KINGS 19:11–12 HCSB

Elijah had just worked with God to show up the god Baal and his prophets. And it was an amazing feat, for at Elijah's request, the One true God sent down fire that consumed a water-soaked offering, stone altar, and wood, and then licked up the water-filled trench! He then had hundreds of the Baal prophets killed.

When Ahab's wife and Baal-worshipper, Queen Jezebel, heard what Elijah had done, she threatened the exhausted prophet's life. "Then Elijah became afraid and immediately ran for his life" (1 Kings 19:3 HCSB).

Elijah headed into the wilderness, sat down under a tree, and prayed for God to take his life, telling Him, "I have had enough!" (1 Kings 19:4 HCSB). Then, exhausted, Elijah fell asleep.

Have you ever been there? You had a mountaintop experience. It couldn't have gone better. But afterward you were exhausted. Then someone or something threatened your well-being. Not having enough energy to defend yourself, you ran and hid. You sought solace somewhere safe. There you hoped against hope that no one would find you or bother you. It's there that you rested, a bit

confused, wondering how you could have gone from one extreme to another so quickly. But it was also there, in that quiet, that you found the stillness you needed. It was there that God sent His angel to provide you with food and water. And it's there that you found God. Heard His voice. Came to your senses.

God beckoned you on further, as He did Elijah. He asked you what you were doing there. You explained, but now your excuse seems pretty lame. Even as you spoke, you realized your tired mind may have been making you leap to conclusions, perhaps even deviate from reality.

Yet God gave you the chance to get all the wrong thinking out of your system. He wanted you to linger there with Him, in His presence. And finally, like Elijah, you heard God's voice, a soft whisper. He again asked, "What are you doing here?" (1 Kings 19:13 HCSB). You explained once more. Then God, ever so near and gentle, redirected you once more.

When you're exhausted mentally, physically, emotionally, and spiritually, fear can find a foothold in you. That's when you need to find a place to be alone with God, allowing Him to recharge and redirect you, giving you the courage to walk His way once more.

Be with me while I rest, Lord. Speak to me in Your still, small voice. Amen.

ENTERING INTO PEACE

Daughter, your faith (your confidence and trust in Me) has made you well! Go (enter) into peace (untroubled, undisturbed well-being).

LUKE 8:48 AMPC

Jesus wants you to neither worry nor fear. That's why He left you two precious gifts (see John 14:26–27). The first is the Holy Spirit—the Helper, Comforter, Advocate, Strengthener, and Standby—who'll teach you everything. The second is His peace.

But to make room for that peace, Jesus *commands* you to empty yourself of fear and worry, to "not let your hearts be troubled, neither let them be afraid. [Stop allowing yourselves to be agitated and disturbed; and do not permit yourselves to be fearful and intimidated and cowardly and unsettled]" (John 14:27 AMPC).

To help you in this quest to increase your faith and let go of your fear, your mind must be transformed (see Romans 12:2). You can do that by praying and by reading and meditating on God's Word and by committing it to memory. To start you off, write on your mind and heart the verses below. Read each slowly, allowing the Spirit of God to make clear its meaning. Allow it to soak into your mind. Perhaps write it out on an index card so you can carry it with you and look at it throughout the day. Begin with the verse that speaks loudest to your heart:

- *"It is the* Lord *who goes before you. He will be with you; he will not leave you or forsake you. Do not fear or be dismayed."* (Deuteronomy 31:8 ESV)
- *The Lord is my Helper; I will not be seized with alarm [I will not fear or dread or be terrified].* (Hebrews 13:6 AMPC)
- *Be transformed by the renewing of your mind.* (Romans 12:2 HCSB)
- *"Daughter, your faith has healed you. Go in peace."* (Luke 8:48 NLV)
- *I looked for the Lord, and He answered me. And He took away all my fears.* (Psalm 34:4 NLV)
- *I can do all things through him who strengthens me.* (Philippians 4:13 ESV)
- *Be the arm [of Your servants—their strength and defense] every morning.* (Isaiah 33:2 AMPC)
- *"Do not be frightened, and do not be dismayed, for the* Lord *your God is with you wherever you go."* (Joshua 1:9 ESV)
- *Do not fear, for I am with you; do not be afraid, for I am your God. I will strengthen you; I will help you. . . . Do not fear, I will help you.* (Isaiah 41:10, 13 HCSB)

Woman of God, allow the Spirit of God to dissolve your fears, build your faith, and provide your peace.

Lord, thank You for the gifts of Your Holy Spirit and peace. Give me the courage to live not by sight but by faith. Be with me as I enter into Your rest. Amen.

WITH EVERY BREATH

Let everything that has breath praise the LORD.

PSALM 150:6 NIV

In. Out. In. Out. In. . . Breathing isn't something most of us have to think about. It's not hard to do. It is our body's involuntary response to the air.

But for some, breathing is a struggle. For the asthmatic and those afflicted with certain disorders or diseases, breathing can feel like a battle between your will and your windpipe. Panic rises as a person fights for every molecule of oxygen. Fear fills the mind as the lungs attempt to fill with air. One episode like this can steal a person's energy for an entire day.

Even those of us who are not suffering from any chronic breathing troubles have probably at some time felt out of breath. After strenuous exercise, we may have bent over, huffing and puffing as we tried to regain the normal rhythm of in and out, in and out. Or in a moment of fright, we may have sucked in air rapidly in a gasp and felt our heartbeat speed up. Maybe on a first date with a special someone, we have become acutely aware of the breathing process, reminding ourselves to keep on doing it. . .in and out, in and out. Or during a time of grief, when our body ached with sorrow, we may have sobbed and gulped in great mouthfuls of air that only seemed to add to the heaviness of our thoughts.

Psalm 150 is a song of praise to God. Every line, one after

another, offers praise. Next time you are feeling anxious, try breathing this praise to God in and out. As we praise Him, we can remember why He is worthy to be praised. We praise Him because of who He is, the God of peace in His sanctuary, the God of power in the mighty heavens. And because He is who He is, and because He has given us everything, and because He is in control of everything, we can praise Him with everything—with the sounds of our lives that are soft and calm, like the lullabies we sing over babies, or the breaths of sleeping children. We can praise Him with sounds of celebration, and we can praise Him with our loudness—even in our shouts of surprise, or anger, or sorrow. In all the sounds of our human emotions, we can praise the God who gives us every breath—the God who is with us even before we take in air at birth for our first breath and the God who waits for us as we exhale our last.

Lord of every breath in and every breath out,
I thank You for breathing Your Spirit into me. Amen.

REJOICING EVEN WHEN. . .

We can rejoice, too, when we run into problems and trials, for we know that they help us develop endurance.

ROMANS 5:3 NLT

In the earliest of the Christian communities, it is reported in various places in the New Testament, particularly in Paul's letters and in Acts, that the early disciples were quite pleased to be persecuted for their belief in Jesus and their adherence to His teaching. Paul sees well that at that moment in time, they are justified by faith and faith alone, since there really is nothing else. Their belief in Jesus is what marks them; their belief in Jesus is what is integral for them. Their belief in Jesus centers them both from within and from without. To be persecuted is to be recognized for just what they are: true believers.

Boasting of their afflictions, then, is a decided celebration of their faith. But their afflictions have another result for them besides being marks of their faith. Their sufferings have the effect of building within them a stronger will and greater endurance. This stronger will and greater endurance then amount to a kind of deepening of their faith and a broadcasting of their faith. Now they have faith, and through their sufferings, they also have greater strength and endurance.

Endurance itself points to the way in which faith is amplified into hope. Endurance appears to be oriented toward the future.

The faith-filled follower of Jesus is willing to bear the buffeting that she gets from the world for the sake of going out tomorrow and continuing to do the will of the Savior. She goes out with a proven character that is produced, Paul tells us, by endurance. She goes out into the world with a character that produces hope. Endurance and character produce a hope that "does not put us to shame, because God's love has been poured out into our hearts through the Holy Spirit, who has been given to us" (Romans 5:5 NIV).

Stella was a public school teacher, and so she was unable to pray as she wished with her Christian students. The school district had become increasingly strict over the years. When she prayed with a group of students after class in one of the classrooms, it was stopped because they were on public school property. So when the weather was warm, at least, they would pray outside just off the property. Stella and the students grew closer to one another as they prayed together, and she was certain they grew closer to God. Moreover, her hope assured her of a tomorrow when the face of her good Lord would shine a light through the darkness of laws prohibiting prayer.

Lord, help me to persevere and deliver hope wherever I go. Amen.

HOW MUCH MORE

How much more, then, will the blood of Christ, who through the eternal Spirit offered himself unblemished to God, cleanse our consciences from acts that lead to death, so that we may serve the living God!

HEBREWS 9:14 NIV

The dog hides in the corner, head down, tail nervously wagging. In the kitchen, the remains of last night's dinner, pulled out of the trash and strewn about the newly mopped floor, wait to welcome the dog's master home.

"Bad dog. What did you do?"

The big pup pushes into the corner a little more tightly, acting for all the world as if he knows he is guilty. And perhaps he does. We cannot really know what goes on in the minds of animals. We cannot read their thoughts. Some pets seem to understand the connection, at least in the short term, of their actions with habitual consequences. That is, good behavior gets rewarded with treats; bad behavior gets punished by time-out in the corner or by a verbal reprimand. But even the smartest dogs do not seem to carry around with them the weight of years of mistakes and sins—doggy guilt.

But we do. Many of us find that one of the hardest tasks as Christians is to truly believe that we are forgiven—that our records can be wiped clean. Instead, we make daily sacrifices, supposed

deals with our Lord and Savior that are more like New Year's resolutions (with just about as much follow-through success): "If I pray every day, God will forgive me for being a rebellious child." Or "I will read my Bible and volunteer at church, then God will overlook all my little white lies."

Some of us just go ahead and put ourselves in the corner. We dole out our own punishments—taking ourselves out of certain opportunities or holding back from being fully alive in Christ. We tuck our tails and hide, fearful of our Master's voice.

But nothing we do can cleanse our hearts. It's worth saying that again: *Nothing we do can cleanse our hearts.* Only Jesus can do that. Only His sacrifice can atone for us. But what a sacrifice! And what a Savior! He can do so much more for us than just relieve us from guilt. He can do so much more than we could ever hope to achieve through our self-rebuke. He can equip us and empower us to serve the living God!

Lord Jesus, help me to believe in You more and more.
Help me to trust that Your blood was enough for me. Amen.

BELIEVING THE IMPOSSIBLE

I have begun shaking with fear. Fear has power over me. . . . I will call on God and the Lord will save me. . . . Give all your cares to the Lord and He will give you strength. He will never let those who are right with Him be shaken.

PSALM 55:5, 16, 22 NLV

Although fear and anxiety are closely linked, they are different. Fear is one's response to a very real, known, and present threat. Anxiety is a response to an unknown threat. What links them is that they both produce a stress response.

In 2 Kings 4:1–7, a poor woman, both anxious and fearful, was doubly stressed. She, the widow of a prophet, had two sons. But because of a debt, she was soon going to lose them both to a creditor who was going to enslave them. The creditor's intentions, a very real and present threat, loomed before her. Concerns over her now unknown future—one to be lived without the support and love of her sons—fueled her anxiety.

In such a state, the widow cried out to the prophet Elisha, a man of God, pouring out her problems. He asked her what she had on hand. She replied, "Your servant has nothing in the house except a jar of oil" (2 Kings 4:2 HCSB). So Elisha told her to borrow from all her neighbors all the empty containers she could find, go home and shut the door, and begin pouring oil into them until they were full. This might sound a tad crazy to some people but not to

this widow. She had faith. So she did as Elisha told her, allowing God to increase the little she already had. When she had filled all the containers, the oil stopped.

When the widow reported back to Elisha, he instructed her to sell the oil, pay her debt, and live on the rest with her sons. Her fear and anxiety were dealt with, and a crisis was averted.

Instead of allowing her anxieties and fears to overtake her, this woman called on the God of Elisha. She unburdened her heart to him and opened it, allowing God to perform a miracle. Then, garnering God-given strength, she obeyed Elisha's instructions, using what little assets she had on hand. In doing so, she not only saved her sons but herself as well.

When fear and anxiety threaten to overtake you, cry out to God. Open your heart. Give God what you have. Believe for the impossible. Garner God's strength. Obey God's instructions. And you too will witness a miracle.

God, as fear and anxiety threaten me, I come to You. I tell You all, I give You all I am and have, open to Your Word, will, and way. Amen.

NO CONDEMNATION

There is therefore now no condemnation to those who are in Christ Jesus, who do not walk according to the flesh, but according to the Spirit.

ROMANS 8:1 NKJV

Remember that first time you were caught red-handed—maybe with your hand actually stuck right down in that cookie jar? Maybe you were teasing the cat, and that last pull to the tail led to you being marked with a claw-written signature you wouldn't soon forget. Maybe you were caught in a lie, wound up in the sticky mess of your own deceit. Or maybe you were caught hurting someone else, and the pain on their face told the whole story before you could even get out a "But. . ."

No condemnation? Not likely, right? Not in your corner of the world. When you got caught, you received a quick judgment and sentence, complete with disapproving stare from your mom or dad or that mean old babysitter.

We're used to being judged. Maybe that's why we so easily fall into judging others. But we are not, in general, well suited to that job. We bring with us too many prejudices, too many experiences that color our conclusions. Too many times we judge in ignorance, without getting the full picture. And what's even worse, we judge without mercy.

The only One who is perfectly qualified to be our judge is Jesus.

And yet He is the One who spares us the punishment we actually deserve. Instead of finding us guilty, as He rightfully could do, He takes on our guilt. Instead of pointing out our faults, He takes on our wounds. Instead of showering us with a barrage of rebuke and condemnation, He rains down blessing through the Spirit.

Jesus Christ, who has no earthly reason to show us mercy, demonstrates for us the perfect power of heavenly thinking. He loves without condition. He gives without getting. He offers without being asked. He pardons without punishing.

No condemnation. Consider those words to be your life slogan. How is your life different, or how should it be different, with the knowledge that you are free from condemnation? You never have to face hell, because Jesus faced it for you. You can know without a doubt that your life here on earth is just a dot on an eternal line, and you get to live out the rest of that line in the freedom and glory of heaven.

No condemnation. How does that knowledge shape the way you look at others? How can you extend the mercy Jesus has shown you and share the freedom of those two words with someone else today?

Lord, I know I may get in all kinds of trouble, but praise God that You offer me no condemnation. Amen.

TREASURES OF RESTLESSNESS

"I have no rest; only trouble comes."

JOB 3:26 NLT

Sometimes we need to be shaken. It's true. Life gets far too easy, and we get way too comfortable sitting down in our circumstances. We get so comfy, we forget why we're here. We lose track of days and years and forget all about going out and loving others and telling them about the love of Christ. We get so busy just living in the day-to-day that we forget about the eternal tomorrow that is waiting for us. We forget all about really following God's Word and doing His work and learning how to be who He created us to be.

It's not that we should go looking for suffering on purpose. No one needs to do that. We should not be pain-seekers. But when trials come, we need to remember that being troubled is perfectly normal and even a good thing. Being troubled shows us that we are familiar with peace. Being troubled shows us that we do have good things in our lives and reasons to be thankful. Being troubled reminds us who is really in control.

Job was a man in trouble. Extreme trouble. He'd had almost everything he cared about stripped from him—his family members, his property, even his own health. And in his suffering and pain, he wished he had never been born. His worst fears had come true. He had no peace and no quiet. Only trouble. (See Job 3:25–26.)

But through these trials and through the added burden of

having to endure the well-meaning but misguided words of friends, Job met God in a way he never had before. He said, "I had only heard about you before, but now I have seen you with my own eyes. I take back everything I said, and I sit in dust and ashes to show my repentance" (Job 42:5–6 NLT).

Job learned about who God is, but he also learned about himself. He learned that the bottom line to every experience we will ever have is that God is in charge. Only God. He's the only Author of our lives. He's our Creator and our King. And He is good. No matter what we think or do or say, no matter what power we think we might have, no matter how well we think we've got everything figured out, the only One who really understands the big picture is God.

Sometimes we need to be made restless before we can find true rest. Sometimes we need to be brought down low so we can know where to look for help.

You, oh Lord, are everything to me.
Help me remember who You are. Amen.

MAKING ROOM

She said to her husband, "Now I see that this is a holy man of God who is always passing by. Let us make a little room on the second floor. . . ." She said, "It will be all right.". . . "It is well."

2 KINGS 4:9–10, 23, 26 NLV

A well-to-do yet childless woman and her husband lived in Shunem. At her suggestion, they made a small room in their house for Elisha, the man of God she had often seen passing by.

In repayment for the woman's kindness, Elisha foretold that God would give her a child. When she did give birth, her world was even more complete. But years later the youth was struck with a headache while out in the field with his father. Servants carried the boy to his mother. She held him in her arms until noon, after which he died.

The woman carried the child upstairs, placed him on Elisha's bed, then told her husband she was going to go see Elisha. When he asked why, she simply responded with "It will be all right" (2 Kings 4:23 NLV). After saddling up a donkey, she told her servant, "Drive on. Do not slow down for me unless I tell you" (2 Kings 4:24 NLV).

When the Shunammite woman arrived at Mount Carmel, Elisha, seeing her approaching, sent his servant Gehazi ahead to see if all was well. Gehazi ran to meet her and asked if all was well with her family, and she said, "It is well" (2 Kings 4:26 NLV).

When the woman finally saw Elisha face-to-face, she never

said her son had died. All she told him was "Did I ask you for a son? Did I not say, 'Do not lie to me'?" (2 Kings 4:28 NLV). That was enough for Elisha. He read the meaning behind her words and sent Gehazi ahead to heal the boy. Left alone with the prophet, the mother, determined to see all made right, said to Elisha, "As the Lord lives and as you yourself live, I will not leave you" (2 Kings 4:30 NLV). Such a determined statement prompted Elisha to start heading to her house. When Gehazi's efforts to revive the child failed, Elisha himself brought the youth back to life and turned him over to his mother, who, on her knees, brimmed with gratefulness.

What courage and perseverance! How did this Shunammite woman do it? How did she maintain such a positive attitude and garner the courage to face this trial alone? It began with her opening her eyes, home, and heart to God. For the closer she grew to Him, the more courage, perseverance, and positivity grew in her. Her trust in God laid the foundation for courage and allowed her to remain calm.

Lord, help me make room in my heart for You. Help me have a positive attitude, knowing that no matter what happens, with You all is well. Amen.

EXPECT OPPOSITION

Consider him who endured such opposition from sinners, so that you will not grow weary and lose heart.

HEBREWS 12:3 NIV

One of the firmest guarantees anyone can make about living the Christian life is that you will encounter trouble. You will face opposition. Whether it's from other humans who don't value your beliefs, or who hate your beliefs, or who simply don't understand what you are doing, or whether it's from life circumstances that are not anyone's fault, you will experience affliction.

But if Jesus could endure the suffering and shame of the cross, we should be able to get through whatever comes our way here on earth.

Indeed, our biggest struggle, the one that haunts us every day and undermines us at every turn and never gives up working against us, is most likely going to be our own wrestling match with our sin. The writer of Hebrews reminds us that "the Lord disciplines the one he loves" (Hebrews 12:6 NIV). We are to "endure hardship as discipline; God is treating you as his children" (Hebrews 12:7 NIV). Moreover, the writer goes on to say that if we don't get disciplined, we should not even consider ourselves legitimate children of God.

But in truth, we are so easily discouraged, aren't we? We try to fight temptation, but it doesn't take all that much for us to cave, relatively speaking. For when you compare our battle with the image

of Jesus sweating blood as He bent His will to His Father's in the garden of Gethsemane, our efforts don't seem all that forceful, do they? Or when you compare the faltering steps we take to follow God with the steps of Jesus on His way to Calvary, it seems we would have to walk at least another thousand miles to be able to equal even one of His steps.

But we are in good company. That "great cloud of witnesses" mentioned at the beginning of Hebrews 12 (and described in chapter 11) knew what it was like to face opposition. And they knew what it was like to fail. The whole point of this list of Bible characters is not that they were perfect people, but that they were instead real people who sometimes made a real mess of things. But God can redeem our messes, and He can use our trials to teach us.

We should expect opposition, especially when we've recently recovered from a bout of temptation or are purposely aiming to walk the straight and narrow path. There will be bumps in the road and even whole roadblocks. Have patience. Keep pushing. Keep fighting. Keep reading God's Word. Keep praying. Keep the faith. Run the race.

Lord, I can keep going when I know You are with me. Amen.

LIKE A LITTLE CHILD

A little girl from the land of Israel. . .served Naaman's wife. And she said to her owner, "I wish that my owner's husband were with the man of God who is in Samaria! Then he would heal his bad skin disease."

2 KINGS 5:2–3 NLV

A little girl had been taken from Israel and now served the wife of Naaman, a well-respected Syrian commander who had leprosy. Although now serving in enemy territory, this child not only continued to be filled with faith in God but harbored compassion in her heart for her master and his condition. So one day she told her mistress how keenly she desired her master to see Elisha in Samaria. For there, Naaman would be cured of his leprosy.

Naaman's wife relayed the girl's message to her husband, and off Naaman went. Taking with him a lot of money, the commander mounted his chariot and rode up to Elisha's house. While Naaman stood at the door, Elisha sent his messenger to tell him to dip himself in the Jordan River seven times and then his skin would be restored.

Unfortunately, Naaman, who had expected the prophet to meet with him face-to-face, was angry. Elisha's obvious lack of respect would not do! As Naaman turned to leave, his servants talked him into trying Elisha's remedy. So the commander dipped himself in the Jordan River seven times and "his flesh was made

as well as the flesh of a little child" (2 Kings 5:14 NLV). Filled with joy, Naaman went back to Elisha, saying, "Now I know that there is no God in all the earth but in Israel" (2 Kings 5:15 NLV).

After all she had been through—being taken away from her homeland, her parents, everything she knew—the little maid from Israel held no grudge or anger against her captors. Instead, quietly, politely, lovingly, and bravely, she did what she could to lead her master—and who knows how many others—to her God.

God is continually turning things on their heads. In this instance, a great commander had a problem that a little girl helped him solve. But that solution could only be had when he himself became as a little child.

Jesus said, "Unless you have a change of heart and become like a little child, you will not get into the holy nation of heaven" (Matthew 18:3 NLV). When Naaman dipped himself in the Jordan, his flesh and his heart were healed; both became like that of a little child. But neither would have happened if it hadn't been for the courage of a little servant girl.

Lord, help me become like a little child. Change my heart and mind so that I can find a way to help not hinder, to love not loathe, to have courage not cower. Amen.

BELONGING

"I will grant peace in the land, and you will lie down and no one will make you afraid."
LEVITICUS 26:6 NIV

Do you remember what it was like to walk into a new classroom for the first time? Butterflies bounced around in your belly and crawled up your windpipe, threatening to steal your breath away. Somehow excitement and anxiety and surprise and fear and confusion and wonder all whirled into a tornado inside of you that seemed as if it might burst out at any minute, knocking all those colorful educational posters right off the cement block wall.

And all you wanted to see was someone who knew you. Someone who could see you and recognize you. Someone whose eyes would light up when they saw you and who would call out your name. You wanted to belong. You wanted someone to be your partner.

In Leviticus, God gives His people, the Israelites, many commands to follow—commands to worship Him as their God and serve Him only, commands to remind them who they are and to whom they belong. And if they don't follow those commands and forget who they are, He gives them ways to come back to Him again.

God tells His people quite simply that if they follow His commands, all will be well. They will receive what they need. They will have all the food they want and live in safety (Leviticus 26:5). God

will keep them secure physically by removing wild beasts from the land and by keeping war from breaking out in their country. He will give them power over their enemies, and the numbers of the Israelites will grow and grow (Leviticus 26:6–9).

But more than that, God makes them promises that set their hearts at rest. He says He will keep His covenant with them. He says He will dwell among them and walk among them and be their God. "And you will be my people" (Leviticus 26:12 NIV). He reminds them that He knows them—He was the One who brought them out of Egypt. He has not forgotten them.

Whenever we walk into an uncomfortable situation, we can be assured of one thing. No matter how anxious or confused or scared we might feel, we can know for certain that when we look around the room, God is there. He is there with us. He is there for us. And He is lighting up, delighted to see us and ready to call out our name.

Lord, I'm nervous about entering a new situation. Help me to remember that You are looking out for me. Amen.

LOST AND FOUND

"And when she finds it, she calls her friends and neighbors together and says, 'Rejoice with me; I have found my lost coin.' "

LUKE 15:9 NIV

Keys. Socks. Homework. Bills. Ten dollars. Grocery list. Your marbles.

Undoubtedly, this could be a list of lost things in many people's households. Why do we lose things so easily? We're headed out the door in the morning, bag on shoulder, coffee in hand, to-do list in mind, and then suddenly we stop. *Keys. Where are the keys?* They were in our hands just a minute ago. We can see them in our mind's eye, but our real eyes can't seem to find them. The frantic search of the whole house begins. Couch cushions turned over. Papers lifted up. Purses and pockets turned inside out. Cupboards checked—just for good measure. And then, where do we find them? Right on the key hook, where they always are.

Perhaps this scene is familiar to you. Or maybe it reminds you of something else you misplace often. Or maybe it reminds you of someone else in your household.

Are you the loser or the finder of things? When something is lost in your house, does everyone come to you, expecting you to find whatever it is? Or when something is lost, do fingers point at you, blaming you for hiding some object that you never even knew existed before this moment?

That experience of sudden realization of the absence of some necessary (or at least significant) item is pretty common to the human experience. Surely each one of us has lost things. Maybe we've even lost something very important to us—either a thing that has sentimental value or a thing that is needed as a practical matter. We all know that frustration, that sense of momentary helplessness, that irritation with ourselves because we can't make things appear at will. Moreover, we probably all know the annoyance or even grief at having lost something important that we cannot recover.

In those moments, when we've searched absolutely everywhere we can think of and still come up empty, we can feel a little empty ourselves. We can feel a little like we are the lost things. And we want to be found. We want to be restored to a place where we know who we are, and we know what we've done, and we know where we are going next.

Thanks to God, we can never be lost in His kingdom. Even when we try to hide, He comes to us. He restores us. He reminds us exactly how important we are to Him. And He leads us back to where we need to be going.

Lord of the lost, keep finding me. Amen.

OPEN EYES

"Don't be afraid, for those who are with us outnumber those who are with them." Then Elisha prayed, "LORD, please open his eyes and let him see." So the LORD opened the servant's eyes. He looked and saw that the mountain was covered with horses and chariots of fire.

2 KINGS 6:16–17 HCSB

Do you ever feel outnumbered? Elisha's servant did.

It all started when Elisha the prophet kept managing to reveal the Syrians' secret plans of attack to the king of Israel. To stifle the spiritual informant, the furious king of Syria decided to do away with Elisha, who happened to be in Dothan. The king sent his army with horses and chariots to that city, surrounding it under cover of darkness.

The next morning, Elisha's servant rose early, went out, and was stunned to see such a powerful army surrounding the city. Terrified, he turned to his master, asking, "Alas, my master! What shall we do?" (2 Kings 6:15 ESV).

Elijah told the man not to worry or be afraid. He said, "Those who are with us outnumber those who are with them." Then, to further comfort his servant, Elisha prayed for God to open his eyes so that he could see the vast supernatural army that was on their side. God answered that prayer. The man's eyes were opened to see a mountain covered with horses and blazing chariots.

When the Syrians finally did begin their attack, Elisha prayed once more, asking God to strike them blind. God once more responded, removing their sight, allowing Elisha to lead them away to Samaria. There Elisha prayed for a third time, asking God to open the Syrians' eyes. And for the third time within this story, God responded.

You may have a time when you feel as if you're surrounded by enemies and see no way out, no solution. As anxiety and fear start to bubble up in your heart, despair seems to be lurking just around the corner.

This is when you need to be an Elisha. To pray to God—perhaps not just once but twice, maybe even three times—to remember that God has a big army, an array of angels, that, although invisible, are there.

Jeremy Taylor wrote, "It is impossible for that [woman] to despair who remembers that [her] Helper is omnipotent." So, woman of God, don't despair. There's no problem too great, no situation so dire that God cannot handle it. For your God is "the Almighty [Whose power no foe can withstand]" (Psalm 91:1 AMPC).

"Oh, Lord GOD! You Yourself made the heavens and earth by Your great power and with Your outstretched arm. Nothing is too difficult for You!" (Jeremiah 32:17 HCSB). Amen.

DELIGHT IN MERCY

Who is a God like you, who pardons sin and forgives the transgression of the remnant of his inheritance? You do not stay angry forever but delight to show mercy.

MICAH 7:18 NIV

Karen looked at her phone for the tenth time that morning. She picked it up, pushed the button to see the screen come to life, checked for new messages, and then put the phone down again.

It's only been one night, she reminded herself.

She felt her heart sink. They'd had such an awful fight the previous day. They had both dredged up long-past sins and mistakes, calling each other to account for things that had been dealt with and buried. Karen tried to replay the afternoon in her head, trying to figure out what had gone wrong. Who had said what first? There were so many things she couldn't remember. But some words had stung so badly, she knew she'd never forget them.

But could she forgive? Last night, she had vowed she wouldn't. Why should she? She felt justified. Those accusations were wrong and unfair. And the names she had been called! There was no reason for that. No reason at all. Why would she forgive anyone who had deliberately tried to hurt her feelings? Even *her*.

But as she tried to kindle the angry flames she had felt inside several hours before, she found that she didn't feel angry anymore. She was just sad. And hurt. And afraid.

What if I call her, but she won't answer? Karen imagined. She didn't think she could stand that. Far better not to call at all than to face that kind of rejection. No, she'd just have to wait it out.

As she waited, she flipped open her Bible. Her eyes fell on a verse from Micah 7:6 (NIV) "For a son dishonors his father, a daughter rises up against her mother, a daughter-in-law against her mother-in-law—a man's enemies are the members of his own household".

You got that right, Micah.

But as she read further, she realized the verses were being spoken about the nation of Israel. This nation of rescued slaves, who had endured so much and been given so much by God, so often chose to turn away from Him. God deserved their praise and honor, yet they often gifted Him with bitterness and rebellion instead.

But God did not stay angry with His people forever. Instead, He took delight in—He actually enjoyed—showing mercy to them. He hurled all their wrongs into the depths of the sea. If God could do that with the Israelites, maybe she could do it too.

"Hello, honey? It's Mama. Can we talk?"

Lord, help me not to hold grudges but to delight in offering mercy and forgiveness. Amen.

STEADY PRAYER

Peter was kept in prison, but prayer was being made earnestly to God for him by the church. . . . Before Herod was to bring him out for execution, Peter, bound with two chains, was sleeping between two soldiers. . . . Suddenly an angel of the Lord appeared.

ACTS 12:5–7 HCSB

To all eyes, the situation appeared dire. King Herod Agrippa had already been persecuting followers of the Way. Then he had murdered James, the brother of John, one of Jesus' disciples. When Herod saw how much James's execution had pleased the Jews, he seized Peter. After Peter's arrest, Herod threw him in prison and ordered four squads of soldiers to guard him. The only thing standing between Peter and death was prayer, "fervent prayer. . .persistently made to God by the church" (Acts 12:5 AMPC).

The night before his execution, Peter was sleeping between two soldiers, and two chains tethered him to the spot. Guards stood at the door of the prison.

And then it happened. An angel of the Lord appeared. He stood right beside Peter. Light streamed into the cell, illuminating everything. The angel shook Peter's shoulders, waking him up. He told Peter to get up quickly. That's when Peter's chains just fell off.

The angel told him to get dressed, put on his shoes, grab his coat, and follow him out the door. So Peter did. But he thought he

was imagining all this, sleepwalking.

Peter and the angel passed the first guard post then the second. The gate leading into the city opened to them—all by itself. They went out the gate, and after passing one street, *poof!* The angel was gone.

Peter shook his head and realized he wasn't having a dream. He was free! He said to himself, "Now I know for certain that the Lord has sent His angel and rescued me" (Acts 12:11 HCSB).

When he arrived at the house of Mary (John Mark's mom), where he knew many had come together to pray, he knocked on the door. The servant girl Rhoda answered it. She was so shocked to hear Peter's voice that she left him on the doorstep while she ran to tell the others. When she had finally convinced them it was Peter, they ran back to the door, opened it, saw him, and were stunned. Their prayers had been answered! Why? Because, as author E. M. Bounds wrote, "God hears prayer, God heeds prayer, God answers prayer, and God delivers by prayer." If you live your life keeping those four things and this story in mind, fear will find no foothold in your life.

Lord, teach me to pray, for that is my best weapon against fear. Amen.

SPEAK TRUTH

Therefore each of you must put off falsehood and speak truthfully to your neighbor, for we are all members of one body.

EPHESIANS 4:25 NIV

It would have been enough if Paul had put the period after "neighbor." Certainly, we all understand the command to speak truthfully to one another. We have known since we were small children that telling a fib is a bad thing. We know it's wrong to lie. We know it's wrong to carry around falsehood with us and wear it like a robe. Or do we?

Spending even a little time on social media sites is enough to see that wearing falsehood is the latest style. People put on fake smiles to go with their fake hair and fake makeup as they stand in front of the one cleaned-up corner of one fake room and pretend that their whole house looks just like that—giving off a vibe of casual yet elegant organization. People "get real" by revealing their somewhat colorful thoughts about one small aspect of life—but only such opinions that they feel absolutely certain will obtain a large number of "likes" from their eagerly waiting social media audience.

Let's be honest with each other here for a moment, friends. We aren't really all that honest, are we? We aren't really committed to putting off falsehood and wearing truth instead. But here's the reason we need to stop messing around and start getting good at it—today.

"We are all members of one body."

Think about it. What happens when you lie to yourself for a long time? Let's take one small lie—like lying to yourself that those extra thirty (or forty, fifty, sixty. . .) pounds you are carrying around really don't matter. You are just as healthy, even if the stupid scale says you are overweight. Sure, you haven't thought about exercise much lately (or this century), but you feel great—right? Until the doctor tells you your cholesterol is way too high and explains what that does to your vital organs.

You can't lie to yourself without experiencing negative consequences. Your mind and heart will get split into two, or you will become a walking display of falsehood, or you will get sick. Or you will hurt somebody else.

And that is the problem. If you believe we are all part of one body—we are all in this thing called life together—then you must realize that what you do, even in the privacy of your own home, matters. What you say to and about yourself matters. What you say to and about your neighbor matters.

Lord, help me to tell true stories about You through the way I live my life every day. Amen.

COUNT THE STARS

"Look up at the sky and count the stars—if indeed you can count them." Then he said to him, "So shall your offspring be."

GENESIS 15:5 NIV

Abram must have been tired. He had just made it through a rather hard battle—fighting off four kings and their armies in order to rescue his nephew Lot. He must have been taking a moment to try to process it all. As night fell, he sat in his tent and wondered what God had in mind for him next.

He didn't have to wonder for long.

God answered Abram's questioning about his future, about his family. He brought Abram outside. Abram walked away from the campfire, away from the other tents. He stood under the vast night sky—the same piece of sky that one day Ruth would sleep under as she lay in the protection of her kinsman, Boaz. The same piece of sky that someday a boy named David would be singing under as he watched his sheep. The same piece of sky in which, one day far away, a new star would appear, shining down a path to the new Savior of the world.

God brought Abram out under this blanket of night filled with thousands upon thousands of pinpricks of light, and He said, "Count the stars." Abram raised his gray head and stared into the galaxy. Once again, God was asking him to do something impossible. *Have a baby when you're a hundred, Abram. Count the millions of stars,*

Abram. Who did God think Abram was, anyway?

But God *did* know who Abram was. He was keenly aware of Abram's limitations, of his humanity. God was never asking Abram to do impossible things. He was never setting Abram up to fail. He was always asking Abram to do just one thing—trust Him. And Abram did. He believed God. He believed God's promises were true, and this was credited to Abram as righteousness (see Genesis 15:6).

What impossible task has God set before you? Has He asked you to count the grains of salt in a shaker, or the number of times your children have said your name in the last twenty-four hours? In what ways has God been nudging you, asking you to trust Him more?

When night comes, go out and sit under the sky. Ask God where He is sending you. Talk to Him about His promises that you read in His Word. Then look up into the vast field of stars and start counting. And with every star, begin to trust God just a little bit more.

Lord who formed the stars and set each one into the sky, thank You for Your promises. Amen.

SINKING FAITH

But when he saw the strength of the wind, he was afraid, and beginning to sink he cried out, "Lord, save me!"
MATTHEW 14:30 CSB

How simple it had seemed to Sam when he set out on his life's journey to be a pastor. How fervent was his faith in Jesus, fervent in the face of all worldly unbelief! His was a faith that could move mountains. He remembered the excitement he felt when he was in seminary. The future seemed so full of promise. But now, these days he was living out seemed so far away from all that excitement and anticipation. Now, there were bills to be paid, a family that was poorer than anything he had envisioned, and a flock to be ministered to. He had never considered the extreme efforts that he would have to make to keep body and soul together. The realities were truly awful when measured against his dreams.

But when he came to this passage one morning, he thought about Peter imploring the Lord in the night: "Lord, if it's you . . . command me to come to you on the water" (Matthew 14: 28 CSB).

And Sam realized that Peter, Jesus' rock, had also experienced a time in his life when he thought his faith would carry him through, only to find himself sinking. He reflected that perhaps he was now having his "Peter moment"; he too had believed that his faith in Jesus would carry him against everything the world could bring to bear, would keep him from sinking into the waves

and enable him to walk on water. And now, just like Peter, he was being overcome by the waves.

Then he took hold of the final three words Peter called out to Jesus: "Lord, save me." He saw that in the very moment Peter lost faith, he also recovered it. At the same time that he lost faith in his ability to walk on water, he turned to Jesus to keep him from sinking and drowning.

We too live in a world in which Jesus becomes harder and harder to see and recognize, like Jesus in the night on the sea. How often do the challenges of the world obscure the face of Jesus? And when we would make headway, when we think that we see Jesus—when we think that Jesus is calling us onto the water, and we set out with all confidence and faith—how often do we find ourselves quailing on the waters, frightened like Peter into thinking that sinking is a likelier bet than keeping our feet? "O ye of little faith," keep your eyes on Jesus. That is His will for us.

Lord, save me. Amen.

ALLIANCES

Jehu the son of Hanani. . .said to King Jehoshaphat, "Should you help the wicked and love those who hate the LORD? Because of this, wrath has gone out against you from the LORD. Nevertheless, some good is found in you, for you. . .have set your heart to seek God."

2 CHRONICLES 19:2–3 ESV

Judah's Jehoshaphat was a good king. He was a God seeker who walked in the ways of King David. He also took down the "high places" where idols were worshipped. He even sent teachers of God's law into the cities of Judah to educate the people.

Jehoshaphat seemed to be the perfect king, yet there was this one thing: "Jehoshaphat, who needed no one's help to achieve greatness, acted as though he depended upon other people for success" (*HCSB Study Bible*, note at 2 Chronicles 18:1). Such was the case when King Jehoshaphat formed an alliance with King Ahab of Israel by arranging for his (Jehoshaphat's) son Jehoram to marry Athaliah, Ahab's daughter. Perhaps Jehoshaphat thought such an alliance would assure peace between the usually contentious kingdoms.

Nevertheless, because of this "unholy" alliance, Jehoshaphat found himself aligning with Ahab in other ways. When Ahab asked if he would go with him to war against Ramoth-gilead, Jehoshaphat responded, "I am as you are, my people as your people. We will be with you in the war" (2 Chronicles 18:3 ESV). And to war they went. But at least King Jehoshaphat insisted on consulting God about it before they stepped onto the battlefield.

In the end, both kings went into battle, but only one survived: Jehoshaphat. Yet when he got home, his seer, Jehu, admonished him before Jehoshaphat could even get through the door! Jehu told the king that God had been angered because Jehoshaphat had made efforts to ally himself with wicked King Ahab. Nevertheless, because God saw so much good in Jehoshaphat and because he had set his heart to seek the Lord, God would stick with him.

From a human perspective, it may have been wise politically for Jehoshaphat to form an alliance with Ahab, via intermarriage and joint battle plans. Such moves held the possibilities of providing peace and making room for victories between the two nations. At the same time, it indicated a certain fear on Jehoshaphat's side: that God might not be able to keep the peace and protect the kingdom, that to ensure success, siding with evil may be the only option.

God makes it clear that one's present and future success lie in relying on and trusting in God alone. Evil has no part with good. And any alliance with it is dust in the wind.

Lord, I want my motivator to be faith not fear.
I trust in and serve You alone. Amen.

REFUGE

The LORD is a refuge for the oppressed,
a stronghold in times of trouble.
PSALM 9:9 NIV

We can look around us, through the lenses of journalists and reporters, and see so many hurting people all around the world. So many thousands and thousands of people have had to flee their homes. So many have been waiting even years now for relief. So many seem not to have a voice. So many are fighting for justice. So many seem to be just struggling to survive.

But God promises us over and over again in scripture that He will "never forget the needy; the hope of the afflicted will never perish" (Psalm 9:18 NIV). The Bible is filled with stories of God rescuing those who were treated unfairly. From the Israelites being led out of slavery to the followers of Jesus being released from the bondage of sin through repentance and baptism, God has been saving people from the forces of darkness since darkness first entered the world.

God, the perfect Judge, "rules the world in righteousness and judges the people with equity" (Psalm 9:8 NIV). Some of this judgment we see come to pass, when corrupt men get arrested and tried for their crimes or when victims receive restitution. But sometimes we don't get to see righteousness come about in ways that are obvious to us. In those times, we have to trust that God's

Word is still just as true and faithful. We have to believe in His promises. We have to remember all that He has done—all the good in the world we have already witnessed come about.

And we also can be a part of His goodness. We can be the hands and feet of Jesus, bringing relief to those who are suffering and hope to those who have been disappointed. We can bring love to those who need to be held. We can speak truth to those who are confused and wondering. We can give medicine and food and shelter to those who are in need. We can comfort those who are mourning. And we can remind every person that God sees them, God knows them by name, and He has "never forsaken those who seek [Him]" (Psalm 9:10 NIV).

And because God remembers them and knows them by name, we have to get to know them too and never forget those who are in trouble, whether it's the family down the street who lost their home in a fire or the family across the ocean who is trying to turn a rescue tent into a home.

Lord of the lonely and hurting and afraid, help me to be Your helper. Help me to stand for justice. Help me to be a voice for the oppressed. Amen.

CONSIDER YOUR HEART

"What's wrong?" they asked. "Do you come in peace?"

1 SAMUEL 16:4 NLT

Pastor Jim was a good man. His spirit exuded warmth and goodness. He made people feel good when he was around them. And he was not afraid to speak the truth.

It was that last thing that sometimes made people walk the other way when they saw Pastor Jim coming. People who were struggling to do right, who were battling temptation, who were knowingly giving in to their desires—these people tended to disappear when Pastor Jim came around.

This avoidance frustrated the good man. It wasn't as if he didn't know what was going on. He was a godly man not a gullible one. Though he never participated in the spreading of rumors, it was easy to pick up on the latest news (it was a small town and a small congregation).

Besides that, he prayed daily for God to open his eyes to the needs of those around him. And God often did. Jim could see when people were wrestling with spiritual problems. He wanted to tell these poor souls that they weren't fooling anyone and they certainly weren't fooling God. Mostly, he wanted to tell people that God didn't care that they felt ashamed or embarrassed or unworthy; God still wanted to love them anyway, no matter what kind of mess they'd entangled themselves in. He wanted to tell

them that God knew their hearts.

Like Jim, Samuel was a good man, a prophet of the Lord. He tried to do what God told him to do. And he was an adviser to the king of Israel. Because of his position before God, people were a little skittish when they saw Samuel coming. After all, when Samuel opened his mouth, sometimes God's words would come out. And God's words to His people often were not complimentary.

It's no wonder then that the elders of Bethlehem came with trembling to meet Samuel. What was he going to say? What had they done wrong? But Samuel had come to anoint a king for God. He had come to anoint, in fact, the king who would stand in the line of the King of kings and Lord of lords.

As the prophet looked at the sons of Jesse, God reminded Samuel not to judge as people often did—by appearances. "People judge by outward appearance, but the LORD looks at the heart" (1 Samuel 16:7 NLT).

How does your heart look today? Would you come trembling before Samuel, or would you walk the other way? If you've been avoiding godly truth, consider your heart. But for goodness' sake, come to God anyway.

Lord, examine my heart. Instruct me in Your way. Amen.

GOD FOCUS: PART 1

We have no might to stand against this great company that is coming against us. We do not know what to do, but our eyes are upon You.

2 CHRONICLES 20:12 AMPC

Since being admonished by Jehu (see 2 Chronicles 19:2–3), the good king Jehoshaphat became even better. He took the seer's constructive criticism and learned from it (see Proverbs 3:11–12; 15:5). Jehoshaphat made even more reforms, bringing His people back to God, appointing judges and priests, and imparting this wisdom to the latter: "Be strong; may the LORD be with those who do what is good" (2 Chronicles 19:11 HCSB).

But then Jehoshaphat received some bad news. Enemy armies were coming against him and were already very near. "Jehoshaphat feared, and set himself [determinedly, as his vital need] to seek the Lord; he proclaimed a fast in all Judah" (2 Chronicles 20:3 AMPC). The king and his people sought God with all their hearts, minds, souls, and strength. Before all the people, the king stood and prayed. He began by reminding all who God was, the power He wielded, and the promises He had given them. Jehoshaphat then told God what was happening, explaining the challenge at hand, ending his prayer with "We're helpless. . . . We don't know what to do; we're looking to you" (2 Chronicles 20:12 MSG).

The king and all his people just stood there, "all present and attentive to God" (2 Chronicles 20:13 MSG). Then the Spirit of God moved Jahaziel to speak: "This is what the LORD says: 'Do not be afraid or discouraged because of this vast number, for the battle is not yours, but God's. . . . You do not have to fight this battle. Position yourselves, stand still, and see the salvation of the LORD. He is with you' " (2 Chronicles 20:15, 17 HCSB).

What do you do when you're afraid? Where do you turn?

Fear is a natural reaction that keeps us safe from harm, but a problem arises when we give in to fear, when we turn to someone other than God for help.

When you first begin to feel afraid, get on the Jehoshaphat track. Seek God. Make it your first and only priority. Be determined to settle for nothing less than time in God's presence. Then get on your knees and pray. Remind Him and yourself of His promises and power. Admit to Him your helplessness. Tell Him that your eyes are on Him alone—and then actually *look* to Him alone! Focus on God by being present *with* Him. Concentrate on Him, looking to see—knowing that you *will* see—Him move on your behalf.

Lord, instead of giving in to fear, I'm focusing on You, fixing my attention there, knowing that You will move on my behalf. Amen.

GOD FOCUS: PART 2

"Do not be afraid or discouraged. Tomorrow, go out to face them, for Yahweh is with you."
2 CHRONICLES 20:17 HCSB

When we last left King Jehoshaphat, he had admitted to God that he and his people were helpless before the enemy horde coming against them. He and his kingdom had no idea what to do. They were looking to Him for everything.

As Jehoshaphat and his people stood waiting for a word from God, it came. Jahaziel delivered God's message, telling them not to be afraid for God was with them. Besides, this battle wasn't theirs, it was God's. All they had to do was stand still and watch to see how God would save them.

Hearing these words, Jehoshaphat bowed to God, and all the people did the same. Right then and there they worshipped Yahweh.

To nonbelievers, this whole idea of going out to meet the enemy, just to watch what God was going to do—well, it sounded pretty unnerving. In fact, it sounded insane. Yet the next morning, God's people got up. And just before they headed out, King Jehoshaphat gave them wisdom into which they could sink their teeth: "Believe in the Lord your God and you shall be established; believe *and* remain steadfast to His prophets and you shall prosper" (2 Chronicles 20:20 AMPC).

Afterward, Jehoshaphat organized a choir that marched ahead

of his army, singing and shouting their praises to God. It was then that God began setting ambushes against the enemy armies, which ended up attacking each other, leaving Judah to pick up the vast spoils left behind. Judah needed three days to haul away the invading armies' plunder. And then on the fourth day, everybody got together in the valley of spoils, which was now being called the Valley of Blessing! From there, King Jehoshaphat led a praise parade back to Jerusalem.

What a journey! King Jehoshaphat and his people had gone from fear to prayer to focus to faith to praise!

When fear first threatens to tear down the walls of your peace, be sure to follow Jehoshaphat's example. Turn to God in prayer. Keep your eyes focused on Him alone. Then muster all your faith, knowing that your Lord is the God of the impossible and improbable. Believe He will make a way where there seems to be none. And begin to praise God—no matter how things look or what others say. Know that He will do something beyond your imagination, greatest hopes, and desires. He will transform what looks bad for your good.

God, transform my fear to faith as I praise You while awaiting the impossible. Amen.

EYES UP

I lift up my eyes to the mountains—
where does my help come from?
PSALM 121:1 NIV

Look up. What do you see? Put down the book. Put down your phone. Put down your schedule. Put down your fears. Put down your stress. Put down the to-do list. Put down all the distractions and temptations and self-recriminations.

Look up. Eyes up, neck bent back, shoulders relaxed, fingers stretching toward the ground, mouth wide open—breathe deeply. What do you see?

Maybe you see a blank ceiling. A clean space. A space with no mistakes in it. Imagine the Creator God beginning to paint on this blank canvas. And with each stroke, a new part of creation appears. A lion leaps out on the plains of Africa. A whale bursts through the surface of the blue ocean. What do you see? Watch the Maker of heaven and earth at work. What do you notice about the colors and the textures and the details that He creates? What can you tell from the care He takes with every stroke?

Maybe you look up into the blue expanse above. What do you see? Is the sun shining? What do you hear? Look at every cloud, every leaf, every squirrel, every feather. What surprises you? What can you hear now that you couldn't before? Take time to look and listen. Look for the Creator's hand; listen for the Maker's commands.

He who once said, "Let there be light," is now speaking something into being in your life: "Let there be. . ." What is it that you are welcoming into your life from the Maker's hands? What is it you are trying to push away? Breathe in the air and realize there is space in you for whatever God has for you to do. He designed that space. He has known about it all along. He has been preparing good works for you to do.

Maybe you look up and see the night sky. Reach up. Let your fingers play among the stars. Imagine reaching higher and higher. Reach up to your Maker and don't be afraid. He will not let you slip. All through the night, He will hang on to you. He will not slumber. He will not fall asleep on the job. He will watch over you all through this night and all through any darkness you have to travel. He will bring you out of that blackness with the light of the sun, or the light of the moon, or even with the Light of His Son. He will watch you come and go, come and go, today and tomorrow and forever.

Maker and Helper, thank You for watching over me. Amen.

MIXED EMOTIONS

Even in laughter the heart may ache,
and rejoicing may end in grief.
PROVERBS 14:13 NIV

What a confusing place is the human heart! One minute we are in love, and the next we are bitterly angry. At one turn we are happy and whole, and around another corner come distress and emptiness. We are lonely; we are suffocated by other souls. We are afraid; we are taking risks. We are desperately longing for love and care; we are rejecting friends and shutting down.

The human heart is changeable and even at times deceitful. It can fool us into thinking things that are not so—into seeing mountains where there is only mist.

And when we are journeying through grief, we may find it hard to understand the sea of feelings we must swim through day after day. At one moment, we might find satisfaction and contentment in knowing our loved ones have gone (or are going) to live eternally with God. In the next moment, we may feel angry about being left on earth alone. One day, we may feel too weary to cry another drop. And then in another hour, a silly commercial jingle can trigger a memory that leaves us reeling with huge, shuddering sobs.

The feelings of grief can surprise us. They can leap upon us without notice, being conjured up from a glimpse of a house through a car window, from the sight of a picture on a wall, or

from the vision of our loved ones visiting us in our dreams. These heavy feelings can rest on our shoulders when we hear a particular saying or the chorus of a familiar song. These feelings can stop us in our tracks when someone asks a simple question such as "How's your dad doing?"

One of the hardest things about traveling through grief is feeling that there is some sort of right way to do it. We sometimes think there's a correct way to grieve, and if our feelings don't line up with that way, we must be doing it wrong. But there is no standard road map through grief. Everyone's trip is different, even though some of the signs along the way are familiar.

The writer of this proverb understood this truth. There is wisdom in knowing that some things are just inexplicable. There is no reason for the mysterious ability to laugh even when our hearts are aching. There is no logic to a moment of rejoicing turning into an expression of sorrow. But the God who made us knows all the mysterious revolutions of the human heart, and He will help us navigate the journey of grief.

God of sorrows, You understand my pain better than anyone. Please help me. Amen.

THE SILENCE OF GOD

LORD, I call to You; my rock, do not be deaf to me. If You remain silent to me, I will be like those going down to the Pit. . . . May the LORD be praised, for He has heard the sound of my pleading. . . . My heart trusts in Him, and I am helped.

PSALM 28:1, 6–7 HCSB

Only twice in scripture did Jesus praise people because of their great faith. The first person was the centurion who asked Jesus to heal his servant (see Matthew 8:5–13). The second was the woman called the Canaanite or Syrophoenician woman who asked Jesus to rid her daughter of a demon (Matthew 15:21–28; Mark 7:24–30). These two people had four things in common: they were Gentiles; they were intercessors; the people they were pleading for were healed from a distance; and they had the courage to approach Jesus. Yet the woman appeared even more courageous. Why? Because Jesus challenged both her faith and her persistence.

Jesus was walking with His disciples when the Canaanite woman kept crying out, "Take pity on me, Lord, Son of David! My daughter has a demon and is much troubled" (Matthew 15:22 NLV). But Jesus didn't say a word to her. His silence was deafening. His disciples began pleading with Him, saying, "Now she's bothering us. Would you please take care of her? She's driving us crazy" (Matthew 15:23 MSG).

Jesus had an unlikely response to their plea, telling them He already had His hands full with the children of Israel He came to save.

The woman overheard Jesus' remark but didn't allow it to discourage her. Instead, she followed Jesus into a house, got down on her knees, and renewed her begging, saying, "Master, help me" (Matthew 15:25 MSG).

As if He was testing her faith, Jesus responded with a metaphor: "It's not right to take bread out of children's mouths and throw it to dogs" (Matthew 15:26 MSG). But once again, the woman was undeterred, replying, "You're right, Master, but beggar dogs do get scraps from the master's table" (Matthew 15:27 MSG).

Finally, the woman heard Jesus' wonder-filled words: "O woman, great is your faith! Be it done for you as you desire" (Matthew 15:28 ESV). At that moment her daughter was healed.

Perhaps you have had moments when you felt your prayers, your pleadings, your words were bouncing off a wall of silence. Woman, take courage. Keep approaching God with your pleas.

Give me the courage and faith I need, Lord, to keep coming to You until I hear Your richest speech. Amen.

THE WOMAN WHO RESCUED THE RESCUER'S RESCUER

The daughter of Pharaoh came down to bathe at the river, and. . .she saw the ark among the rushes and sent her maid to fetch it. When she opened it, she saw the child; and behold, the baby cried. And she took pity on him.

EXODUS 2:5–6 AMPC

Because brave midwives defied the Egyptian king's command to kill newborn Hebrew boys, Moses survived his birth. He was then hidden by his courageous mother, Jochebed. When hiding the child proved to be hazardous, Jochebed made a watertight basket, laid Moses in it, and set it in the reeds in the crocodile-infested Nile River. His older sister, Miriam, watched and waited to see what would happen to her baby brother.

Enter a cruel ruler's daughter. Coming down to the Nile with her friends to bathe, Pharaoh's daughter saw the basket and its contents. The baby cried. Her heart was melted by such a tender child. The princess decided she would hire a Hebrew woman to nurse the child, then have her return him when he was weaned. Miriam ran to find her a nurse for the baby and returned with Jochebed, the infant's mother, in tow. The princess told her to take the boy away, nurse him, and then bring him to her when he was weaned. She would pay the nurse for her services.

When the boy was weaned, the nurse handed him over to the

princess. He, the one Pharaoh's daughter named Moses, became her son and the grandson of Pharaoh.

We have no more details about the princess and this story. But there are a few things we could surmise. The steps she took in saving Moses ran counter to what her father had commanded: *all* male Hebrew babies were to be annihilated. They were a threat to the stability and future of Egypt. Yet the princess not only disregarded her father's edict but adopted the child, raising him in luxury, giving him an education, keeping him safe from her father's designs. What courage this must have taken! She saved the man who would end up bringing plagues on her people, including the death of the Egyptian firstborn. She rescued the boy who would one day grow into a rescuer himself, having been trained up and sent by the ultimate Rescuer. Only God could so successfully orchestrate these events.

Too often we may judge people based on their nationality or parentage. Yet God would have us be courageous enough to evaluate people, including babies, on their own merit.

Lord, help me to be brave enough to take chances, to not make rash judgments, to evaluate people on their own merits. In Jesus' name I pray. Amen.

NEVER TOO LATE, NEVER TOO OLD

"I'll be with you," God said.

EXODUS 3:12 MSG

God saw the plight of His enslaved people in Egypt. Their cries had reached His ears. So, He visited Moses.

The adopted son of Pharaoh's daughter, Moses had been raised in privilege yet still maintained his Hebrew roots. So, when he saw one of his own being beaten by an Egyptian, he stepped in to save the man by murdering his attacker. The next day, stories of the incident had become common knowledge. This prompted the forty-year-old Moses to run to Midian (see Acts 7:23). There he met and married a girl and became a shepherd.

Moses spent the next forty years tending his father-in-law's sheep. That's when God showed up in a burning bush (see Acts 7:30). The eighty-year-old Moses heard God call his name, and a dialogue began. God wanted Moses to free His people from Egypt. To go back to his birthplace, back into the court in which he was raised, and tell the reigning pharaoh to let His people go.

Yet Moses didn't jump at the chance. Why leave his comfort zone and change careers at this point of his life? So, Moses started looking for reasons why this plan of God's wouldn't work.

First, Moses, thinking himself ill-equipped for the task, asked God, "What makes You think I can do this?" God answered Moses, "I'll be with you" (Exodus 3:12 MSG). God was saying, "Who *you* are

doesn't matter. The fact that *I'm with you* does." Second, Moses told God, "I don't even know who to say sent me." God told him, "Tell the People of Israel, 'I-AM sent me to you' " (Exodus 3:14 MSG). Third, Moses wondered how the Israelites would believe him or listen to him. After all, he was nothing but a murderer and a shepherd. God showed him how to use his staff to work miracles. Fourth, Moses admitted he was not a very good speaker. God said He would help Moses speak and teach him what to say (see Exodus 3:11–12).

Finally, Moses said, "Oh, Master, please! Send somebody else!" (Exodus 4:13 MSG). And at that, God's anger erupted, yet He didn't give up on Moses. God reminded him about his brother, Aaron, who spoke eloquently and added that Aaron was already "at this very moment. . .on his way to meet [him]" (Exodus 3:14 MSG).

With God, it's never too late and you're never too old to answer His call. All you need is courage and the faithful determination to walk with Him. For as Warren Wiersbe wrote, "The will of God will never lead you where the power of God can't enable you."

Thank You, Lord, for the reminder that I need not fear when You call me. For it's never too late for me to serve; I'm never too old—if I have You! Amen.

ALL THINGS

For from him and through him and for him are all things.
ROMANS 11:36 NIV

"Oh, the depth of the riches of the wisdom and knowledge of God!" (Romans 11:33 NIV).

Just consider the range of subjects that our God and Father understands. Nothing is beyond His comprehension. Nothing is below His consideration. Even our smallest needs and the flitting thoughts of our distracted brains are known to Him. There is nothing that we should feel is too trivial to bring to Him. We can talk with Him about anything we feel, anything we see, anything we hear. We can talk with Him about controversies and complicated relationships. We can talk with him about problems that we can't seem to wrap our heads around.

"How unsearchable his judgments, and his paths beyond tracing out!" (Romans 11:33 NIV).

God is the only perfect judge in the world. We are warned not to judge others—not just because we don't have the mind of God but because when we place ourselves in the seat of judgment, we put ourselves at risk of also being judged. But even worse than that, what we really put at risk is the ability to have real relationships with people. It's easy to put people in boxes and slap on labels. It's difficult to have actual conversations with people and get to know their stories.

We will never be able to understand all the judgments of God. The paths that lead to where He sits are not known to us—we cannot see from His point of view. But we can be assured that what God is doing is for our good.

"Who has known the mind of the Lord? Or who has been his counselor?" (Romans 11:34 NIV).

How good it is to know that no one on earth or in the heavenly realms understands the infinite mind of God! Our God is limitless. Our God is beyond definitions. Our God is bigger, grander, deeper than anything we could ever hope to imagine. And yet He wants us—smaller, lesser, shallower—to be with Him.

"Who has ever given to God, that God should repay them? For from him and through him and for him are all things" (Romans 11:35–36 NIV).

God does not need our gifts. God does not need anything. But we need to give to Him. We need to be placed in that position of gratitude—to practice offering up something of ourselves for something that is bigger than us. We need to practice letting go of our things and to be reminded that we are more than the things we own.

"To him be the glory forever! Amen" (Romans 11:36 NIV).

Lord, all glory and honor belong to You. Amen.

WAVES

Deep calls to deep in the roar of your waterfalls;
all your waves and breakers have swept over me.
PSALM 42:7 NIV

Crashing, falling, rushing. Enormous power channeled into curves and curls moves rapidly down the river, hurrying to the edge of the land as if an important appointment is waiting on the other side. The water leaps out and then falls forcefully into the pool below—a faucet that is never shut off.

Grief is like that sometimes. It seems like it will never end. Just when you feel you are over it, another wave comes, welling up inside you until it feels like your chest will explode with the pressure. Some days it grabs you all of a sudden—a memory rises up in your mind and you see the familiar scene play out like a movie. You watch the characters interact, you hear their lines, and you see them play their roles, but then comes the devastating realization that you will never be able to live that scene again. You'll never be able to hear that voice. You'll never be able to touch that hand.

And there you are, in the grip of grief. Air sucked out of your lungs. Mind swept of whatever thing you were supposed to be focusing on. Body frozen as you struggle to keep the tears from falling.

Grief lives deep inside you—underneath all day-to-day activities that you use to try to stay busy. You put one foot in front of another and keep walking, but grief makes each step a little

heavier. It's like the beat of a song that no one wants to sing. It's the experience of your heart breaking again and again. Grief is exhausting.

And down in the depths of your weary sorrow, God is there, calling to you, deep to deep. By day, as you work and try to think a clear path through the fog, He directs His love toward you, surrounding you with comfort. At night, God sings over you, like a mother singing a lullaby to her frightened child. God reminds you that you are never ever alone.

And with that promise, hope comes. And with hope, healing. And eventually, someday, you'll be able to have the memories without the mourning. You'll be able to replay those scenes and rejoice in the love you were blessed to have.

Lord, I put my hope in You. I trust that You are preparing a place where all of us can live and love together with You. Amen.

AN AMAZING ESCAPE

Jehosheba, daughter of King Jehoram and sister of Ahaziah, took Ahaziah's son Joash and kidnapped him from among the king's sons slated for slaughter. She hid him and his nurse in a private room away from Athaliah.

2 KINGS 11:1–2 MSG

After the good Jehoshaphat, king of Judah, died, his son Jehoram became king. To strengthen his position as ruler, the not-so-good Jehoram killed all his brothers. Apparently, Jehoram—who had married Ahab and Jezebel's daughter, Athaliah—had decided to follow in the footsteps of his father-in-law, the evil Ahab of Israel, instead of his own father.

Eight years later, Jehoram "departed with no one's regret" (2 Chronicles 21:20 ESV), and his youngest son, Ahaziah, became king. Ahaziah didn't have to kill any of his brothers because an invasion of Arabs had already done that. Ahaziah also followed in Grandpa Ahab's footsteps perhaps because his adviser was his mom, Athaliah.

Wounded in battle, Ahaziah died a year after taking the throne. Her son now dead, the queen mother, Athaliah, killed off the rest of the royal family of Judah—including her own grandsons! Although not of the line of David and therefore having no legitimate claim to the throne of Judah, Athaliah made herself queen. Yet unknown to her, one heir to the throne had been saved: Joash, Ahaziah's son.

Who saved the baby? Ahaziah's courageous half-sister,

Jehosheba. Few details are given about the rescue. Some say the child may have been lying among those already slaughtered when his aunt found him alive amid corpses. Whatever the particulars, the brave Jehosheba found the child. She hid him and his nurse in a bedroom, saving him from her murderous stepmother, Athaliah. Later, after consulting with her husband, the high priest Jehoiada, Jehosheba moved the boy to the temple, where she kept him safe for six years.

"Then, in the seventh year, Jehoiada summoned his courage" (2 Chronicles 23:1 HCSB). He presented Joash to the leaders of Judah. Together they brought out the legitimate heir to David's throne, put the crown on his head, and made him king.

When she heard the "Long live the king!" chants, the treasonous Athaliah screamed, "Treason, treason!" Nevertheless, her voice was soon silenced.

Although Jehosheba was a sister of an evil king (Ahaziah) and a granddaughter of an evil queen (Jezebel), she herself took a different path. Staying true to God, she was able to summon her courage and risk her life to rescue and shelter God's king.

What you make of your life is your own. What will you make of yours?

I want to be courageous and faithful to You, Lord. Be with me as I focus on You and Your ways no matter who or what may be trying to influence me. Amen.

LETTING GO

When she could no longer hide him, she took for him an ark or basket made of bulrushes or papyrus [making it watertight by] daubing it with bitumen and pitch. Then she put the child in it and laid it among the rushes by the brink of the river [Nile].

EXODUS 2:3 AMPC

Jochebed is one of those biblical women who has no dialogue in her story (see Exodus 2:1–10). Nor is she named in this account. Yet her courageous actions speak so much louder than any words could have.

Jochebed, a Levite, was married to Amram, a man from the house of Levi. She and her husband already had two children, Miriam and Aaron (see Numbers 26:59). And now, when newly born Hebrew boys were on Pharaoh's most-wanted-dead list, Jochebed gave birth to a son. Seeing how special he was, she hid him from prying eyes and somehow kept his cries from enemy ears.

When she could no longer hide the boy, she began to craftily create a watertight vessel for the babe. She then put the child in it and laid it in the reeds by the riverbank. Then she sent her daughter, Miriam, to stand by, at a distance, to see what became of him as his makeshift cradle floated in the Nile's crocodile-infested waters.

Imagine Jochebed's state while she awaited word about the welfare of her child. She must have been praying, on her knees, rocking back and forth, asking her Lord to protect this precious cargo floating on His waters.

As God would have it, Pharaoh's daughter came down to the river to bathe, discovered the floating basket, and sent her maid to fetch it. When she opened the vessel and saw the Hebrew baby, he began to cry, winning her heart. Miriam asked the princess if she would like her to call a Hebrew woman to nurse the child. With the princess's consent, Miriam ran off and soon came back with Jochebed. "Then Pharaoh's daughter said to her, 'Take this child away and nurse him for me. And I will pay you' " (Exodus 2:9 NLV).

Her precious son back in her arms, Jochebed nursed him. Once weaned, she brought him back to the princess, who adopted him as her son, giving him the name "Moses (Pulled-Out), saying, 'I pulled him out of the water' " (Exodus 2:10 MSG).

The immense courage and faith of Jochebed is seen in not just the survival of her children but in who those children became: Moses, one of the greatest leaders ever born; Aaron, the first of God's high priests and the founder of a priesthood; and Miriam, a gifted singer, dancer, musician, and prophet.

Lord, help me to have the courage to let go of those things and people close to my heart and to put them into Your care. Amen.

BETTER

"Mary has chosen what is better, and it will not be taken away from her."

LUKE 10:42 NIV

She had started off well. Offering hospitality like a champ, Martha had welcomed in the unexpected visitors. But then. . .there was a meal to be made, and floors to clean, and furniture to move, and drinks to be fetched, and. . .what was that smell?

Martha just couldn't be still. There were so many things to be done. And if she didn't do them, who would?

She looked over at her sister, Mary. *Not her, that's for sure*, Martha thought. From the moment Jesus had entered the house, Mary hadn't left His side. She hung on His every word. We can imagine that Martha had tried in vain to get her sister's attention. Maybe she had cleared her throat loudly and lifted her eyebrows so severely that she almost frightened them right off her forehead. She might have tried staring down her sister with a glare that spoke volumes—at least a few choice paragraphs. She even might have crept up close to give Mary a loving nudge in the side. But it was no use. Mary wasn't budging.

Finally, the exasperated Martha just couldn't take it. Can't you just picture her in your mind? Coming away from the cooking fire, sweat dripping, hair curling around her neck, stains on her best dress—having lost her patience and her temper and her composure,

she marched up to the Rabbi: "Lord, don't You care?" One wonders how she had finished that question in her head. *Don't You care at all that I'm doing all these things for You? Don't You care about how much work this is for me? Don't You care about me too, Lord? You haven't even asked what's for dinner! Don't You care?*

But what she said was, "Don't you care that my sister has left me to do the work by myself? Tell her to help me!" (Luke 10:40 NIV). It must be said: Martha had guts.

Ever full of grace, Jesus quieted Martha's worries. He took Martha's cares and distilled them down into what was important. He heard her, but He also knew what she needed to hear. She needed to know she was wrong. "Mary has chosen what is better, and it will not be taken away from her" (Luke 10:42 NIV).

It was better to listen. It was better to be near Jesus. It was better not to be so caught up in the things of this world that she missed the presence of God. Right there in her own living room. What are you doing that's keeping you from the better choice?

Lord, don't let me forget that what matters most is You. Amen.

SPEAKER OF TRUTH

Hilkiah the priest, Ahikam, Acbor, Shaphan, and Asaiah went straight to Huldah the prophetess. . . . The five men consulted with her. . . . The men took her message back to the king.

2 KINGS 22:14, 20 MSG

Good King Josiah of Judah did what was right in God's eyes. When he was sixteen, he began to seek God, to purge Judah of idolatry. At his orders, repairs were made to the temple. It was there that Hilkiah, the high priest, found the Book of the Law and gave it to Shaphan, the king's scribe, who read it to the king.

When Josiah heard God's words, he tore his clothes, distraught over how far he and his people had veered from God's ways. He ordered Hilkiah, Shaphan, and others, "Go, ask the Lord for me and all Judah about the words of this book. . . . For the Lord is very angry with us" (2 Kings 22:13 NLV). But instead of going to the temple to talk to God or consulting with a male prophet, such as Jeremiah and Zephaniah, the committee of five men went to see Huldah, "the woman who spoke for God" (2 Kings 22:14 NLV). "She was the wife of Shallum. . .who was in charge of the palace wardrobe. She lived in Jerusalem in the Second Quarter" (2 Kings 22:14 MSG).

They asked. Huldah answered. She prefaced her words by saying, "This is what the Lord God of Israel says" (2 Kings 22:15 NLV). Then she went on to give them two messages. The first one foretold

what was going to happen to the kingdom of Judah. Because the people hadn't been following God's law, His judgment was going to fall on Judah. Every word, every punishment written in the book would become a reality and couldn't be stopped.

Huldah's second message was to the king himself. God had seen Josiah as one who had a good heart and loved the Lord. Because of that, God would first gather Josiah to his grave in peace so that Josiah wouldn't be around to see the doom that was coming. When Josiah heard Huldah's messages, he became even more determined to bring his people back to God.

God had seen His people and sometimes their leaders turning away from Him. But Huldah, the wife of a man in charge of clothing, had not turned away from God. Her heart had always followed Him. She was a trusted prophet, known to speak God's truth. With courage, she delivered the words of God, regardless of how difficult the news was to deliver.

As a follower of God, you too must speak the truth. Do so with the courage of Huldah.

God, give me the courage to speak Your truth. Amen.

A HEALTHY RESPECT

Blessed man, blessed woman, who fear GOD, who cherish and relish his commandments. . . . Unfazed by rumor and gossip, heart ready, trusting in GOD, spirit firm, unperturbed, ever blessed, relaxed among enemies.

PSALM 112:1, 7–8 MSG

God doesn't want you to be afraid of people, circumstances, and situations. But what He does want is for you to have a healthy respect of Him. To understand that He's the One in control of all things. He's the One you'll have to answer to someday. He's the One who not only made the world but moves and sustains it. This fear, or awesome respect, of God is something the midwives Shiphrah and Puah could attest to.

Back in the day, Jacob's son Joseph had once been the Egyptian king's number two man. Now he had died, but the people of Israel continued to live in Egypt and had dramatically grown in population.

The new reigning pharaoh didn't know Joseph or how or why Joseph's entire family had been permitted to live and thrive in Egypt. On top of that, Pharaoh felt threatened by the Israelites increasing in number for they might become too many and too mighty.

Pharaoh's first plan was to enslave God's people, putting over them cruel and demanding taskmasters. But the harder he made things for them, the more the Israelites grew in number. Something

else had to be done.

So Pharaoh spoke to the chief midwives, Shiphrah and Puah. He told them to kill male Hebrews at birth but to allow the females to live. Yet, as Pharaoh later discovered, this wasn't going to work either because "the midwives feared God." And because of that fear, they "did not do as the king of Egypt commanded, but let the male babies live" (Exodus 1:17 AMPC). And those midwives under Shiphrah and Puah's authority did the same.

When Pharaoh asked why they let the sons of the Hebrews live, Shiphrah and Puah said what may or may not have been an untruth: "Because the Hebrew women are not like the Egyptian women; they are vigorous and quickly delivered; their babies are born before the midwife comes to them" (Exodus 1:19 AMPC).

Two God-fearing women stood up to their cruel ruler, *choosing* to continue bringing life into the world as befit their calling and their God. As a reward, God gave them families of their own.

When faced with cruel rulers, lawmakers, or other people in authority, do not let fear of them hold you back. Instead, allow your respect for God to move you to do what He would have you do. And God will reward your courage and obedience.

Give me the courage, Lord, to follow
the awesome You and no other. Amen.

RISING ABOVE SHADOWS

Jabez was more honorable than his brothers. His mother named him Jabez and said, "I gave birth to him in pain." Jabez called out to the God of Israel: "If only You would bless me, extend my border, let Your hand be with me, and keep me from harm, so that I will not cause any pain." And God granted his request.

1 CHRONICLES 4:9–10 HCSB

Family genealogies are pretty dry. When reading name after name after name, staying awake can be difficult. But then you come across 1 Chronicles 4:9–10. Like an oasis in the middle of a desert, these verses appear, piquing your curiosity, prompting you to ask more questions than they can answer.

It's uncertain what kind of pain Jabez's mother had experienced. Perhaps his father had just died or some other traumatic event had occurred, leaving her depressed; perhaps the delivery of this son was exceptionally painful; maybe she was suffering from postpartum depression. Regardless of the specifics, the fact remains that a child was born, and his mother called him Pain.

That's a hard name to rise above, to shake off, to ignore. Growing up, Jabez must have found it difficult to get out from underneath the shadow cast by this appellation. It was a constant reminder that, from day one, his birth had somehow caused his mother pain—physically or mentally. Yet perhaps it was because he was named Pain that he was extra careful that he *not* live up to his name. Perhaps that's what made Jabez "more honorable than his brothers." Some things we'll never really know.

Yet we can surmise that Jabez's mother must have raised her son to know and recognize God, for his prayer is heartfelt and powerful. He would like God to bless him, increase his land holdings, and have His guidance and protection in all things. But most of all, Jabez wanted God to keep him from being hurt so that he wouldn't cause anyone else pain. Ever.

Jabez must have needed great courage to offer such a plea. Somehow he must have known that, although he couldn't change the circumstances of his birth, he could change his attitude toward his name. Jabez didn't ask for his name to be changed; he was still called Pain. But what he did want, what he had the courage to do, to aspire to, to ask for, was a way out from underneath this ill omen of a misnomer and get under God's protection, power, and provision.

When an adverse circumstance brings a shadow over your life, be as brave and wise as Jabez. Call on God. Ask for His help and light—and He will grant your request.

Lord, give me the courage to bring
my shadows into Your light. Amen.

HIDING PLACES

You are my hiding place; you protect me from trouble.

PSALM 32:7 CSB

"Eighteen. . .nineteen. . .twenty! Ready or not, here I come!" And off he runs, searching for his hidden friends. The friends wait in eager anticipation, ready to spring out from behind trees and bushes to make a dash for home base. Because as much fun as it is to hide, it's still more fun to be found. To come out in the open and join the crowd and compare notes on who had the best hiding place, who was found first, and so on. The real fun of the game only happens in community. You can't play hide-and-seek alone.

It is a blessing to be out in the open and free—to feel as though you can be yourself without having to cover up any blemishes or faults. To feel that whatever wrong things you have done have been revealed and forgiven and can now be put behind you. To know you have learned and grown and changed and can now hope for better days.

The psalmist spoke of the damaging effects of hidden sin: "When I kept silent, my bones became brittle from my groaning all day long. . . . My strength was drained as in the summer's heat" (Psalm 32:3–4 CSB). Once our sin is confessed and forgiven, we can stop hiding away from God and instead turn and hide within God's protection—safe from trouble.

Hiding there with God, we can be protected by knowledge.

God teaches us and provides wise counsel, showing the way we need to go to become the people He created us to be. With God, we can be surrounded by love—by the love of God that never fails and never fades, that doesn't require us to pretend to be anything different from what we are but rather calls us to be honest and true. With God, we can be encouraged and lifted up by the joy of the Lord—and by the feeling of standing upright before Him!

God doesn't expect us to always make right choices. After all, He made us, and He has observed human behavior since the beginning. God is not surprised when we fail. So why hide? Come out, come out, wherever you are, and share your story. You'll be glad you did, and you'll help those who are listening to share their stories too.

Most holy God, please forgive all the ungodly parts of me. I place myself in Your care. Hide me in Your love. Amen.

DO YOU SEE?

The angel said, "I am Gabriel, the sentinel of God, sent especially to bring you this glad news. But because you won't believe me, you'll be unable to say a word until the day of your son's birth. Every word I've spoken to you will come true on time—God's time."

LUKE 1:19–20 MSG

Zechariah and Elizabeth were a happily married couple, both very godly, walking blamelessly, following all of God's commands. Zechariah was a priest, and Elizabeth was descended from the line of Aaron. They were also old and childless.

Then one day, while Zechariah was at the temple offering incense, the angel of the Lord appeared to him. Zechariah was not just troubled about what this angel might want; he was also afraid, wondering what this angel might want from *him*.

Picking up on the mortal's rising fear, the angel told him not to be afraid. Zechariah's prayer had been heard by God, and Elizabeth was going to give him a son that he would name John. The angel then detailed John's mission and future.

After hearing all the angel had to say, Zechariah disbelievingly said, "Do you expect me to believe this? I'm an old man and my wife is an old woman" (Luke 1:18 MSG).

The angel then introduced himself as Gabriel, the one specially sent to bring Zechariah this good news. And because Zechariah

didn't believe him and his message, the priest would be mute, unable to say a single syllable until his son was born. "Every word I've spoken to you will come true on time—*God's* time." Gabriel made clear that what he wanted from Zechariah was for him to believe the impossible.

When his priestly duties were over, the now mute Zechariah went home. Somehow he must have shared the angel's message with his wife, because soon after Zechariah's return, Elizabeth conceived. In doing so, she proved the truth of the angel's words spoken to her cousin Mary: "Nothing, you see, is impossible with God" (Luke 1:37 MSG).

Eventually, Elizabeth gave birth to a boy and named him John. And he, John the Baptist, filled with the Holy Spirit, went out to announce the coming of the Lord. All just as promised and predicted by the angel of the Lord.

God's promises to you may at times seem impossible of fulfillment, but God wants you to believe them. No matter how long it takes for Him to bring the miracle about, have faith that He will—in His time. And while you're waiting, allow what you perceive as a delay to deepen your faith not destroy it. Keep praying. Keep believing. Keep expecting. And God will do the impossible in your life.

Lord, write this truth indelibly upon my heart and mind: "Nothing is impossible with God." Amen.

THREE GOOD REASONS

Joseph was well-built and handsome. After some time his master's wife looked longingly at Joseph and said, "Sleep with me." But he refused. . . . "How could I do such a great evil and sin against God?"

GENESIS 39:6–9 HCSB

Joseph, the eleventh son of Jacob, was also his father's favorite. Prompted by their jealousy of him, Joseph's brothers got rid of him. They threw him into a pit then sold him to some traders passing by. From there Joseph ended up a slave in the house of an Egyptian officer named Potiphar.

Joseph did the best he could in the situation he was in. As the days went by, his master realized "the LORD was with [Joseph] and that the LORD made everything he did successful" (Genesis 39:3 HCSB). So Potiphar put him in charge of his house. It was there that Potiphar's wife constantly invited Joseph to sleep with her. Joseph refused for three good reasons: (1) she was his boss's wife; (2) he didn't want to violate the trust his boss had in him; and (3) he knew God would not approve.

Still, day after day, Potiphar's wife pleaded with Joseph to go to bed with her. Then one day she grabbed him by his coat, demanding he sleep with her. But he tore himself loose and escaped her clutches, leaving his coat in her hands. She used that coat as evidence that Joseph had tried to seduce her. "When he heard me

screaming for help, he left his garment with me and ran outside" (Genesis 39:15 HCSB).

When Potiphar heard his wife's story, he had Joseph thrown into the dungeon. But even there "the LORD was with him and the LORD made everything that he did successful" (Genesis 39:23 HCSB).

No matter how bad things got, Joseph never succumbed to depression, despair, or destruction, nor did he deviate from his walk with God. He never looked for the easy way out. With courage, patience, strength, and fortitude, he faced every difficulty, knowing that God would be with him no matter where he wound up.

You too have the courage, patience, strength, and fortitude within you to walk where and how God would have you walk. Choose the high road, the right way, no matter how enticing the temptation or shortcut that comes your way, for God is with you just as He was with Joseph. And as you keep in step with Him, refusing to get sidelined by fear or temptation, God will make all you do successful.

Help me, Lord, to do my best no matter what the situation. Help me keep my eyes on You, knowing that You are with me all day and in all ways. Amen.

THE PRICE OF FORGIVENESS

"But God sent me ahead of you to preserve for you a remnant on earth and to save your lives by a great deliverance."

GENESIS 45:7 NIV

If you didn't know the whole story, he would seem pretty cruel. Joseph, once a prisoner and slave, now second-in-command to Pharaoh, put his brothers through some psychological torture when they came to him seeking food. His brothers, those same men who at one time had contemplated killing him, didn't recognize Joseph. They weren't looking for him. Last time they saw him, he was sitting on the back of an Ishmaelite merchant wagon sold as a slave.

Now he stood before them, full of power and holding the strings to their survival. And he seemed to be playing them like a puppet master with his marionettes. He gave them tasks to do, but he set them up to fail. He gave an appearance of being threatening, even when they had no knowledge of what they had done wrong.

Was he bitter? Vengeful? Just out of his head?

None of those seem to be adequate explanations given what happened next—when Joseph could no longer hold in his emotions. It seems what was really running through Joseph's mind that whole time, his real feelings on seeing his family after so many years of being forgotten by them, was just. . .love.

It seems likely that Joseph all along was just trying to get all

of his brothers together in one place and to get them used to being around him. Perhaps he wanted them to see and realize what power he had—not to lord it over them, but so he could later assure them that they were safe with him.

Of course, Joseph had every right to hold a grudge. No one would have been surprised if Joseph had wanted to exact some kind of revenge on his brothers. No one would have been shocked at all if he at least had been angry with them. But Joseph just wanted his family back. He gave up on retribution in order to have reconciliation. He gave up on punishment in order to have fellowship. He gave up personal pride in order to rejoice in family pride.

We sometimes have to let go of our own dreams about how things should be or what ought to be said in order to be open to the possibility of restored relationships. Forgiveness often costs us something. But the rewards are worth every penny.

Lord, help me to let go of what I think is due me and to accept all You have for me. Amen.

IN THE DETAILS

"Don't be hypercritical; use your head—and heart!—to discern what is right, to test what is authentically right."

JOHN 7:24 MSG

Those poor people. They were just trying to figure this puzzle out. Now, to be fair, one would have thought that seeing Jesus heal the sick, feed the hungry, and raise people back to life would be enough to convince them that He was the One they had been waiting for. They heard Him teach with authority because He was the author of the Word. They had the proof—why were they still questioning who Jesus really was?

They got stuck in the details. Where Jesus came from versus what the scriptures had to say about the origin of the Messiah. And why didn't He act like they expected the Messiah to act? And why didn't He follow the letter of the Law? We read in John 7:5, "Even his own brothers did not believe in him" (NIV).

They were blinded by a hundred little things they pictured Jesus would be for them and do for them. And there Jesus was, walking, talking, living, and breathing in front of them, and they were missing it.

We do this all the time though, don't we? Before we judge those Jews living at the time of Jesus, let's stop and take a look at ourselves. Have you ever missed seeing what God was doing in your life because you were busy thinking you'd be called in a

different way?

Have you ever missed the goodness of a relationship because you were busy waiting for it to come with the violins and romance and roses you thought you needed?

Have you ever missed the beauty of a gift because you didn't like the way it was handed to you?

Have you ever negated the satisfaction of a meal because the food didn't taste like you imagined this dish was supposed to taste?

Have you ever missed out on a second chance because you were too busy mourning that first chance you failed to take advantage of?

Have you ever been so sure about how a person following Jesus should look and sound that you missed out on gleaning wisdom from some amazing Christians?

Use your head *and* your heart. Be discerning. Hang on to the truth instead of letting yourself drown in the details. Don't miss out on what God has for you simply because you believe you know exactly how and what God is going to give. Be open to the mystery of the living and breathing Lord of all.

Lord, I don't want to lose You in my own expectations and limitations. Help me to imagine more. Amen.

CHAIN OF ENCOURAGEMENT

I was very much afraid. I said to the king, "Let the king live forever. Why should my face not be sad when the city, the place of my fathers' graves, lies waste and its gates destroyed by fire?" Then the king said to me, "What are you asking for?" So I prayed to the God of heaven.

NEHEMIAH 2:2–4 NLV

Nehemiah was an exiled Jew and cupbearer serving King Artaxerxes of Persia. After hearing that Jerusalem's walls and gates had been badly damaged, Nehemiah mourned for days. Then he began fasting and praying to God about the situation.

For months, Nehemiah had been trying to hide his feelings from the king, but Artaxerxes couldn't be fooled. One day he asked Nehemiah why he was so sad. The king could see that Nehemiah wasn't physically sick, so the problem must be sadness within Nehemiah's heart.

These words struck terror in the cupbearer for two reasons. The first was that he had obviously failed to be upbeat, positive, and encouraging, which was a must in the king's presence. The second was that now God had presented Nehemiah with an opportunity, one in which he was going to have to risk pleading for his people. But he had no idea how the king would react.

Sometimes the only way out is to go forward. So the fearful cupbearer did. He eased into his response by praising the king.

Then he asked Artaxerxes how he, Nehemiah, could be happy knowing that Jerusalem, his home city, lay in ruins.

The wise Artaxerxes cut to the chase: "What are you requesting?" he asked. This prompted Nehemiah to send a quick yet powerful prayer to God. Then, and only then, did Nehemiah ask if he could go to Judah to help rebuild Jerusalem.

The king graciously approved Nehemiah's initial request and then two more: letters from Artaxerxes to local officials and leaders so Nehemiah would have safe passage to Judah; and another letter to "Asaph, keeper of the king's forest" (Nehemiah 2:8 HCSB) so Nehemiah would have timber to rebuild Jerusalem's wall. Nehemiah wrote, "The king granted my requests, for I was graciously strengthened by my God" (Nehemiah 2:8 HCSB).

Once in Jerusalem, Nehemiah motivated workers to rebuild the city wall by telling them "how God was supporting [him] and how the king was backing [him] up" (Nehemiah 2:18 MSG). Only then were the men "encouraged to do this good work" (Nehemiah 2:18 HCSB).

Your prayers can provide all the strength, courage, and hope you need to follow God's leading. Whether lengthy prayers or short arrow prayers, your request to God should be shared to help inspire others. Doing so sets off a chain of encouragement.

Help me strengthen and encourage myself and others, Lord, with prayer. Amen.

DETERMINED TO RIGHT WRONGS

Judah identified [his signet ring, cord, and staff] and said, "She is more righteous than I."

GENESIS 38:26 ESV

Judah had three sons—Er, Onan, and Shelah. Anxious to continue his ancestral line, Judah found a wife for Er, his oldest boy. Her name was Tamar. But Er was evil, so God cut his life short.

Then Judah told his son Onan to marry his brother's widow, live with her, and raise up her children for his late brother. Doing so in those days was normal. It was part of Old Testament law (see Deuteronomy 25:5–6). But Onan didn't like siring sons for his brother. "So whenever he went in to his brother's wife he would waste the semen on the ground" (Genesis 38:9 ESV). Offended by his behavior, God took Onan's life as well.

Judah had only one son left: Shelah. Afraid for his youngest's life, Judah told Tamar to go back home to her father's house until Shelah was grown. So she did. There she waited. And waited. Until one day she realized she was never going to be married to Shelah.

When Tamar heard her father-in-law was coming to Timnah, she decided to take action. She summoned up all her courage and changed out of her widow's clothes. She put on a veil to conceal her identity and sat on the side of the road. It was there the now widowed Judah found her. Assuming she was a prostitute, he asked to come in to her, promising to send her a goat for that privilege.

As a pledge for payment, Tamar asked for Judah's signet ring, cord, and staff, which he willingly put in her hands. After Judah slept with Tamar, she became pregnant, removed her veil, and put on her widow's clothes once more.

Later, when Judah heard his daughter-in-law was pregnant, he sent for her, intending to have her burned to death in accordance with Levitical law. When they brought her out, she sent Judah the signet ring, cord, and staff with the message, "I'm pregnant by the man who owns these things" (Genesis 38:25 MSG). It was then Judah realized he had done her wrong. Tamar had been more righteous and just than he had been.

What courage it must have taken Tamar to stand up for what was hers in this patriarchal society. How amazing that because of her determination to right the wrongs done her, she not only continued her father-in-law's line but became an ancestor of Jesus and, as such, is listed in His genealogy: "And Judah the father of Perez and Zerah by Tamar, and Perez the father of Hezron" (Matthew 1:3 ESV).

Lord, give me the courage to make things right when I and others have been wronged. Amen.

QUICK, SLOW, SLOW

Understand this, my dear brothers and sisters: You must all be quick to listen, slow to speak, and slow to get angry. Human anger does not produce the righteousness God desires.

JAMES 1:19–20 NLT

You get in the car and start the morning commute. *Wham!* You slam on the brakes as some person with an apparent death wish decides to cut in front of you in their extremely big hurry to. . .wait for it. . .the very next exit. After your heart stops pounding, you continue but miss the turn you've taken every day for the last ten years because you just realized that you also slammed your coffee cup out of the holder and onto the floor, just out of reach of your fingertips.

And all the while you've been muttering various choice words, the little ears in the backseat have been listening to every single syllable. You look at your young son in the rearview mirror and say, "Sorry, Jacob! Mommy's having a hard morning."

"So it's okay to say things like that when it's a bad day?" Jacob can always be counted on to put things in perspective.

"No, it's not okay, buddy. I'm sorry. I just let my words come out too fast. I'll try harder."

"That's okay, Mommy. Daddy does it too."

Quick to listen. Slow to speak. Slow to get angry. It sounds pretty easy, doesn't it? But to whom should we listen? And what

should we be speaking? What will produce righteousness, after all?

We should be quick to listen to God and to His Word, which we should have planted in our hearts. Especially in heated moments when we are prone to anger, we should listen to God reminding us to be patient, to think things through, to consider others above ourselves.

Be slow to speak. Slow to speak the first thing that comes to your mind. Those first things hardly ever represent the truth of who you are or even the truth of what you really think.

Be slow to get angry. God's anger comes from the place where all good things come from. God loves us with a pure form of love that always has our best interests at heart. His anger is incurred when His children are treated unjustly or when they disobey Him and hurt one another. But humans get angry for all sorts of reasons that have very little to do with love. Yet if we follow God's example, we can find the way to righteousness and keep ourselves from being a bad example to the kids in the back seat.

Lord, slow my tongue and quicken my heart to be aligned with Yours. Amen.

A WORD ABOUT MIDWIVES

[Rachel] had hard labor. And when her labor was at its hardest, the midwife said to her, "Do not fear, for you have another son."

GENESIS 35:16–17 ESV

In her book *Bible Women: All Their Words and Why They Matter*, Lindsay Hardin Freeman writes, "By our count, using the New Revised Standard Version of the Bible in English, about 14,000 words are spoken by women." Since that amounts to roughly 1.2 percent of the total words found in the Bible, one thing is certain: when biblical women speak, we should be paying very close attention.

In Genesis 35, labor came upon Rachel as she and her family were traveling. During this birth of her second child, things weren't going well. You can imagine her cries, her screams, her tears, her panting as she pushed and pushed the child from her womb. As her son was making his way down the birth canal, Rachel began bleeding uncontrollably.

To help distract, encourage, and comfort Rachel, perhaps to help even herself bear up under the strain, Rachel's midwife said, "Don't be afraid." These are the three most strengthening words any woman in Rachel's situation can hear, especially from another woman. Then the midwife added, "You have another baby boy." In those days, having a boy was a great blessing because a son meant the family line would continue and also meant that if the mother became widowed, she had a better chance of survival and protection.

When she had been childless, Rachel had witnessed her sister, Leah, giving Jacob four sons. Angered and frustrated, Rachel demanded her husband, Jacob, "Give me children, or else I die!" (Genesis 30:1 NKJV). Later, God listened to Rachel's request and granted it, allowing her to conceive and give birth to her first son, whom she named Joseph, meaning "The LORD shall add to me another son" (Genesis 30:24 NKJV).

This second boy, Benjamin, was an answer to Rachel's deep desire to provide her loving husband, Jacob, with another son. Yet it was during this birth that as she gave life, her life gave out.

Thousands of years ago, childbirth was risky business. Since then things have improved somewhat, yet women still must navigate many dangers when bringing a child into this world. Yet how wonderful and precious are the encouraging words "Don't be afraid; don't fear" from another woman, midwife or otherwise.

Perhaps there's a woman—premenstrual, pregnant, menopausal, whatever stage—who needs to hear those words from you today. Don't spare them. Share them.

Show me, Lord, who needs to hear the words "Don't be afraid." Then give me the courage to say them. Amen.

GREAT AND AWESOME

They. . .decided to fight against Jerusalem and create as much trouble as they could. We countered with prayer to our God and set a round-the-clock guard against them. . . . I stood up and spoke. . ."Don't be afraid of them. Put your minds on the Master, great and awesome, and then fight."

NEHEMIAH 4:8–9, 14 MSG

Nehemiah was determined to rebuild and repair the wall in Jerusalem. But to do so he needed more than workmen and tools. He needed prayer, faith, and focus.

Certain leaders in the nearby nations, not wanting to see the building project succeed, started mocking the Jews. To counter their jeers, Nehemiah prayed that God would "boomerang their ridicule on their heads" (Nehemiah 4:4 MSG). And the building continued.

When the enemy leaders' anger and harassment grew, Nehemiah countered with more prayers to God. But he didn't stop there. He himself took action. He set a twenty-four-hour guard to protect his workers.

In spite of all his determination and efforts, negative rumors started going around in Judah among the people: "The builders are pooped, the rubbish piles up; we're in over our heads, we can't build this wall" (Nehemiah 4:10 MSG). At the same time, death threats from the Jews' enemies ramped up. Their neighbors began panicking as well, afraid they would soon be attacked.

Once again, Nehemiah took action, adding more men to guard the most vulnerable spots in the wall. He then gave the people great advice on how to handle their enemies and their threats, saying, "Don't be afraid of them. Put your minds on the Master, great and awesome, and then fight for your brothers, your sons, your daughters, your wives, and your homes" (Nehemiah 4:14 MSG).

In the end, God frustrated the plans of Judah's enemies. And after fifty-two days, the wall was finished (Nehemiah 6:15). Nehemiah wrote, "When all our enemies heard the news and all the surrounding nations saw it, our enemies totally lost their nerve. They knew that God was behind this work" (Nehemiah 6:16 MSG).

When God calls you to take on a task, you too will need at least several things to see it through. Determine within yourself to stay the course. Pray to counteract the plans of those trying to thwart your efforts. Take whatever action may be necessary to move the project forward. Instead of giving in to negative statements within and without, encourage yourself and others by remembering the many "great and awesome" things God has done for His people. Take courage, knowing that God is behind your work, helping you to succeed.

Lord, tell me what You would have me do for You. Then give me determination, power of prayer, faith, focus, and courage to see it through, remembering that with You I can do anything. Amen.

WHENEVER AND WHEREVER

"This is from the LORD; we have no choice in the matter. . . . Take [Rebekah] and go, and let her be a wife for your master's son." . . . So they said, "Let's call the girl and ask her opinion." They called Rebekah and said to her, "Will you go with this man?" She replied, "I will go."

GENESIS 24:50–51, 57–58 HCSB

Abraham, now a widower, sent his servant to find a wife for his son Isaac. She had to be from Abraham's brother Nahor's town and family. Abraham told his servant, "[God] will send His angel before you" (Genesis 24:7 HCSB). The servant swore that he would perform this duty then headed out to find a bride for Isaac, his master's son.

Arriving in Nahor, the servant lifted up a prayer to God, asking for success in his mission and for God to pick out the perfect match for Isaac. She would be the one who not only drew water for the servant but for his camels as well.

Before the servant finished his prayer, Nahor's beautiful granddaughter Rebekah appeared. This young woman was not only happy to help water man and beasts but offered Abraham's servant bed and board for himself and his camels. The servant, discovering she was related to Abraham, immediately worshipped God, thanking Him for answering his prayer.

Flush with success, the servant followed Rebekah home,

where he explained his mission and God's answer to his prayer. He then asked her father, Bethuel, and brother, Laban, if they would allow Rebekah to travel back to Abraham's home so she might marry Isaac.

Laban and Bethuel said, "This is from the LORD; we have no choice in the matter. . . . Take her and go" (Genesis 24:50–51 HCSB). The servant once more praised God and distributed the gifts he had brought with him.

The next morning, the servant was anxious to get going because his master, Abraham, was old and sick, and the journey back was five hundred miles. Rebekah's family was hoping she would spend ten days with them before she left for a new land and husband. When the servant asked them not to hinder his departure, Rebekah's family decided to ask her if she would go. She responded with three simple, straight, definite, and direct words: "I will go."

Rebekah set the example for what to do when we're sure God is calling us out of our comfort zone and into a new place, a new life. God wants us to have faith in Him and courageously say, "I will go," knowing that as we do so, we're not only following God but may be answering someone else's prayer.

Wherever and whenever You call me, Lord, I will go! Amen.

OFFER UP

Use your whole body as an instrument to do what is right for the glory of God.

ROMANS 6:13 NLT

Caroline stretched out her arm and traced the blue lines of her veins from her shoulder down to her wrist. Her skin had always been so pale. She remembered once, a long time ago, tracing her own mother's veins in the same way and asking her why she had made blue marker lines on her skin. Her mother had laughed.

That was long before the bruises started appearing on the inside of her mother's wrist in the size and shape of tightly gripping fingers. Long before the constant yelling. Long before her father finally left the house and didn't come back. And long before Caroline started self-medicating with whatever alcohol she could find.

But today felt different. Today Caroline felt like she was standing on the edge of some invisible cliff, ready to leap off into a new part of her life. She wanted to be "dead to sin" and "alive to God," as she had heard the speaker say in the group meeting the other night. She wanted that as badly as she had ever wanted another buzz. She wanted to put behind her a past that was filled with decisions made based solely on temporary, selfish wants. And she wanted not to want things that would only hurt her or other people. But could she achieve this? Not on her own, that was for certain.

So why am I here now? Caroline wondered, as the stranger

stretched the rubbery strip around her arm and pressed softly on her flesh, feeling for the vein. *Why do this now?*

The needle went in quickly with just a slight sting. Caroline relaxed and laid her head back. She smiled. She knew why. Because it felt good to be doing something good with her body. It felt good to offer herself up to a path that led toward life. To offer someone else a bit of life-giving force.

"Thanks so much for your donation, Caroline," the nurse said, handing Caroline some informational sheets. "Take it easy today, okay?"

Yes, easy, thought Caroline. *It's not been an easy road to get here, but it's easy to want to offer every part of me up to God.* She walked out under the huge Blood Drive Today sign, eating the last bites of her complementary cookie and smiling from ear to ear.

Lord God, thank You for allowing me to start with a new slate. Help me know how to use every part of me to glorify You. Amen.

ROOTED

"But since they have no root, they last only a short time. When trouble or persecution comes because of the word, they quickly fall away."

MARK 4:17 NIV

The parable of the sower must be right up there on the Top 5 list of Parables Jesus Taught That People Know About. It's a well-crafted story that still speaks to us today, even if we haven't ever sown a seed in our entire lives. We get it. Of course, it helps that we have such a good Teacher who goes to great lengths to explain things to us.

We can all see ourselves in this story, and at different times in our lives, we might identify with different kinds of seeds. Many of us know what it is to be a seed sown in a rocky place. We know what Jesus means about having no root. But what does it look like to be rooted? And how do we get there?

If you've ever been a child or had a child or known a child, it's likely that at some point you have been engaged in some version of a seed-growing experiment. They've brought that bean seed home in a see-through container of some sort, and then the seed must be observed, and the observations of growth must be noted. And what do we see about roots? They grow. They curl around, looking for a source of food. They keep growing and stretching, always seeking more food and water.

Another thing about those roots is that they were not stuck

on at the last minute. Those roots were ready to come out of that seed because the information needed to make them grow was already in there.

We become rooted when we let our roots grow. We become rooted by immersing ourselves in the Word of God—listening to what He has to say to us. We become rooted when we not only read His Word but live it out. We become rooted when we allow His Word to feed us every day.

We also become rooted through the generations. Maybe your family has no faith traditions in your history. Maybe you are the first in a long line to try following Christ. But now you can start your own traditions. You can become part of a family of believers and know that you have people such as Paul and Mary and Ruth and David and Peter in your family tree. And you can pass on your faith practices to the next generation. You can make sure that they are rooted in the Word from birth.

Lord, I want my roots to be firmly planted in Your Word. Help me to grow. Amen.

WHO KNOWS?

"Who knows, perhaps you have come to your royal position for such a time as this."

ESTHER 4:14 HCSB

During the Jewish exile, Mordecai and his beautiful young cousin, Esther, lived in Susa. So, when King Ahasuerus (or Xerxes) was looking for a new queen, Esther was one of many young girls rounded up and brought to the palace, where she became part of a harem. When Esther's turn came to spend a night with the king, Ahasuerus was so pleased with her that she was made queen. She did not tell him that she was Jewish.

Soon afterward, Mordecai overheard of a plot to assassinate the king. He reported it to Esther, who, in turn, told the king. After an investigation by the king's men, the plan was verified and the conspirators hanged.

Later, Haman, a man on Ahasuerus's staff, was promoted by the king. The king ordered that all bow down to Haman. But Mordecai, a Jew, would not. For this infraction, Haman began to plot against the Jews. He convinced Ahasuerus that the Jews living in his kingdom should be annihilated. Ahasuerus agreed, and an edict from the king was delivered to all the provinces.

When Mordecai heard of Haman's evil plan, he sent word to Esther, detailing what their people faced. He suggested she go before her husband and talk to him about it.

Esther sent word back to Mordecai, saying that if she went to the king without first being called, she could be put to death. Mordecai responded by telling her not to keep silent. She had to go to the king and save her people or else she herself might lose her life. Then he said perhaps she was where she was "for such a time as this."

Esther agreed to go before the king before being called—to put her life on the line. But she first asked for Mordecai to gather the Jews together to fast and pray for her for three days and nights. She and her female servants would do the same. Then Esther would go to see the king. "If I perish, I perish" (Esther 4:16 HCSB), she said.

Esther saw the king. She lived. He ensured the safety of the Jewish people. Haman was hanged. Mordecai was honored.

Esther showed true courage and handled the situation with great finesse. Because of her and Mordecai's dependence on and faith in God, many Jewish lives were saved. Tables were turned. Good dismantled works of evil.

God has called each of us to live out His purpose for us. Perhaps this is your moment, your reminder, to pray for the courage you'll need for such a time as this.

Here I am, Lord. Give me the courage
I need for such a time as this. Amen.

MAKING THINGS RIGHT

"If you enter your place of worship and, about to make an offering, you suddenly remember a grudge a friend has against you, abandon your offering, leave immediately, go to this friend and make things right. Then and only then, come back and work things out with God."

MATTHEW 5:23–24 MSG

When you come to God ready to worship, to offer yourself to Him, He wants you pure, open, free, and clear of shame, angst, anger, unforgiveness, bitterness, and worry. That's why Jesus tells you to search your heart, soul, mind, and spirit before you offer anything to Father God. If you are in your place of worship and remember that someone has a grudge against you, God wants you to leave by the nearest exit and go and make things right.

You may have to apologize, forgive or be forgiven, perhaps even forget the wrong you have done or the wrong done against you. For most of us, this can be an enormous challenge.

Someone once said, "The first to apologize is the bravest. The first to forgive is the strongest. And the first to forget is the happiest." These statements have a ring of truth about them.

Apologizing often takes a lot of courage, especially when you don't think an apology is needed. Even worse is when you think the other person should be apologizing to *you*, not the other way around. In any case, God wants you to be the most forgiving and

peace-seeking person you can be. Find a way to let the words *I'm sorry* cross your lips. Be sincere when you speak them. Gird yourself with courage, arm yourself with humility and understanding, and make things right.

At the same time, God wants you to be strong and emboldened enough to forgive all those who have wronged you. Go even further and forget the wrong if you can. For you know you'll be happier when you do. Why? Because the last thing God wants you to do is sink into a mire of bitterness. Bitterness is like drinking poison and waiting for the other person to die.

When you're reconciled with all sisters and brothers, take a moment to check within one more time. Search yourself and see if there's anything you need to forgive *yourself* for. And do so. Then and only then, make your way back to God. Offer your gift with a pure heart, one now easy, calmed with the peace of reconciliation.

Search my heart and mind, Lord. Show me who I need to apologize to and to ask forgiveness of so that I can make things right with them and You. In Jesus' name I pray. Amen.

HOW SMALL

If you falter in a time of trouble, how small is your strength!
PROVERBS 24:10 NIV

Picture in your mind for just a moment the strongest person you've ever seen or heard of—the person who you think has the most physical strength. Perhaps you are thinking of a bodybuilder, or a guy in the circus who can hold up ten other guys, or some amazing duodecahexathlete (yes, that might not be a real word).

How did that person get to be so strong? Surely no one comes out of the womb lifting cars or running twenty-five miles or sporting muscles that bulge out of their diapers. Strong men and women have to work up to that level. They start with small challenges and gradually work up to bigger ones until those bigger ones seem small to them. Along the way, they have setbacks. And they have to stay disciplined and keep eating good food and resting and working their bodies.

In order to be strong and stay strong, they have to keep practicing being strong. They have to keep envisioning what it looks like to be even stronger. And when sickness or injuries come, they have to allow time to heal, and then they have to get right back at the work of growing stronger.

The writer of this proverb presents a scenario: we see some type of injustice, and instead of doing anything about it, we pretend not to see it (Proverbs 24:11–12). We falter. We feel afraid to speak

up, so we just shrink back from the opportunity.

There may be all kinds of good reasons to be afraid. It may be that speaking up will cost us—maybe even put our own lives at risk. It may be that we don't think we can actually help. But being *afraid* to do what is right is not the problem here. Being afraid is normal. Being afraid can even be good. Being *led* by fear away from the truth is when trouble really hits us.

This is the faltering that is happening in the scenario presented by the writer of this proverb. It's not about being afraid. It's about being dishonest. It's about forgetting who we are and turning away from what is good. It's about deceiving ourselves.

To be strong, even in times of trouble, we have to practice being strong. We have to discipline ourselves to seek truth every day. We have to envision what it looks like to be a person following God's truth. At first our strength—and our faith—may be small, but with practice and discipline, it can grow into something that can stand up under enormous amounts of pressure.

Lord, challenge my strength so I can be strong like You. Amen.

UNDERGROUND FEARS

The thing which I greatly fear comes upon me, and that of which I am afraid befalls me. I was not or am not at ease, nor had I or have I rest, nor was I or am I quiet, yet trouble came and still comes [upon me].

JOB 3:25–26 AMPC

The healthy and wealthy Job had been faithfully following the Lord. Then Satan went before God and asked to test Job's faith, first by taking away most of his material things and second by taking away his health. In both cases, God gave Satan the go-ahead. God's only caveat was that Satan could not take Job's life.

Round 1: Satan took away Job's ten children, 7,000 sheep, 3,000 camels, 500 yoke of oxen, and 500 female donkeys. All Job's servants—except the four who escaped to bring the news to him of each calamity—were taken as well.

In response, Job stood, tore his clothing, cut his hair, then fell to the ground and worshipped God, saying, " 'The Lord gave and the Lord has taken away. Praise the name of the Lord.' In all this Job did not sin or blame God" (Job 1:21–22 NLV).

Round 2: Satan infected Job with boils from head to toe. In misery, Job sat down in a trash pile, using a piece of broken pottery to scrape his wounds. His wife then discouraged him even further with her advice: "Curse God and die!" (Job 2:9 NLV). But once more Job held steady, telling her that she was being foolish,

adding, "Should we receive good from God and not receive trouble?" (Job 2:10 NLV). Even with the loss of his health, Job didn't sin in what he said.

Then Job's three friends came to mourn with him. For seven days they sat with Job in silence. But then the tide seemed to turn a bit as Job asked a lot of *Why?* questions (Job 3). At the end of his monologue, Job said all the things he once feared had now happened—and in rapid succession.

Like Job, many of us have deep-seated worries and underground fears, ones we voice to no one for fear that by speaking them, they'll come to fruition. Yet God invites us to bring all of our troubles—real or imaginary—to Him. Jesus says, "Come to Me, all you who labor and are heavy-laden and overburdened, and I will cause you to rest. [I will ease and relieve and refresh your souls]" (Matthew 11:28 AMPC).

Dig deep today. Release all your burdens and fears—real and imaginary—to Jesus. Then bask in the peace and quiet you find in Him.

Jesus, I give You all my fears. I rest in the peace of Your presence. Amen.

SOUL PURPOSE

Even to your old age I am He, and even to hair white with age will I carry you. I have made, and I will bear; yes, I will carry and will save you.

ISAIAH 46:4 AMPC

Childhood can be amazing. Teenage years are an exploration in wonder along with confusion. Then there are the decades that follow. In your twenties, you're just beginning to find your path, career, calling. The thirties come, sometimes with marriage and children, sometimes not. Either way, you're now more settled. When the forties arrive, you can finally relax a bit—maybe. Then one day you wake up, and you are in your sixties, seventies, eighties, or nineties!

You're not sure how it happened, but you feel as if you're a young person trapped in an aging body. You shrink back from the AARP mailers now coming to your door. Yet at the same time, you realize you have been slowing down a bit. You wonder, *What, if anything, can I do for God this late in life?*

Instead of being afraid of aging, look at some of the biblical women who were still going strong, living and loving for God, though others may have considered them "elderly."

Sarah had a child at age ninety. She is mentioned in the Hebrews Hall of Fame: "Because Sarah had faith, she was able to have a child long after she was past the age to have children.

She had faith to believe that God would do what He promised" (Hebrews 11:11 NLV).

The widowed Naomi mentored her young, newly widowed daughter-in-law Ruth, taking Ruth with her back to Israel, guiding her into marriage and motherhood. In this way, Naomi found her way back into a family, assuming the role of grandmother to Ruth's son Obed.

In the New Testament, God helps the elderly Elizabeth conceive. Nine months later, she presents her husband, Zechariah, with a son, John (see Luke 1:57–63).

And last but not least, there's the ever-patient Anna, a prophet who was "of a great age" and "was a widow of about eighty-four years" (Luke 2:36–37 NKJV). She had been living in the temple, serving God day and night, praying and fasting, looking for the arrival of the Messiah. Her perseverance was rewarded when Mary and Joseph brought the baby Jesus to the temple for his dedication. "She told the people in Jerusalem about Jesus. They were looking for the One to save them from the punishment of their sins and to set them free" (Luke 2:38 NLV).

No matter what your age, you'll always be a child of the God who made you and has promised to carry you. Today and every day, live your life unafraid and with the soul purpose of loving and serving your Creator and Savior in this life and the next.

Father God, lead me wherever,
whenever, and I will follow. Amen.

GLORIOUS SIGHT

"Rabbi, I want to see."
MARK 10:51 NIV

Many of us have experienced the wonder of some beautiful sight. It could be something as commonplace as a beautiful sunrise or sunset, a dogwood or a rosebush in full bloom. At those times, we find ourselves treasuring the world around us and spontaneously rendering praise to God for the gift of His creation. But most days there is none of that. We merely walk through the world apathetic and unseeing. We walk through the world as if there were something inconsequential or insignificant about the things we observe. At those times, we are blind to the world, and our power of sight is unavailing to us. We not only fail to see the beauty around us; we fail to see what a gift God has granted to us in the very power of sight, our way into the corridors of God's splendor.

There is hardly need to speculate about Bartimaeus, the blind man in Mark's Gospel, and the visual experience of the world that he had after Jesus healed him. How glorious the colors must have seemed to him! How bright! How deep! How rich! The passage tells us that after he gained his sight, he followed Jesus. How grateful he must have been to Jesus, who through His power had revealed the glory of God's creation to him.

We are not completely unlike Bartimaeus. We too want to see. But what do we want to see? Is it just another curio, another

bauble, another chestnut for our catalog of lovely things? Or do we want to see the world that the cured blind man saw? Do we want to see the world God has given to us in all its splendor, not worn down and exhausted and drained by overfamiliarity, overexposure, and careless attention, but fresh and vibrant and burgeoning with vitality?

We are unlike the blind man in one crucial way. Most of us have never been blind; we have never had to struggle in that way, and so we take for granted our sight and the sights. In Mark's passage, Jesus has pity on the blind man. He asks him what he wants Jesus to do for him. "Master, I want to see," comes his plea.

Jesus is asking each of us too, "What do you want Me to do for you?" We might answer, "Master, I want to see the world that Bartimaeus the blind man saw. I too want to see a world so full of God's glory that all I want to do is follow You."

Lord, grant me the ability to see and appreciate all the beauty You have created for us. Amen.

BELOVED SHEPHERD

My beloved [shepherd]. . . [I can feel] his left hand under my head and his right hand embraces me!

SONG OF SOLOMON 2:3, 6 AMPC

Throughout the Bible, you find verses telling you that God is your shelter and sanctuary. Psalm 46:1–2 (AMPC) says, "God is our Refuge and Strength [mighty and impenetrable to temptation], a very present and well-proved help in trouble. Therefore we will not fear, though the earth should change and though the mountains be shaken into the midst of the seas."

Those powerful words tell us *who* God is. Yet just as important are verses telling you *where* He is and how we are to experience Him: "The Lord of hosts is with us. . . . Let be and be still, and know (recognize and understand) that I am God" (Psalm 46:7, 10–11 AMPC).

Hmm. . . "Be still"? That's hard to do these days. There seems to be so much going on within and without, it's hard to find a moment to yourself much less one without distractions. But if you're going to live a life with less fear and more faith, spending time in God's presence, sitting quietly and still before Him, is a must.

To help you get there from here, begin by finding a quiet place, one where you won't be disturbed. Put on some soothing music or just bask in the silence. Then consider meditating on some verses from the Song of Solomon, words you can use to snuggle

up to your Beloved.

Spend several minutes imagining that Jesus, your Beloved Shepherd, is with you. Feel His left hand under your head as His right hand embraces you, tenderly sheltering you. Allow your body to relax as you rest in His arms.

Then hear your Beloved speaking to you, saying, "Rise up, my love, my fair one, and come away" (Song of Solomon 2:10 AMPC). Imagine climbing ever higher with Him. Let God's words sink in deep:

> *[My beloved shepherd said to me] O my dove, [while you are here]. . .in the sheltered and secret place. . .let me see your face, let me hear your voice; for your voice is sweet, and your face is lovely.*
>
> *[My heart was touched and I fervently sang to him my desire].*
>
> Song of Solomon 2:14–15 AMPC

As you take this time to snuggle up to Jesus, to become more intimate with Him, telling Him all your desires, you'll become stronger, feel more worthy, just by being with Him. Your fears will fade as your faith blooms. . .in Him.

My Beloved Shepherd, I come to You. I can feel Your left hand under my head and Your right hand embrace me! Amen.

ABUNDANT WATERS

"What's wrong, Hagar? Don't be afraid. God has heard the boy and knows the fix he's in. Up now; go get the boy. Hold him tight. I'm going to make of him a great nation." Just then God opened her eyes. She looked. She saw a well of water.

GENESIS 21:17–19 MSG

Even though Hagar was a slave and a foreigner, without friends and family, she was also a woman of amazing firsts. She was recorded as the first person—not the first woman but the first *person*—to talk to and see the Angel of God, and as the *only* person to give God a name, *El Roi*, the God who sees (see Genesis 16:13).

At the end of Genesis 16, Hagar had obeyed God's orders to go back to and submit to Sarah. She had also given birth to the eighty-six-year-old Abraham's first son, whom they named Ishmael, just as God had commanded.

The next time we meet up with Hagar is in Genesis 21. The chapter begins with Sarah giving birth to Isaac, just as God had promised. The proud father, Abraham, was now one hundred years old. And things seemed to be fine—until one day when Sarah saw Ishmael making fun of her Isaac. So she told Abraham, "Get rid of this slave woman and her son" (Genesis 21:10 MSG).

Abraham, who loved Ishmael, found it hard to drive the boy away. But God told him not to worry; all would be well. So, albeit reluctantly, Abraham gave Hagar bread and a bottle of water and

sent the pair off into the wilderness.

After some wilderness wandering, Hagar realized the water bottle was empty. She left her dehydrated son in the shade then sat down nearby, saying, " 'I can't watch my son die.' As she sat, she broke into sobs" (Genesis 21:16 MSG). Another first. Yes, Hagar was the first person recorded crying in the Bible.

That's when the Angel of God came through for Hagar once more, telling her not to fear for God had seen what was happening. He told her to hold Ishmael tight. God would make him into a great nation. Then God opened Hagar's eyes, and she saw a well of water.

Refreshed and renewed, Hagar and Ishmael continued their journey, God walking with the boy every step of the way.

When you're in the wilderness, out of resources, including courage, look to God. Know that He sees what's happening. He hears your cries. He'll give you everything you need to continue. And He won't just refill your drinking bottle; He will open your eyes to a well of abundant waters.

Thank You, Lord, for seeing me, hearing me. Give me courage to go on. Open my eyes to Your abundant resources. Be with me as I walk on in You. Amen.

FIRE WALKERS

"The God we serve can rescue us from your roaring furnace and anything else you might cook up, O king. But even if he doesn't, it wouldn't make a bit of difference, O king. We still wouldn't serve your gods or worship the gold statue you set up."

DANIEL 3:17–18 MSG

Nebuchadnezzar, king of Babylon, came to Jerusalem and took back with him some noble youths. Four of these young exiles who were to be trained and educated in Babylonian culture were Daniel, Shadrach, Meshach, and Abednego.

When Daniel proved his ability to interpret King Nebuchadnezzar's dream, the king not only gave him many honors and gifts but promoted Daniel and his friends Shadrach, Meshach, and Abednego.

Sometime later, Nebuchadnezzar made a gold statue that stood ninety feet in height and nine feet in width. All people were to bow down to this image whenever the band began playing. If anyone did not bow down and worship the statue, he or she would immediately be thrown into a blazing furnace.

Amazingly, three people refused to bow to Nebuchadnezzar's idol: Shadrach, Meshach, and Abednego. When the king found out about their refusal, he became enraged. He called them to him, questioned them, even gave them another chance to bow to his creation and all would be forgiven. But once more they refused,

knowing the consequences yet having no fear. The king's threat meant nothing to them—because they trusted their God.

Now even more enraged, King Nebuchadnezzar ordered the furnace temperature be increased seven times hotter than usual. He ordered the three men to be tied up and thrown into the furnace. The king watched flames rage all around the three men. But wait! There were no longer three men in the furnace! Nebuchadnezzar said, "I see four men, walking around freely in the fire, completely unharmed! And the fourth man looks like a son of the gods!" (Daniel 3:25 MSG). The king then called Shadrach, Meshach, and Abednego to come out of the furnace. When they did, the king and his officials noticed that not only were they no longer bound but their clothes and hair remained intact. They didn't even smell like fire!

Because of their refusal to worship an idol and their wholehearted trust in God, Shadrach, Meshach, and Abednego were joined in the fire by another supernatural being. And all three were saved.

Whenever you're challenged or in distress, remember that you too can trust God's promise: "I will be with you when you pass through the waters, and when you pass through the rivers, they will not overwhelm you. You will not be scorched when you walk through the fire, and the flame will not burn you" (Isaiah 43:2 HCSB).

I will not fear because I trust You'll be with me, Lord, through flood and fire. Amen.

AGAINST GOD

"How then could I do such a wicked thing and sin against God?"

GENESIS 39:9 NIV

The one factor in Joseph's life that made all the difference in the way he lived—that allowed him to move up the ranks of Egyptian society from slave to second-in-command—was his recognition of the fact that God was with him.

God was with him in the bottom of the pit where his brothers had thrown him. God was with him when he was sold as a slave. God was with him when he was placed in Potiphar's house. God was with him in prison. God was with him when he was called to stand before Pharaoh. God was with him in his visions. God was with him in his decisions. God was always with Joseph.

But if Joseph had not known this and been grateful for it, his life might have turned out very differently.

When Joseph was bought by Potiphar, he probably didn't even realize how powerful his master was at first. Potiphar was an official in the Egyptian ruling class—he was captain of the guard. He was used to people following his orders. And he was good at spotting leaders. Potiphar saw a leader in Joseph. He trusted Joseph. Potiphar could see that Joseph was favored by God. And Joseph knew that God was blessing him in everything he did. The more he realized God's favor, no doubt the more Joseph wanted to serve the Lord and honor and obey Him.

So when Joseph found himself in a tricky situation with his master's wife, Joseph knew what he had to do. He refused to be with the woman even though she commanded him to sleep with her.

Joseph knew that if he did this thing, it would not just be a breach of trust with his master. It would not just be a bad thing to do to the man who had trusted him with everything he owned. It would in fact be a sin against God.

Sometimes we find ourselves in sticky situations. It can be very difficult to decide what to do. Sometimes it might even seem as though we can't escape temptation. But one thing that can help us get out of this kind of trouble is the knowledge and certainty of the fact that God is with us. God is the reason we are where we are. God is the reason that any good thing has happened to us at all. If we give in to temptation and commit acts of sin, we are not just doing bad things to others or ourselves, we are sinning against God.

Lord, help me. I don't ever want to sin against You. Amen.

ENCOURAGING HOPE

Then we will be with the Lord forever.
So encourage each other with these words.
1 THESSALONIANS 4:17–18 NLT

Sometimes living on this planet is just hard to bear. We look around and become weighed down by the gravity of the grave. People are shot and killed every day for reasons of vengefulness and hatred and wickedness—and sometimes for no reason at all. People do horrible things to each other in the name of desire or some twisted version of what they call love. And they don't even know it's twisted, because it's impossible for them to see a straight path—much less walk one. People do terrible, sickening things to weak, helpless individuals, and one wonders if evil is winning after all. Perhaps the demons have the upper hand.

But that's not how it is. Not at all. And we must not let ourselves be so absorbed in seeing evil that we forget to look for the light. The light is always there. The light is always shining. The light is, in fact, the reason we feel so appalled at the darkness.

So when we grieve, we can know that, yes, it is okay to be sad. When people we love leave this world, it is perfectly acceptable to miss them. But we should not despair—as if the leaving of one good man or woman somehow subtracts that amount of goodness from our environment. We have not lost their goodness. We have not really even lost them—they are simply away from us for a while.

As Christians, we can be sure that those who have accepted Jesus as their Savior will truly be saved. They will be saved from the darkness of this world, but they will also be saved from the darkness of death. They will not disappear. We all can have this hope. Whether we have already passed before Jesus comes again or whether we are still standing on this ground when He returns. We all will be caught up together with Jesus. We all will rise. We all will be freed from suffering and selfishness and the sin of this dark world. We will start new stories with Jesus. We will learn new songs. We will see what happens when goodness rules in every corner of the universe.

It is this hope that we live in. It is this hope we can take with us as we live and work and breathe in this world. It is this hope we can be secure in, even when we are sitting in a funeral service. Darkness has not won. Look for the light.

Lord, I want to encourage others with the hope that I have. Help me find the words to do that. Amen.

PLUNGING INTO PROMISES

[Abraham] didn't tiptoe around God's promise asking cautiously skeptical questions. He plunged into the promise and came up strong, ready for God, sure that God would make good on what he had said.

ROMANS 4:20–21 MSG

Leymah Gbowee, a Nobel Peace Prize–winning Christian woman, says, "You can never leave footprints that last if you are always walking on tiptoe." Just as Leymah plunged in to help lead a nonviolent struggle for the safety and rights of women in Liberia, determined not to tiptoe around the ravages of war and abuse of women, Abraham didn't tiptoe around God's promises. He took them to heart, body, mind, spirit, and soul.

The Message puts it this way: "Abraham didn't focus on his own impotence and say, 'It's hopeless. This hundred-year-old body could never father a child.' Nor did he survey Sarah's decades of infertility and give up" (Romans 4:19 MSG). Instead, he trusted God. "When everything was hopeless, Abraham believed anyway, deciding to live not on the basis of what he saw he *couldn't* do but on what God said he *would* do" (Romans 4:18 MSG). Because of Abraham's outlook and perspective, because of his complete and utter trust in God, he was declared to be in right and good standing with the Lord.

Just as Abraham was made right with God, God will make

you right with Him—if you believe in and totally trust God (see Romans 4:24), the One who can "with a word make something out of nothing" (Romans 4:17 MSG).

At one time, only your God existed. Nothing else. And then He spoke. God said, "Let there be light" (see Genesis 1:3). And there was light. This God, this Maker and Mover of your world, the Being who with one word creates something out of nothing, was Abraham's God. And Abraham's God is your God. You can trust Him just as Abraham did.

No matter what your situation, no matter how big your mess or circumstances, you need never fear anything. For if you totally trust in God, you too can hope, even when everything looks hopeless. You too can decide to live not looking at what only *you* can't do but at what God has promised *He* will do.

Begin living unafraid. Stop tiptoeing around what-ifs and maybes. Get in there, immerse yourself in God's promises, then come up in the power of Christ ready, willing, and able to wait, watch, and expect God to make good on His Word. And you'll be right with God.

Lord, show me to hope against hope. To make mighty footprints as I take in Your promises— heart, body, mind, spirit, and soul. Amen.

A WISE QUEEN MOTHER

Because of the outcry of the king and his nobles, the queen came to the banquet hall. "May the king live forever," she said. "Don't let your thoughts terrify you. . . . There is a man in your kingdom who has the spirit of the holy gods in him. . . . Summon Daniel, and he will give the interpretation."

DANIEL 5:10–12 HCSB

Sometimes your imagination can run away with you, causing you to inflate the challenges before you, making them and your fears balloon out of proportion to reality. Then there are other times when your fears are based on a bizarre yet very real occurrence, something beyond your imagination that's happening right before your eyes, that puts you into a panic. In both scenarios, your thoughts need to be reined in and your fears ignored, tamped down, or eliminated so that things can be seen for what they are. So that you can determine how best to face the challenge before you.

King Belshazzar, Nebuchadnezzar's successor, was having a party. He called for the servants to bring in the gold and silver cups from the Jerusalem temple, which his predecessors had sacked. He and his pagan lords and ladies then drank wine out of them, praising their man-made gods.

As they did so, a man's hand appeared and wrote "MENE, MENE, TEKEL, PARSIN" (Daniel 5:25) on the king's palace wall. "As the king watched the hand that was writing, his face turned pale, and his thoughts so terrified him that his hip joints shook and his knees knocked together" (Daniel 5:5–6 HCSB). None of his mediums, astrologers, or wise men could tell him what the words meant.

The king became even more terrified. That's when his mom, the queen mother, stepped in with some calming words of wisdom. After her long-live-the-king salutation, she went right to the heart of the matter, saying, "Don't let your thoughts terrify you." Then she came up with a name, a person who might be able to help the king know what the words meant.

Daniel was summoned and interpreted the words: "MENE means that God has numbered the days of your kingdom and brought it to an end. TEKEL means that you have been weighed in the balance and found deficient. PERES means that your kingdom has been divided and given to the Medes and Persians" (Daniel 5:26–28 HCSB).

Before the night was over, Daniel was again promoted, Belshazzar was killed, and Darius the Mede was made king.

We don't hear about the queen mother again. But we can take her words and wisdom to heart. "Don't let your thoughts terrify you." Instead, calm down, see things for what they are, and seek the wisdom of others.

Lord, when I'm afraid, help me rein in my thoughts, seek Your calm, and pray for wisdom. Amen.

NOT ABOUT YOU

"But when you give to the needy, do not let your left hand know what your right hand is doing, so that your giving may be in secret. Then your Father, who sees what is done in secret, will reward you."

MATTHEW 6:3–4 NIV

In Matthew 6, Jesus teaches about several behaviors of those who would seek to follow Him. This whole part of the Sermon on the Mount easily could have been labeled "It's Not about You."

He tells us to give in secret—not to be seen. Why? Because it's not about you. It's not about how much you have to give or how generous you are. It's not about your righteousness. It's about honoring God by taking care of His people.

Jesus tells us to pray in secret—not out on the street corners to be heard by every passerby. Why not? Isn't it a good thing to pray in public? Sure—but this is not about you. Your daily prayer life should be about the time you spend in intimate relationship with God. It's not about making a speech. It's not about showing others how well you can pray or how holy you are. There's no word count quota. God knows what you need and want. He just wants to spend time with you.

Similarly, fasting should not be done as a show of suffering. Only God needs to know about what you are giving and for how long and why. When you commit to depending on Him, really

commit to depending on Him not on your own image.

Jesus goes on to warn us about where we store our treasures—are we serving our stuff or are we serving our Savior? Are we piling up things to show our success? Or are we concerned instead about being successful citizens of heaven?

Lastly, worry does not appear at first as a form of pride, but it is. When you worry about the things of this life, you take your eyes off God. You worry because on some level you think you can figure out all the answers—you can supply your own needs. But God wants you to depend on Him. He wants you to lean on Him. It's just not about you. And it's not about just you. It's about where you are with God.

Lord, help me to remember that whatever I do to follow You, I should be following You and not trying to lead my own way. Help me to depend on You above all else. Amen.

CLING-FREE

"If you don't go all the way with me, through thick and thin, you don't deserve me. If your first concern is to look after yourself, you'll never find yourself. But if you forget about yourself and look to me, you'll find both yourself and me."

MATTHEW 10:38–39 MSG

Sodom was such a disreputable city that God decided to destroy it. When Abraham got wind of its upcoming demise, he was concerned for his nephew, Lot. So he convinced God to spare Sodom from destruction if He found at least ten decent people there (see Genesis 18:32).

When God's two angels arrived in Sodom, they found the righteous Lot living amid an overwhelming number of evildoers. Their vileness ensured the destruction of the city, but Lot and his family would be spared. The angels warned Lot about God's intentions. They urged him to gather his wife, daughters, and soon-to-be sons-in-law, for the next day they would have to leave. In spite of the warning, Lot's sons-in-law opted to stay behind. The rest of the family began gathering their belongings.

When dawn broke, the angels dragged out of Sodom Lot, his wife, and his two daughters. As they made their way beyond the city limits, one angel said, "Run for your lives! Don't look back and don't stop anywhere on the plain. . .or you will be swept away!" (Genesis 19:17 HCSB).

Then, just when Lot and his family finally reached a place of safety, God began the city's destruction. Whew! It looked as if the sole survivors had managed to escape the rain of ruin. But wait. "[Lot's] wife looked back from behind him, and she became a pillar of salt" (Genesis 19:26 AMPC). More afraid of losing what she had in the past than moving forward into an uncertain future, Mrs. Lot disobeyed the angel's orders, to her demise. More concerned about her material treasures than her very life, Lot's wife lost both.

How about you? Where do your treasures lie? What might you be afraid of losing? Consider Jesus' words: "Remember what happened to Lot's wife! If you grasp and cling to life on your terms, you'll lose it, but if you let that life go, you'll get life on God's terms" (Luke 17:32–33 MSG).

Realize that your treasures in heaven are much more valuable than those on earth. The best thing you can do for yourself, your family, and God is to be courageous enough to forget about your life and focus on Jesus. In doing so, you'll gain both.

Give me the wisdom and courage I need, Lord, to keep my eyes on You. To look to Jesus above all else. To keep You and Your Word my sole treasures—in heaven and on earth. Amen.

NEITHER MAN NOR BEAST

When Daniel learned that the document had been signed, he went into his house. The windows in its upper room opened toward Jerusalem, and three times a day he got down on his knees, prayed, and gave thanks to his God, just as he had done before.

DANIEL 6:10 HCSB

Author Leonard Ravenhill said, "A man who is intimate with God will never be intimidated by men." Such a man was Daniel.

Daniel had such an amazingly extraordinary spirit that King Darius of Persia planned to put him in charge of the entire kingdom. This, of course, was not well received by the other officials serving the king. So they began looking closely at Daniel, trying to find something they could charge him with. But because he was so faithful and trustworthy, they found nothing.

The jealous officials' next idea was to create an obstacle by which to trip up Daniel. They went to the king and had him sign and issue a decree: for the next thirty days, no one could pray to any god or man except King Darius. Anyone disobeying the law would be thrown into the lions' den.

When Daniel found out that the new law had been signed and publicized, he still prayed to Yahweh. With his upstairs windows open toward Jerusalem, Daniel knelt and prayed three times a day, giving thanks to and praising his God, just as he had always

done before.

When the king was told of Daniel's breaking the law, that he had ignored the king's decree, the king was very distressed for he liked Daniel. Although he kept trying to find a way to rescue Daniel, he couldn't come up with any way to save him from punishment. So the king ordered Daniel to be thrown into the lions' den, saying, "May your God, whom you serve continually, rescue you!" (Daniel 6:16 HCSB).

With Daniel in the den, the king went back home and fasted. After a sleepless night, the king rose at dawn and went to the lions' den. He yelled, asking Daniel if his God had saved him, hoping to hear Daniel's answer. And Daniel did answer, saying, "My God sent His angel and shut the lions' mouths. They haven't hurt me, for I was found innocent before Him" (Daniel 6:22 HCSB). Fearing neither man nor beast but having "trusted in his God" (Daniel 6:23 HCSB), Daniel came out unscathed.

Spend time in God's presence. Trust Him for all things. Then you too will fear neither man nor beast.

Lord, "what a stack of blessing you have piled up for those who worship you, ready and waiting for all who run to you to escape an unkind world" (Psalm 31:19 MSG). In You alone I trust. Amen.

IN ALL THINGS

And we know that in all things God works for the good of those who love him, who have been called according to his purpose.
ROMANS 8:28 NIV

In all things. We tend to apply that phrase to, quite literally, all things. We say God is working for good when it's raining and we show up for that big presentation sopping wet and with mascara running, only to find that some extra-special visitors will unexpectedly be attending the meeting today—including the CEO and chairman of the board.

In all things. When we are trying to impress our children while at the same time trying to make ourselves feel a little younger, and we hop on that skateboard for all of two minutes before we fall and break an elbow, we say surely we can figure out how God is working for good in this experience. Like maybe how it allowed you to get to know the emergency nurses or how you'll be spending more time with your children since they will have to help with all the chores—is that how God is working for good in this thing?

In all things. Sometimes we struggle to find God in all things. When a child is murdered by a relative and through some fluke of the court system that person goes free, we find it hard to see God working in all things.

When a community that was already recently ravaged by flooding now experiences a horrific tornado that takes many lives,

we try hard to find God in anything.

But the passage never promises we'll see God working. In fact, if you read the verses leading up to this bit, you'll see that the exact opposite is stated. Paul speaks to the Romans about a hope we cannot see, a time that creation itself has been waiting for, when the children of God will be revealed, and when the glory of God will be revealed. Paul clearly states that we don't have this vison yet, but we are waiting for it: "Hope that is seen is no hope at all" (Romans 8:24 NIV).

We don't even know what we ought to pray for sometimes—that's how clueless we are. We look around at this world and can't figure out where to start. But God knows. The Spirit prays for us—taking what's in our hearts and minds and weaving it together into a wordless whisper of longing and hope to God.

Yes, we can know—we can be sure—that the God who is perfectly good is working for the good of those who love Him. But we won't always be able to see it. And that's okay.

Lord, help me to be certain of You even when I can't see. Amen.

EXPECTING A MIRACLE

"The Holy Spirit will come on you. The power of the Most High will cover you. The holy Child you give birth to will be called the Son of God. . . . For God can do all things." Then Mary said, "I am willing to be used of the Lord. Let it happen to me as you have said."

LUKE 1:35, 37–38 NLV

God was moving in mysterious ways. . . . An angel from God had made the old priest Zechariah mute. His elderly wife, Elizabeth, was pregnant. And now a young betrothed teenage girl named Mary in Nazareth had a celestial visit from the same angel.

The first thing Gabriel said to Mary was flowery with compliments. He told her that she was highly favored by God and that He was with her.

The faithful Mary found these words confusing. Troubling. She was trying to figure out what God might be expecting of her. Wanting to alleviate any possible anxiety on her side, Gabriel immediately told Mary not to be afraid; she had found favor with God.

Yet after those two major assurances, the angel now laid out God's plan: Mary was going to have a child whom she would name Jesus. He would be God's Son, who would reign from David's throne forever.

Mary took in all that information then came up with a good question: "How's this going to work? After all, I'm a virgin."

What Gabriel said next sounded a bit fantastic. He told Mary that God's Holy Spirit would come over her, and she would later give birth to this holiest of children who would be called the Son of God.

The angel then told Mary about her cousin Elizabeth. How that even though she was old and well past childbearing age, she was six months' pregnant! If God could do that for Elizabeth, He could surely do this for Mary. With God, everything and anything are possible.

Mary courageously responded, "I am willing to be used of the Lord. Let it happen to me as you have said" (Luke 1:38 NLV).

How could this young girl be so willing to become part of this amazing plan? What was it about her that made her suitable to be the mother of God's Son? What gave her the courage to simply say, "Let it be just as you've said"? Did God have a backup plan in case this didn't work?

We may never know the answer to those questions, but we do know this: many men—Lot (Genesis 19), Moses (Exodus 3), Jonah (Jonah 1), Ananias (Acts 9), Gideon (Judges 6), Jeremiah (Jeremiah 1:6)—had hesitated to take on a God-assigned duty. So how did this teenage girl acquiesce so willingly and courageously?

Simple. She had faith. She trusted God. She was willing. Are you?

Lord, make me Your brave and willing servant. Amen.

PRIMED FOR PROMISES

"Is anything too hard for GOD?"

GENESIS 18:14 MSG

Have you ever come across one of God's promises and thought, *Yeah, right. Like that could ever happen*? Have you ever then had that thought followed by a word from the Holy Spirit? Something like "Why are you fearful, you of little faith?" (Matthew 8:26 HCSB).

Something of that sort happened to Sarah, the one desperate to have a baby. The one to whom God had *promised* a baby. The one who had tried to "fix" her childlessness herself and failed miserably.

Sarah was now ninety years old, and Abraham was one hundred, well past their prime. God came to pay Abraham a visit. Outside the tent, God told him, "I will certainly come back to you in about a year's time, and your wife Sarah will have a son!" (Genesis 18:10 HCSB).

Sarah overheard this proclamation from inside the tent, where she had been eavesdropping. She started laughing, saying to herself, "An old woman like me? Get pregnant? With this old man of a husband?" (Genesis 18:12 MSG).

God, having heard her thoughts, asked Abraham why Sarah would laugh and ask herself such a question. God followed this up with an even more important question—one that we should oft times ask ourselves when we're caught in a web of doubt: "Is anything too hard for GOD?" (Genesis 18:14 MSG).

Sarah answered the questions God addressed to Abraham, but unfortunately she lied: "I didn't laugh." Why? "Because she was afraid." But God is no fool. He knows the truth. In fact, He *is* the truth. So He called her on it, saying, "Yes you did; you laughed" (Genesis 18:15 MSG).

Doubt in what God's Word says and in what God can do in our lives takes us down a road we don't want to travel, for doubt tends to blossom into mistrust. And mistrust breeds fear. And fear opens the door to wrong thoughts, which may quickly turn into outright lies—to ourselves and others, including God.

Whenever you come across what sounds like an impossible promise of God's, take another look. See it using eyes of faith. Remember that God is the doer of the impossible. Nothing in heaven or on earth is beyond His means. He can work a miracle for you, just like He did for Sarah. A year after her laugh and lie (a year during which she grew in faith and confidence in God), Sarah received her promise. She held her own baby in her arms.

Lord, show me Your promises. Help me to see You—the doer of the impossible—with the eyes of faith. Amen.

LOVE COVERS

Above all, love each other deeply, because love covers over a multitude of sins.

1 Peter 4:8 NIV

Dirty socks on the living room floor. The used-up toilet paper roll left on the dispenser. . .again. Crumbs in the bed. Toothpaste globs on the bathroom sink.

Can love cover over all of that? Yes.

Now, to be fair, none of those things in the list above are really sins. But these day-to-day annoyances we deal with when we live with other humans are often the things that lead to sins—sins such as self-centeredness, deceit ("No, I didn't eat the last piece of cake!"), envy, and even hatred. One trivial mistake can lead to an argument that leads to a series of fights that leads to bitterness and resentment and unforgiveness.

Can love cover all of that? Yes.

We know it can because God has forgiven us already of all those things and many other acts and desires and thoughts that we might deem even worse. In His relatively short time walking as a human on this earth, Jesus forgave people for betraying Him, for insulting Him, for giving false testimony about Him, for sinning against His Father, for calling Him crazy, for comparing Him to Satan, for beating Him, and for crucifying Him.

Since God has forgiven us of so much, who are we to refuse

to forgive others of so little?

We have to accept that people are human. People will make mistakes. People will make wrong choices. And if we are going to love humans, things are certainly going to get messy. Not just toothpaste-globs-on-the-sink and hairballs-in-the-bathtub kind of messy. But sometimes the words people say will wound us. The things people do will grieve us. And sometimes even the things they don't do will leave a mark on us.

When you love people deeply, you become vulnerable. That doesn't mean you must subject yourself to abusive or toxic relationships. God doesn't tell us that we have to put ourselves in harm's way deliberately so that we can show love to abusers. We have to recognize that some people need to be loved in a way that helps them not to hurt others, to become better than what they are.

But loving others also means you open yourself up to the riches of deep understanding, deep intimacy, deep caring, and deep love. Love covers us when it goes deep enough. And then we learn just a bit more about the love God has for us—the love that is so deep and wide and high and long that it can cover a whole planet full of people.

God, thank You for teaching me how to love deeply. Amen.

GENTLE POWER

He gathers the lambs in his arms
and carries them close to his heart.
ISAIAH 40:11 NIV

He had a leathery face, aged by the elements much more than by his years. A somewhat unkempt beard gave him an impression of gruffness, and he generally wore old, tattered clothing when he was out in the fields. In the world of those who are in the position of taking care of little lambs, this shepherd was about as far away as you could imagine from "Mary" of nursery song fame.

But when he gathered up little lambs in his arms, he was gentle and tender as could be. He would smooth down the little lambs' big ears and speak softly to them, warning them to stay close to the flock and not stray too far. Then he would set them back down among the herd and go on his way, but he always kept an eye out for the helpless, silly little lambs.

Our God is like that shepherd—strong and enduring, patient and ever watchful. How reassuring to know that the King of the universe has His eye on us! He will not stop us from stumbling now and then—He knows that we learn great lessons through the mistakes we make. But He will not let us be attacked with no defense.

The God who "measured the waters in the hollow of his hand, or with the breadth of his hand marked off the heavens" (Isaiah 40:12 NIV) is the same God who puts no limits on His love for us.

The God "who has held the dust of the earth in a basket, or weighed the mountains on the scales and the hills in a balance" (Isaiah 40:12 NIV) is the same God who wisely judges our thoughts and actions and yet offers us infinite mercy. The God whose Spirit is unfathomable and whose mind is boundless generously shares with us His wisdom. He understands us better than we understand ourselves, and He offers us perfect counsel for every situation.

The God who "sits enthroned above the circle of the earth" (Isaiah 40:22 NIV) is the One who bows low to serve us. The God who "stretches out the heavens like a canopy" (Isaiah 40:22 NIV) is the One who reaches across the darkness to welcome us into His beautiful light.

The God who has "great power and mighty strength" (Isaiah 40:26 NIV) does not let any one of us go missing—He knows us each by name and calls us to Him. Like a strong shepherd, our God scoops us up when we are far away from Him and holds us tightly to His heart. He whispers to us to stay close and not stray too far. And then He lets us go again.

Lord, I love Your gentle power. Please protect me. Amen.

GOD SEES YOU

O LORD, you have searched me and known me! You know when I sit down and when I rise up; you discern my thoughts from afar.

PSALM 139:1–2 ESV

Hagar is first introduced as Sarah's "woman servant from Egypt" (Genesis 16:1 NLV). But a few verses later, after the barren Sarah promoted Hagar to the position of Abram's second wife and Hagar became pregnant, Hagar's attitude toward Sarah changed. Instead of looking up to her, Hagar "looked with contempt upon her mistress *and* despised her" (Genesis 16:4 AMPC). Things became so bad that Sarah insisted Abram do something about the situation. He told her, "Your maid is in your hands. . .do as you please with her" (Genesis 16:6 AMPC).

So Sarah began to abuse Hagar. It became so bad that Hagar, in fear for her life, ran away. Yet then the Bible presents us with a "but. . ." (Thank God that even in the midst of our fear and despair, God always presents us with a *but*.) "*But* the Angel of the Lord found her by a spring of water in the wilderness" (Genesis 16:7 AMPC, emphasis added). A concerned God revealed Himself to Hagar. He first let her know that He knew exactly who she was: Sarah's maid. Then He asked (a question He also knew the answer to), "Where have you come from and where are you going?" (Genesis 16:8 NLV). Hagar couldn't really tell God where she was going. But she could tell Him why she was where she was. She said, “I am running away from my mistress Sarai” (Genesis 16:8 AMPC). Notice that Hagar didn’t fess up as to *why* she was running (because the woman she had been abusing was now abusing her), just that she—a frightened foreigner, concerned not just for her own welfare but for that of her unborn child—was on the run.

God told her, “Go back to your mistress and [humbly] submit to her control” (Genesis 16:9 AMPC). This may have been a difficult command for Hagar to obey. Yet obey it she would because God added a promise: in God’s plan for her, she would have many descendants, beginning with a son named “Ishmael [God hears], because the Lord has heard *and* paid attention to your affliction” (Genesis 16:11 AMPC).

That’s how this one abused pregnant foreigner, without friend or family to help her, became the only person—not the only *woman* but the only *person*—who gave God a name: “You are a God Who sees” (Genesis 16:13 NLV).

If you find yourself on the run, not sure whether you’re coming or going, take courage: God sees you, hears you, has a plan for you, and will help you.

Lord, because You see me, I’m not afraid. Amen.

PATTERNS

Do not conform to the pattern of this world, but be transformed by the renewing of your mind. Then you will be able to test and approve what God's will is—his good, pleasing and perfect will.

ROMANS 12:2 NIV

Frosty snowflake crystals on a cold window. Symmetrical crowns of petals circling yellow flower heads. Geese flying in Vs through a blue autumn sky. Sunrise and sunset day after day. Waves upon waves crashing onto the shore. Crystal formations deep within the earth.

Nature is filled with beautiful, amazing patterns. We can see evidence of the clever structure and brilliant elegance of God's design everywhere we go.

But often the patterns that people follow are not so pretty. We make mistakes, we hide our mistakes, we lie about our mistakes, we suffer from our mistakes, and we forget them. Then we start that cycle all over again.

We get our feelings hurt, we don't talk about it, we get bitter, we get angry, we get into arguments with people who don't even know what we are talking about. We get hurt again. And we hurt others.

We notice a temptation, we try to control ourselves, we don't talk about it, we get tempted again, we give in, and we hide what we've done. Then it happens all over again.

We say we will do a thing, we get busy, we forget, we do other

things, we don't say we are sorry, and then we blame someone else for our neglectful behavior.

Do you recognize any of these cycles? Are these familiar patterns at play in your world, in your town, in your household?

Paul urges us to change things up. Start over. Start new. Be transformed. Be different. How are we supposed to do this? Through the "renewing of your mind." And how does this happen? We're given a clue in the next sentence—we're told that we'll be able to test and approve what God's will is.

Now, how in the world can we test and approve what God's will is if we don't have anything to test it against?

But we do. We have God's Word. We have the testimony of Jesus. We have the wisdom of God poured out to us through others. We have the ability to ask God about it in prayer. By doing these things, by doing what's required to test and approve what God's will is, we can renew our minds. We can get our minds following different thought patterns. We can make ourselves practice different ways of behaving. We can be transformed.

Lord God, change me. Renew my mind.
Transform my heart. I want to know Your will. Amen.

OVERCOMING UNBELIEF

"I do believe; help me overcome my unbelief!"
MARK 9:24 NIV

Does anything trouble a parent more than a son or daughter with a chronic illness? Moms and dads try to endure the stress of such a situation as best as they can. They try to hide their fears and worries from their children. But it's so hard. Day after day, they have to fight for their child's health. They have to deal with health insurance claims and doctor appointments and medical prescriptions and bills, bills, bills. And sometimes they have to deal with a lot worse—they have to deal with watching their child go through pain.

The father in Mark 9 had caused quite a stir. You can just imagine the lines of desperation on his face. There he is, seeking help from these followers of the Messiah. He's heard about miraculous things—people regaining their sight, paralyzed men walking again, women being restored to good health. But he finally makes it to the potential source of help, and he gets rejected.

Devastation. That must have been what he felt. Where else could he go?

But then Jesus comes. And the Teacher is ready to teach this generation a lesson.

The boy is brought to the Messiah. The father tells again of the sorrow and suffering they have endured together—he and his son.

The words must be hard to get out—how many times would he have to tell this story? How many times must he relive all the horrible moments when he thought his son would be killed by the spirit inside him? They had tried to get help from so many places. Not one of us would blame this father for feeling a bit defeated. "If you can do anything, take pity on us and help us," he said (Mark 9:22 NIV).

If we took Jesus' next words out of context, they might sound harsh. " 'If you can'?" said Jesus. "Everything is possible for one who believes" (Mark 9:23 NIV). But Jesus was not mocking the father. He knew how this story was going to end. No, the Rabbi was simply teaching the crowd. It's as if He was saying, "Look, everyone—you could do this if you would really believe in me. You have access to the power of the living, holy, healing God. You say you believe in this God. But do you?"

Then the father prayed a prayer that any of us can recognize: "I believe, but I don't think I believe enough. God, help me believe even more!"

And Jesus, in His grace and mercy, showed the man and the whole crowd exactly why they could believe even more. We can't overcome our unbelief on our own—we need to come to Jesus.

Lord, I do believe in You. Help me believe even more. Amen.

BELIEVERS BLESSED

When Elizabeth heard Mary's greeting, the baby leaped in her womb, and Elizabeth was filled with and controlled by the Holy Spirit. And she cried out. . . . Blessed. . .is she who believed that there would be a fulfillment of the things that were spoken to her from the Lord.

LUKE 1:41–42, 45 AMPC

At some point after the angel Gabriel departed from her, Mary went to visit Elizabeth, the one person who might accept her and her situation just as it was. Perhaps there, with a woman of like mind and physical condition, Mary might receive the companionship, strength, trust, love, and tenderness both she and her unborn child needed.

And so it was that when Mary walked in the door, the yet-to-be-born John the Baptist leaped inside Elizabeth's womb. Mary's cousin felt the joy of her child, and she herself was "filled with. . .the Holy Spirit."

Through that Spirit and through her unborn son, Elizabeth knew Mary was carrying the Savior of the world within her. Elizabeth cried out, telling Mary she was the most blessed of all women, that her child would be blessed! Elizabeth marveled that this was happening to her, that she, a once-barren old woman, was part of this awesome plan of God. She told Mary how the babe within her leaped for joy at Mary's greeting. Then Elizabeth said, "Blessed is

this woman who believed what God said, that all His words and promises would become a reality" (see Luke 1:45, author paraphrase). Elizabeth was revealing the truth that Mary was not just blessed because she was carrying the Son of God *but because she believed*. She trusted. Not in herself but in God and His words.

Both Mary and Elizabeth were experiencing their first pregnancies. And not just any pregnancies but ones predicted by an angel and ordained by God. And Mary, perhaps for the first time, feeling at ease with the events unfolding in her life that were outside of her control, could not help but burst into song: "The Mighty One has done great things for me, and His name is holy" (Luke 1:49 HCSB).

When you're going through a challenging time and need some comfort, strength, and courage, do as Mary did. Get clarity by asking God questions, as Mary did with Gabriel. If you have any fears, share them with God, knowing that He will immediately reassure you and tell you not to be afraid. Then let God know you're willing to be His servant, to abide by His plan and continue to trust. And you'll be blessed for believing.

Lord, help me believe in Your Word and to ask for courage when I'm afraid. As I am willing to serve You, may I be blessed in believing. Amen.

STAYING THE COURSE

Be like those who stay the course with committed faith and then get everything promised to them.

HEBREWS 6:12 MSG

What do you do when you have waited. . .and waited. . .and waited . . .and still God doesn't come through on His promise? You begin to think He never will. That maybe you misheard Him.

That's doubt. And where there's doubt, fear isn't far behind.

Sarah was in that place. She was beginning to think maybe God needed some help in fulfilling His promise to make her and her husband parents. So she came up with what she thought was a great idea: she should offer Abram her maid, Hagar. She told him, "Maybe I can get a family from her" (Genesis 16:2 MSG). But notice the first word in that sentence: *Maybe.* Because this idea didn't really have God's backing, it was something that might not work. Even worse, it could easily backfire. Yet Abram agreed. Hagar got pregnant, and now the former maid, having received the seed of the leader of the clan and heavy with his child, began to disrespect her mistress.

What a mess! So did Sarah go to God? Did she ask Him for forgiveness? No. She did neither. Instead, she opted to make things worse by playing the blame game. Sarah told her husband, "It's all your fault that I'm suffering this abuse. I put my maid in bed with you and the minute she knows she's pregnant, she treats me like

I'm nothing. May God decide which of us is right" (Genesis 16:5 MSG). Abram threw up his hands and said, "You decide. . . . Your maid is your business" (Genesis 16:6 MSG). So Sarah began abusing Hagar and did it so maliciously that Hagar ran away. Perhaps in fear. Maybe in frustration.

So, Sarah's plan, the remedy she invoked to cure her doubts and fears brought on by what she perceived as God's inaction, did nothing but wreak havoc in her family. Her impatience led to bad family planning, which affects the world even now.

Willingness to wait on God to act is a sign of one walking by faith not by sight. Speaking through Isaiah, God said, "See, I lay in Jerusalem a Stone of great worth to build upon, a tested Stone. Anyone who puts his trust in Him will not be afraid of what will happen" (Isaiah 28:16 NLV).

God has a perfect timetable. His job is to work it out. Yours is to be patient while He does so, steering clear of fear as you stay on the faithful course.

I believe in Your promises, Lord. Help me be patient as I wait, knowing that You'll work in Your time. Amen.

WAVES

Mightier than the thunder of the great waters, mightier than the breakers of the sea—the LORD on high is mighty.

PSALM 93:4 NIV

"The seas have lifted up, LORD" (Psalm 93:3 NIV).

It's one of those days. You know the kind. The schedules are conflicting. The family members are quarreling. The colleagues are circling. The deadlines are overwhelming. And you are barely swimming. Or are you almost drowning?

"The seas have lifted up their voice" (Psalm 93:3 NIV).

What is it that comes to your mind? Echoes of defeatist thinking? Guilt-ridden nightmares of despair? Accusations of unmet expectations? Predictions of failure? Or can you hear words of encouragement yet floating high on the crashing waves? Can you hear truth that comes from the source of all truth? Can you hear that you are loved? That no matter what mess you are swirling in right now, the One who made you has you in His hands?

"The seas have lifted up their pounding waves" (Psalm 93:3 NIV).

Truth is heavy. Praise is weighty. Sometimes accepting the vision God has for you, for your life, is hard to do. It's hard to grasp the idea that someone so big, so important, so amazing, cares so much about what happens to you—on this day, in this town, at this moment, right now. His words come pounding down on us, but we are not left beaten. When ocean waves crash into us, they

may well leave us breathless but not lifeless. On the contrary, when that saltwater comes for us, we feel more alive not less. We want to get up and chase the waves away, far away, to lands unknown beyond the horizon. We want to swim with schools of fish and become friends with dolphins. We want to breathe deeply, know deeply, love deeply.

"Mightier than the thunder of the great waters, mightier than the breakers of the sea—the LORD on high is mighty" (Psalm 93:4 NIV).

Our God is mighty—deep and wide like the ocean. Unpredictable and beyond our control. We cannot fathom Him. We cannot contain Him. We can only begin to grasp the words to describe Him. He reaches into our lives like the tides—sometimes arriving quickly and full-on, with beautiful, high, rushing waves of light. Sometimes He stretches out into our days—steady and strong and serene, teaching us peace and patience and calm.

The seas have lifted up their voice, and we have heard it. And now we can join them in their song: "The Lord, our Lord—our Lord on high is mighty."

Sometimes, Lord, just knowing You are here, as surely as I know the seas will come to shore, is enough to bring me peace. Amen.

JOY OF THE HARVEST

He said to his disciples, "The harvest is great, but the workers are few. So pray to the Lord who is in charge of the harvest; ask him to send more workers into his fields."

MATTHEW 9:37–38 NLT

Harvesttime in many communities is a time of celebration. In days long past, this was even truer. Farmers had worked hard all spring and summer to plow the land and plant the crops and tend their fields. They might have suffered setbacks and hard times, terrible weather and diseases affecting their plants. But at harvesttime, they could all come together and rejoice in the work they had done. And they could be thankful to God for the results of that work.

At harvesttime, after all the usable parts of the crops are gathered in, the workers finally have a chance to rest. The farmers can take a break from worry and stress and sweat. They reap the rewards of their labor in money for their crops, in food for their families, but also in the feeling of satisfaction for a job well done.

But other people celebrate at harvesttime too—people who have not toiled in the fields. People who have never worried about hailstorms and freezing temperatures. People who may have never seen the crack of dawn.

A lot of people want to enjoy the benefits of the harvest. They want the food, but they don't want the work. They want the celebration, but they don't want to perform the service.

When Jesus traveled from town to town, He saw so much work that needed to be done. He saw people who were suffering with all kinds of diseases and illnesses. He met people who were hurting in their hearts. And he heard from people who were seeking answers. He saw that so many people were "confused and helpless" (Matthew 9:36 NLT). They didn't know what to do to make their lives better. They didn't know where to go to ask their questions and get good answers. They didn't know who to follow.

Jesus wanted to help them all. He had compassion on them. But even Jesus couldn't be everywhere at once in His human form. And He knew the people would still have needs long after He had left the earth.

But He also knew that people needed to do the work. They needed to come together and serve one another. They needed to feel compassion. They needed to listen to each other's cares and share each other's sorrows. They needed to ask questions together. And then everyone would really know the joy of the harvest.

Lord, send more workers into the fields. Send me, Lord. Amen.

NOTHING TOO HARD

Alas, Lord God! Behold, You have made the heavens and the earth by Your great power and by Your outstretched arm! There is nothing too hard or too wonderful for You. . . . Behold, I am the Lord, the God of all flesh; is there anything too hard for Me?

JEREMIAH 32:17, 27 AMPC

Many females, girls and women alike, live with the fear that they're not good enough, strong enough, capable enough—that in some way they don't measure up at school, at work, or at home. Yet that sense of "not enough" can change. How? By applying the words of Philippians 4:13 (AMPC) to oneself: "I have strength for all things in Christ Who empowers me [I am ready for anything and equal to anything through Him Who infuses inner strength into me; I am self-sufficient in Christ's sufficiency]."

Those words prove to be even more potent if you understand who God and Christ are, the power They wield, and Their thoughts about and for you. Thankfully, the Bible is filled with verses with which you can build up not only your knowledge but your faith.

Jeremiah the prophet understood God's awesome power, how by simply stretching out His arm, God made the heavens and the earth. He knew that there is nothing too difficult for the Lord to do. God echoed Jeremiah's understanding of Him, agreeing that nothing is too difficult for the God who created us.

Once you understand the power and nature of your God,

you'll know you're worthy, sufficient, strong, and capable enough to do anything!

Christian missionary Amy Carmichael (1867–1951) said, "God delights to meet the faith of one who looks up to Him and says, 'Lord, You know that I cannot do this—but I believe that You can!' " Wouldn't you love to delight God every chance you get? Wouldn't you be less fearful if you believed that because God is who He is, and because you follow Him, you who are in Christ can do all the things He empowers you to do?

Whether you are a single woman or a girl, a wife or a widow, a mother or a daughter, a sister or a friend, you are enough with Christ. With His power pulsing through you, know and believe that you are good enough, strong enough, and capable enough to be His hands and feet on earth, to be a blessing to others, to do whatever He calls you to do here and beyond.

Remember that "nothing is impossible; the word itself says, 'I'm possible!' " (Audrey Hepburn).

Lord, fill me with Your strength. Help me to acknowledge that because of You and Your power, I am enough! Amen.

WHERE YOUR HEART IS

"For where your treasure is, there your heart will be also."

MATTHEW 6:21 NIV

One thing we can ask ourselves about our spiritual lives is exactly what our intentions and goals are in making the appearances that we make and doing the things that we do. Are we proud that we attend services each weekend we make the effort to attend them? Do we boast about it, if only to ourselves? What is there to boast about? Among our friends, is our attendance a badge of honor? What exactly is the honor?

Granted, in a world abounding with scoffers, the temptation is great to boast and to throw our faith and our spiritual constancy in the faces of those who taunt us. But then we might ask ourselves, *To whom am I attending when I am present at services? Toward whom is my focus directed? Am I locked into some earthly battle with earthly adversaries over whom I wish to triumph? About whose praises am I finally concerned, those of the people around me or those of God? And who is it, exactly, that I am worshipping? Is it God or is it me?*

Sal and Alex are two neighborly friends. Alex gets up every day, rain or shine, to get himself to the gym. According to him, his routine is directed at his health more than his "six-pack," although he talks more about his six-pack than his health.

Sal, on the other hand, gets to the gym two or three times a week. But every morning of just about every day, Sal makes it his

business to sit on the back porch or stretch out on the couch with his Bible or his prayer book. He spends forty-five minutes to an hour each morning sustaining and strengthening his relationship with Jesus. He gleans whatever wisdom he can from his reading, and he has a running dialogue with his Lord and Master. He talks to Him about his cares and his worries. He prays for his children and his siblings and for all the people who have no one to pray for them.

Regularly enough, Alex asks Sal to come to the gym with him, and from time to time, Sal accepts the invitation. He always enjoys the physical activity and the camaraderie. But in the end, he asks himself about his limited time and how he should spend it. Should he be worrying about getting fit, or should he be working harder to serve God well? Sal often finds himself thinking that only God knows how we appear; only God knows about our true treasure and where it is that we are trying to store it up.

Lord, help me to make sure that where I'm spending my time and treasure is where You are. Amen.

BUT, YET, NEVERTHELESS, STILL

In my fear I said, "You have closed Your eyes to me!" But You heard my cry for loving-kindness when I called to You. Love the Lord, all you who belong to Him! The Lord keeps the faithful safe. . . . Be strong. Be strong in heart, all you who hope in the Lord.

PSALM 31:22–24 NLV

Thank God for His gifts of *but*, *yet*, *nevertheless*, and *still*.

Even if, in fear, you imagine God has closed His eyes and ears to you, remember His *but*. *But* turns your fear and doubt into celebration because God has heard your cry for the love you need. His *but* brings you to the realization that because you belong to Him and are faithful to Him, He will keep you safe. Because of these things, you can be strong as you continue to hope in Him.

You may have times when you get weary of seeing ne'er-do-wells prosper as you, a God follower, continue to struggle. You begin to feel pangs of jealousy for those who have while you have not. Then God inspires you with a *yet*: "*Yet* I am always with You. You hold me by my right hand. You will lead me by telling me what I should do. And after this, You will bring me into shining-greatness" (Psalm 73:23–24 NLV, emphasis added). Then when you're tired, God gives you another *but*: "My body and my heart may grow weak, *but* God is the strength of my heart and all I need forever" (Psalm 73:26 NLV, emphasis added).

When you look back in Bible history, you can see how God has continued to work with His people no matter how they acted. After all the miracles God performed for His people in Egypt, they still rebelled against Him at the Red Sea. Out of fear of being caught between Pharaoh and the Red Sea, God's people told Moses, "It would have been better for us to serve the Egyptians than to die in the wilderness" (Exodus 14:12 ESV). "*Nevertheless* He saved them for His name's sake [to prove the righteousness of the divine character], that He might make His mighty power known" (Psalm 106:8 AMPC, emphasis added). Even when God was so angry with the Israelites that "he couldn't stand even to look at his people. . . . *Still*, when God saw the trouble they were in and heard their cries for help, He remembered his Covenant with them, and, immense with love, took them by the hand" (Psalm 106:40, 44–45 MSG, emphasis added).

Because of God's immense love, you need not fear anything. Just as God has helped you in the past, have faith He will do so in your future with His myriad gifts of *but*, *yet*, *nevertheless*, and *still*.

Thank You, Lord, for Your constant love and endless gifts. Amen.

THAT KIND OF PEACE

And the peace of God, which transcends all understanding, will guard your hearts and your minds in Christ Jesus.

PHILIPPIANS 4:7 NIV

When a very best friend is sitting with you, everything looks a little better. Even when sad or frustrating things might have brought you together for a time, the comfort of having someone who knows you well close by to care for you is the best feeling in the world. It doesn't really matter what gets said or done; just a squeeze of the hand is a kind of sweet medicine, soothing your soul and giving you strength.

Paul tells us that "the Lord is near" (Philippians 4:5 NIV). Now, for some, that statement could produce fear. For if the Lord is near, then He is close enough to see what we are doing and to hear what we are saying. And why is He so near? Is He here to deliver punishments to us? No, not in this case. The Lord is near because He is always near in this way: He always comes close to those He loves and who love Him.

And with this perfect best friend beside us, we know for sure that we don't have to be afraid of anything. We don't have to be worried. We don't have to stress about how to solve a problem. Through prayer and petition and with thanks, we can present our requests to Him, and He will answer us. Because that's what best friends do. They come when you need help. No matter how far away they are, they offer real, tangible help in some way.

And that's how the peace that is deeper than any other kind of peace arrives. God's peace pours over us, filling us and surrounding us like a gushing stream. Even when the world looks bleak, when we can't see an answer, when we are burdened with stress and worries, God's peace can push through all of that and fill up our hearts—untangling the knots in our minds and soothing our spirits. It's the kind of sure footing we feel when we make a decision that puts us in line with His will. It's the supernatural calm we are able to cling to when storms are roaring all around us. It's the quiet confidence that allows us to step into situations that would otherwise shake us. It's the peace that we don't understand, that we can't describe, and that doesn't make sense. It's that kind of peace.

Lord, I'm so thankful You are near me when troubles come. Bless me with Your impossible peace. Amen.

THE TURN-AROUND

Answer me when I call, O my God Who is right and good! You have made a way for me when I needed help. Be kind to me, and hear my prayer. . . . Know that the Lord has set apart him who is God-like for Himself. . . . I will lie down and sleep in peace. O Lord, You alone keep me safe.

PSALM 4:1, 3, 8 NLV

When you're exhausted, burned out, your faith may easily crumble. Next thing you know, fear has filled the void and you find yourself on the run, trying to outpace feelings of failure and disappointment. With your last ounce of strength, you manage to make it into the wilderness. Perhaps your prayer becomes like that of Elijah: "I've had it, Lord. Nothing is working out like I thought it would. If you want to take me, do so now" (1 Kings 19:4, author paraphrase).

Well, at least now you're in the right place: before God. Now you start doing what you should have done all along: allow Him and His angels to take care of you, nourish you. And then you can sleep. Ah, blessed sleep.

When God created the world, He did so in six days—not seven! For on that day, God performed His final act in his seven-day play: He rested. And you, who were made in His image, are to reenact that act. You too are to rest. But if you have put off rest until you have run yourself down to the ground, chances are it's going to take a while to recover not just physically but emotionally, spiritually, and mentally.

Even Elijah, back on his feet physically, was still having trouble seeing things straight. Filled with discouragement, he told God that he was the only prophet left alive. And now the evil king Ahab and queen Jezebel were hunting him down. That's when God gave Elijah exactly what he needed: His presence and plan. After passing by Elijah, God told him to go back the way he had come and to perform specific duties. Then God told Elijah that He had seven thousand more godly followers through whom God could work. God's gifts of hope and encouragement gave Elijah just what he needed to turn himself around, to adjust his attitude and outlook.

Woman of faith, God loves you, cares for you. He wants you to know that He will do what He can do with and for you. But you need to do what you can do too: take care of yourself, getting the sleep and rest you need every day. Then you will be a wise woman.

Help me to take better care of myself, Lord.
To get the rest I need so that I'll see things with
Your wisdom, using Your perspective. Amen.

BOTTOM

"We shall see what will become of his dreams!"
GENESIS 37:20 NKJV

How in the world did I get here?

Joseph must have been bewildered. At the beginning of this chapter of his life, he is on top of the world, a favorite of his father, respected, and seemingly favored by God. He'd had dreams indicating that even his older brothers and father, members of the family of the great patriarch Abraham, would bow down to him—young Joseph.

And now he was stuck at the bottom of a pit, sitting in the dirt, with literally nowhere to go.

Nowhere to go, that is, but up.

Sometimes we just don't see how God is with us until we've hit bottom. Now, this doesn't mean we should aim for bottom just so we can experience Immanuel ("God with us") even more. As Paul said, "What shall we say then? Shall we continue in sin that grace may abound? Certainly not!" (Romans 6:1–2 NKJV). After all, Joseph never intended to end up in that dry well. He didn't throw himself in there.

But one wonders, as he was down there in the dark, disrobed, listening to the harsh voices of his brothers somewhere overhead, did Joseph wake up to the reality that perhaps he had allowed his own pride to blur his vision? Had he become so content in his

position of favor that he hadn't seen the growing divide between him and his brothers? How had he missed all the signs of their anger?

It's all too easy when things are going well—when we feel as though we are sitting on top of the world—to forget to be sensitive to the perspectives of others. We can't control how people feel about us, but we can try to be better listeners. We don't have to hide when good things happen to us, but we can be sensitive and respectful in the way we share our news, and we can give the glory and our thanks to God.

The grown man we know as Joseph is someone we all look to as an example of great faith, perseverance, and forgiveness. But young Joseph is the picture of a self-absorbed teenager—annoying his family with his ignorance and arrogance.

As Joseph sat there, stripped and bruised, he had limited options. But one thing he could do was pray. He could look up to the light and ask God to be with him in the darkness. And God certainly was there with Joseph. God stayed with Joseph all his life.

And God is with you too—whether you are basking in the light or hunkering in the dark.

Lord, help me to see You with me all the time—
even when it looks like I have nowhere to go. Amen.

FAITH-FILLED ATTITUDE

"Don't panic. I'm with you. There's no need to fear for I'm your God. I'll give you strength. I'll help you. I'll hold you steady, keep a firm grip on you. . . . Because I, your GOD, have a firm grip on you and I'm not letting go. I'm telling you, 'Don't panic. I'm right here to help you.' "

ISAIAH 41:10, 13 MSG

How would your life change if you were to live it firmly and consistently, believing God is with you, helping and guiding you?

In His Word, God repeatedly tells you He is with you and *will always be with you*. No matter who you are, what's happening, when you need Him, where you are, or why you need Him, God is with you. You have no need to fall into fear and plummet into panic. In His care, you can relax.

You may not know how God does it, how He can be with you at the exact same time He can be with trillions of other believers. Don't bother trying to comprehend it. Just believe it. Take it on faith that *God is with you*.

Not only is God *with* you, but He's actively *helping* you. He not only has a grip on you but is shielding you, standing between you and trouble. And He is giving you the strength you need to stand as He holds you steady.

Not only is God with you and helping you, but He's guiding you. He's the One who has called you. Just as God called His sons, He

has called you, His daughter: "I've picked you. I haven't dropped you. Don't panic. I'm with you" (Isaiah 41:9–10 MSG). When you feel the weakest and the most afraid, God says, "I'll help you. I, God, want to reassure you. . . . I'm transforming you from worm to harrow, from insect to iron" (Isaiah 41:14–15 MSG).

In God's hands, you'll be able to do anything, even crush a mountain. "You'll be confident" (Isaiah 41:16 MSG) in God and His power working in your life.

Your faith is what shapes your attitudes. Consider Joseph. What might have happened to him—and the nation of Israel—had Joseph not continued to believe in God when he was sold to traveling traders by his own brothers, resold into slavery, and then put into a dungeon? What if Joseph had become despondent and stopped believing God was with him, helping him, and guiding him? But Joseph did believe in the dreams God had given him. He had confidence in God. And his attitude that God would not let him down lifted Joseph up above his situations, no matter how dire they became.

Thank You, God, for being with me,
helping me, and guiding me. Amen.

GO AND DO

The word of the LORD came to Abram in a vision: Do not be afraid, Abram. I am your shield; your reward will be very great. . . . Abram believed the LORD.

GENESIS 15:1, 6 HCSB

When you need encouragement, the best place to *go* is to God. And the best thing to *do* is to listen to and believe in His Word.

Genesis 15:1 contains two firsts. Here the phrase "the word of the Lord came" appears for the first time in the Bible. And this phrase is directly followed by the first-time appearance of God's command "Do not be afraid." We may have a hard time grasping these four little words when we're on shaky ground. Yet that's just where Abram stood. But before going there, let's take a look at how he got there.

Genesis 14:17 (HCSB) says Abram had won a great victory over "Chedorlaomer and the kings who were with him." Afterward the king of Salem offered Abram a reward. But Abram refused it, saying, "I will not take a thread or sandal strap or anything that belongs to you, so you can never say, 'I made Abram rich' " (Genesis 14:23 HCSB). So, although the battle was won, the human reward was rejected.

Yet afterward Abram was, on the material plane, standing on shaky ground because chances were good that his enemies would return for a rematch. That left him wondering where, when, and

how they would appear. But God had that covered too. He followed up His "Do not be afraid" command with an assurance, a reason Abram need not fear anything. God said, "I am your shield." Here God was making sure that Abram knew that God—the most powerful force in heaven and on earth—would protect him, just as a scaly hide protects a crocodile. Finally, God followed all this with a promise: "Your reward will be very great." God was letting Abram know that He would more than replace the reward Abram had given up for God.

It's great to read about God's commands and assurances. But to conquer your fear and insecurities and to hold on to God's promises, you need to *believe* what He says, putting faith in His Word not in your feelings.

When fear begins to creep into your life, look away from yourself and up to God. There you'll find the commands, assurances, and promises you need. There you can replace your negative thoughts (*I'm not safe*) with God's positive words ("I'm your shield").

Lord, help me abide by Your commands, believe Your assurances, and live by Your promises. In Jesus' name I pray. Amen.

REFUGE OF DESTRUCTION

Come, see the glorious works of the LORD: see how he brings destruction upon the world.

PSALM 46:8 NLT

There's a scene in the film *Superman* (1978) in which the hero throws a green crystal, and out of an Arctic landscape, through crackling glacial slabs, shards of ice burst forth, exploding into a frozen sky. The Fortress of Solitude, the superhero's elaborate (and chilly) man cave, rises up like some kind of fantastic Nordic crown for a giant ice princess.

The fortress is Superman's home base—his palace of refuge. It's a place where he can go to find safety and seclusion. It's a place where he can be reconnected to his source. But this quiet, hidden sanctuary is born out of crashing destruction.

Sometimes, when the certainty of our life circumstances is collapsing around us, and the solid ground we thought we were standing on seems as shifting and unsteady as the sandy shore under the ocean waves, that is when we find our real source of strength. We cannot hold too tightly to the things of this earth—the things that perish and fade away. But we can hold on forever to God and know He will hold on forever to us.

Nations have been in chaos before. Long ago, kingdoms fought one another and castles crumbled to the ground. Governments have fallen apart. But where God dwells, we can take refuge. And

the Lord of Heaven's Armies is right here—here among us.

But this is not a refuge of quiet and calm. This is the place where God brings destruction. "He causes wars to end throughout the earth. He breaks the bow and snaps the spear; he burns the shields with fire" (Psalm 46:9 NLT). The God of peace, who destroys the weapons of violence and rules over nations, calls out to us, "Be still" (Psalm 46:10 NLT). He tells us to be silent in our actions and our speech—but not so we will do nothing at all. Not so we can just be spectators of His might. "Be still, and know that I am God! I will be honored by every nation. I will be honored throughout the world" (Psalm 46:10 NKJV).

How can we know that He is God? We have to ask. We have to do research. We have to search the scriptures and see who God claims to be, what He is like, what He does, and whom He does it to. We have to keep searching and talking about Him in every corner of the world. We can meet others and tell them about Him. And then we can be still—still in the satisfaction of knowing who He is and what He wants from us.

God, please bring peace out of the destruction in our lives. Amen.

CRAVING GOD'S PRESENCE

Hear me, Asa, and all Judah and Benjamin: the Lord is with you while you are with Him. If you seek Him [inquiring for and of Him, craving Him as your soul's first necessity], He will be found by you; but if you [become indifferent and] forsake Him, He will forsake you.

2 CHRONICLES 15:2 AMPC

Listen up, daughter of God, sister of Jesus. God wants you to know that He is near you when you're near Him. If you seek Him, craving His presence, you *will* find Him. What God *doesn't* want is for you to fall into the cycle in which the Israelites continually found themselves. Remember? When things were going well, God's people would neglect, sometimes even abandon, Him. Then, finding themselves in a heap of trouble, they'd return to Him and once more enjoy His blessings. The next thing you knew, they'd walked away from Him again! That's a bad formula for any kind of relationship.

God wants you to stick close to Him through thick *and* thin. He wants your prayer to be like that of Asa's: "LORD, there is no one besides You to help the mighty and those without strength. Help us, LORD our God, for we depend on You" (2 Chronicles 14:11 HCSB). When God hears words like these, He's quick to rout enemies, remove obstacles, and bring victory (see v. 12).

As you read through the Bible, take note of how often God

is only a whisper, a prayer away from His people. If only they'd seek Him, call to Him, reach out with their hearts and souls. God is just waiting for His people to look to Him, to crave His Word and presence above all. For that's when they'll find Him, the One who is always closer than they imagine (see Psalm 119:151; 145:18; Jeremiah 23:23; Acts 17:27).

If you find yourself trembling in fear instead of standing steady in courage, stop. Take a look at where you're standing. Are you with God or without Him? Talk to God. He's there, listening for your voice.

Today, "be strong; don't be discouraged" (2 Chronicles 15:7 HCSB). Commit (or recommit) to seeking the Lord with all your mind and heart. As you do so, you'll find "rest on every side" (2 Chronicles 15:15 HCSB).

As I stand here and whisper Your name, Lord, I feel Your presence, closer than I'd ever imagined. Amen.

MORE THAN BREAD

"I am the bread of life. Whoever comes to me will never be hungry again. Whoever believes in me will never be thirsty."

JOHN 6:35 NLT

We ask for patience. God gives us long lines. We ask for courage. God puts us in situations where we have to face our fears. We ask for more power. God shows us how little we are. We ask for safety. God shows us what we have to risk and how much we must depend on Him.

When we ask God for solutions, we shouldn't be surprised when His answers don't look like they go with our questions. God, in His perfect wisdom, gives us exactly what we need when we need it. But He doesn't always give us what we think we want. And that's a good thing.

The huge crowd had been following Jesus for some time, traveling with Him on the dusty roads over rough terrain. They climbed up a hill to sit around the Teacher, and Jesus looked out over the thousands of faces and knew these people were hungry. They didn't have to ask for a lunch break—Jesus knew what they needed. But they didn't just need lunch. They needed to depend on Him.

Later, after Jesus had fed the crowd miraculously with five loaves of bread and two fish, they came looking for Him again. They weren't just hungry for more fish sandwiches. They wanted

this power Jesus had. They wanted to be able to perform miracles.

And maybe they wanted to be seen as the kind of people who could perform miracles.

They said they wanted to perform "God's works." And Jesus told them they could. All they had to do was believe in Him.

That was all they had to do. Believe that this Jesus—this man who had just turned bread and fish into a feast right in front of them—was sent from God. Believe that He was who He claimed to be. Believe that He was the way to God, the way to live forever with God in heaven.

But many of them just couldn't do it. No matter what they had seen, they couldn't believe that this fellow from Nazareth, this son of a carpenter, could also be the Son of God. Maybe they weren't ready to believe that God really could do anything. Or maybe they weren't ready to obey this God.

Many of them turned away. They had wanted bread. But Jesus wanted to give them much more than the ability to make a meal for a day. Jesus wanted to feed them for life. And they were missing it. Are we?

Jesus, my Lord and King, help me obey whatever You ask me to do. Amen.

WORDS OF WISDOM

Wisdom calls out in the street; she raises her voice in the public squares. She cries out above the commotion. . . . "Whoever listens to me will live securely and be free from the fear of danger."

PROVERBS 1:20–21, 33 HCSB

We're living in the information age, a time when people can access a lot of information and knowledge quickly and easily. Yet much of that "information" can be suspect. Have you ever asked yourself if what you hear is true? Do you consider that some of the things out there may have been planted by a ne'er-do-well, a foreign government, a bad actor, or a liar? Are you checking your sources, making sure the information you see, read, and hear is authentic, true, real, something you can hang your hat on?

In this fast-paced and increasingly complicated world, it can be difficult to know where to go for the truth, how to discern what information is reliable. But there's still one source you can trust, one place where you can find the truth: God's Word. There you'll find incomparable wisdom ready, willing, and able to pour out her spirit on you, to teach you her words (see Proverbs 1:23). She's calling out to you, trying to steer you in the right direction, away from the edge of the cliff. That's her job. *Your* job is simply to open yourself—heart, soul, mind, and spirit—to her voice. To hear her above the mass of misinformation, the din of commo-

tion, the seemingly never-ending falsehoods that surround you. Listen to what she has to say. Have the courage to take her words to heart—*and* keep them in mind. Then, and only then, will you be able to "live securely and be free from the fear of danger."

Throughout your day, keep your ear to God's lips. Be open to His Spirit, listening for His counsel and guidance in everything you do. Ask God to direct your every step as you endeavor to do what He would have you do, be who He would have you be.

Know that as you do all these things, not just seeking out God's wisdom but heeding His voice and walking His way, you'll not only be able to more clearly find your way but help others find theirs as well.

I come to You today, Lord, seeking what You would have me know. Speak to me through Your Word. Help me apply what I hear so that I will be kept free from deceit and danger. Amen.

FOR US

What, then, shall we say in response to these things?
If God is for us, who can be against us?
ROMANS 8:31 NIV

Ever feel as if the whole world is against you? It seems like that at times, doesn't it? You run out of milk, get to the store, realize you left your wallet at home, leave the store, and discover someone "bumped" into your parked car. You go to call your insurance company but then realize your cell phone is dead.

Doesn't it seem like someone is out to get you? For what reason is unclear. Perhaps they are trying to discourage you from doing some greater good. Perhaps all of it is some grand distraction from your true life purpose. But there are definitely times when it feels as if God went on vacation and left mischievous substitutes in charge.

But even though it may feel this way at times, we can know for certain that God has not left us alone. God is for us. In thousands of ways, through all the centuries, and through every page of His Word, we see that God is for us. God promised He would be for us, reminding us of this promise with His rainbow in the sky. God was for us in the wilderness, leading His people with cloud and fire, providing for them every step of the way. God was for us in His temple, coming near to dwell among His children. God was for us one night in Bethlehem, when He sent our Savior to be swaddled and laid to sleep in an animal's feeding trough. God was for us as

He healed us and fed us and taught us and led us. And God was for us as He hung on the cross.

God was for us in every second of the stories of our lives, and He is for us now. He gives us everything we need and so much more than we deserve. He justifies us—forgiving us and setting things to rights so that we can be freed from our lives of sin and start again.

Nothing can separate us from His love. No difficult schedules, no difficult people, no difficult financial situation, no difficult relationships. There is no bad day so awful that we cannot recover from it, because there is no bad day with God not in it.

God is for us. No one can really be against us because no one can stand against God. Thank You, Lord.

Lord God, I am so glad You are here for me.
Thank You for being my very best friend. Amen.

SCRIPTURE INDEX